$1/—

D1132969

GARDENING
IN CALIFORNIA

Early May in the Berkeley garden of the author, an Iris enthusiast. Dozens of varieties, yet planted for garden effect, not in rows. White Omphalodes linifolia and lavender Nepeta mussini edge the paths of this sunny hillside garden.

GARDENING
IN CALIFORNIA

*A Guide for the Amateur
on the Pacific Slope*

BY
SYDNEY B. MITCHELL

GARDEN CITY   NEW YORK
DOUBLEDAY, DORAN & COMPANY, INC.
1936

COPYRIGHT, 1923, BY DOUBLEDAY, PAGE
& COMPANY. ALL RIGHTS RESERVED.
PRINTED IN THE UNITED STATES AT THE
COUNTRY LIFE PRESS, GARDEN CITY, N. Y.

TO

R. F. M.

WITHOUT WHOSE ABLE ASSISTANCE
THIS BOOK WOULD NOT HAVE
BEEN WRITTEN

CONTENTS

Contents

ix

LIST OF ILLUSTRATIONS

GARDENING IN CALIFORNIA

CHAPTER I

Introducing the California Climate

IN CALIFORNIA everyone seems to feel a personal responsibility for the climate. It is loved, praised, lied about, misunderstood. The last is hardly excusable in the native gardener, as climate is the most important factor in his success, but it is understandable in one who has come from such different conditions as those on the Atlantic coast. For his sake a few explanatory words may be an assistance. They deal with the general phenomena of our weather, not with the vagaries of single seasons, which show wide deviations from the normal in regard to temperature and particularly in amount of annual rainfall.

There are but two seasons, the rainy one from October to May and the dry one covering the remaining months. It should be understood that the rainy months are merely those during which rain normally falls, the dry ones those during which moisture heavy enough to be of any garden value is rarely precipitated. The rains are not continuous but come as storms, the spells of fine weather in between often lasting for weeks. These circling storms originate in the north Pacific Ocean and move southeasterly, revolving from right to left, the opposite of the direction of the hands of the clock, so that the windy rains come from the south to us. Many of the storms reach only the northern California coast; some of them get to the San Francisco Bay region; fewer go as far south as Los Angeles, and only the very occasional one gets to San Diego. In other words, the annual rainfall at Eureka will often run up to fifty inches; in San Francisco about half that amount; in Los Angeles a third, and at San Diego sometimes only a sixth.

It will be understood that these are general figures, and that local conditions, in particular the proximity of mountains, greatly increases the precipitation. It is enough, however, to show why Rhododendrons, Azaleas, and Daffodils are so much happier on the north Pacific coast than they are a thousand miles south. The first rains are not to be considered as the coming of winter, but of spring, for the wise gardener will want to take advantage of the natural moisture, and, following nature, will sow many of his seeds at that time; and before they end in April or May he will have done the great bulk of his planting.

The California coast is nearly a thousand miles long, covering latitudes the equal of Boston in the north and Savannah in the south, but without their great differences of winter cold. It is difficult for the newcomer to realize the tremendous moderating and equalizing character of the Pacific Ocean and the winds which blow from it across the land. It will suffice to say that at Eureka the minimum temperature reported is twenty degrees Fahrenheit, and at San Diego thirty-two degrees, a difference of only twelve degrees. The coldest places in California will then be those in the interior, especially on the foothills of the Sierras which bound California to the east.

In the long dry summer great heat would naturally be expected, especially in the south. Here again we encounter the moderating effects of the ocean, the west wind blowing in from it the summer fogs which throughout the length of California keep the coast cool and in places where they are most frequent will often make July and August positively cold. But in the interior, whether it be in the south at San Bernardino or Bakersfield, or in the north at Chico or Sacramento, the summers will be almost equally hot, not on account of their latitude but because the cooling fogs rarely get more than a few miles inland. To sum up, the distance north or south is of comparatively little importance in determining winter or summer temperature. The great factor is the distance from the ocean. Isothermal lines tend to run north and south along the coast or inland, not across the state.

A further consideration is the percentage of humidity in summer. The general low average is responsible for the fact that high inland temperatures can be endured without great suffering. This absence of moisture is, however, responsible for the difficulty of growing many plants and flowers during the warm summers of the Sacramento and San Joaquin valleys.

While accepting these general truths about the climate of California it must also be recognized that especially in the coast valleys there are many local climates, modifications due to the varying aspects, protection from summer fogs, the cold north winds of the rainy months or the warm, dry north winds of the summer. These variations add greatly to the interest of gardening, as a move of only a few miles may make a good deal of difference in the adaptability of certain plants to the location.

Compare, for example, the garden possibilities of Santa Monica and Pasadena, of San Francisco and San Jose, comparatively neighboring places. In the summer fog of Del Monte or San Francisco the Dahlia is far happier than in the continual sunshine of Fresno, but with the Zinnia or the Canna the odds are all in favor of the warmer place, provided plenty of water be given. Fogs are kindly to Fuchsias, but to achieve success with the Crape Myrtle or the Oleander one must get away from the fog belt. Many broad-leaved evergreen trees and shrubs need the moderating influence of the warm winter ocean to bring them through our coldest months, but in the same sections the summer heat is not enough to produce the rapid and luxuriant growth which coniferous evergreens will make in the warm interior valleys.

A favored district, Santa Barbara, facing south and protected by high mountains to the north, was credited a few years ago in an English horticultural magazine with being the place in the whole world where the greatest variety of plants might be grown. We cannot all live there, but in our own localities we can by the experience of others and our own trials learn what will be best, and, if our gardens are to be truly successful, depend chiefly on such plants. But many will also want the joy of the occasional success or of that which comes with a difficult plant raised after years of endeavor. To these we say, Good luck.

One further suggestion should be made, that is that in general we use those plant materials which come from climates similar to our own. A comparison will show that, though there are differences, the climate of the Pacific slope bears many resemblances to the west coast of Europe and, in its southern part, to the Mediterranean countries. From Vancouver Island down through Washington and Oregon to northern California the similar conditions favor the planting of those things which do well in the south of Ireland or England, while from central California south our most successful cultivated plants are strikingly similar to those of the Riviera, Italy, north Africa, and also Madeira. It is not surprising that the Bearded Irises from Dalmatia or Cyprus, *Iris ochroleuca* from Asia Minor, and *Iris unguicularis* from Algiers, are happier here than elsewhere on the continent of North America, for they have come from countries with wet and dry seasons similar to ours. Other countries with a kinship of climate are South Africa and Australia, hence the ease with which we grow South African bulbous flowers and naturalize Australian trees, shrubs, and vines. The Eucalyptus, best known of importations from Australia, has become one of the most characteristic features of the California landscape.

CHAPTER II

AS THE average amateur does not make the nature of the soil the first consideration when selecting his home, he must take it as he finds it. But he does not have to keep it so, for all soils are susceptible of improvement. First of all, he will seek to better its mechanical condition. If it is too stiff he will do his best to lighten it; if it is too dry and sandy he will try to make it heavier and more retentive of moisture. As very much can be done for the soil merely by plowing or digging, this should be first attended to.

We are prone to expect far too much from our soils, when we consider how shallow is any digging which most gardens get. If the place is large enough it will pay to have it plowed, and it will be far better if it is gone over a second time with a subsoil plow, so as to loosen up the ground as deeply as possible. When it is in proper condition, that is, not wet, it may be harrowed to break up clods and to level it. Where time will allow, the ground should be left rough for a while between these operations. A small garden should be dug by hand.

Most of the day-laborers who in our country mas-

querade as gardeners are quite satisfied to dig only the
depth of a spade, and prefer to lighten their work by
holding this tool at such an angle that the depth reached
is far less than if it were held vertically. They should
learn what the old-country gardener calls trenching.
This consists in removing the surface soil of a given
patch of garden to the depth of a spade and putting it
aside, then loosening up the subsoil—this will often
require the use of a pick—then taking the surface from
the adjacent section of the bed and throwing it over the
already loosened subsoil. This will uncover further
subsoil, and the operation is continued until all has
been dug, when the first lot of top soil will be used
to cover up the last patch of subsoil. It is not claimed
that successful gardening may never be carried out
without this careful preparation, but such initial work
undoubtedly makes for fine and permanent gardening,
as it allows roots to go farther in search of food and
water.

DIGGING AND CULTIVATION

This digging and the later surface cultivation do
much to improve the mechanical condition of the soil,
but some soils will be further helped in this respect by
the addition of some other substance. Heavy soils,
such as adobe and clay, are often quite sufficiently rich
in plant food, but their close texture prevents this
being always available. They need loosening up so
that the necessary air may permeate the soil to the
roots of the plants. The addition of leaf-mold, strawy

manure, rotted vegetable refuse, sand, or even coal-ashes will be of great assistance. The three first mentioned will furnish humus, while the two last have no fertilizing value whatever. Heavy soils are also helped by spreading on them and digging in old builder's plaster which has been pulverized, or lime. This will be of special value where the soil is lacking in this constituent. Sandy soil, on the other hand, generally needs both plant food and such additions as will make it more retentive of moisture. Here again humus is needed, though the mixing in of heavier soil will in itself improve the condition.

HUMUS AND FERTILIZERS

With this recognition of the value of humus, not merely for fertilizing, but as a help to the physical condition of the soil, gardeners should not need further counsel as to the importance of having at hand as large a supply of it as possible. As horse and cow-manure are becoming more expensive and more difficult to obtain, we must conserve leaves, grass clippings, the stems and tops of green plants, green weeds, and vegetable trimmings. The easiest way to handle such material is to dig a trench or pit at some distance from the house into which it may be thrown. An occasional shovel of soil and during the dry season a watering now and then will assist it in rotting. Such humus is also very useful to have for mixing with soil for potting.

The use of commercial fertilizers to obtain results

proportionate to their cost requires a knowledge of the chemistry of soils which is beyond most amateur gardeners.   Until he learns more about them, the gardener can only experiment.   Bone-meal and bone-flour are safe and proven allies in the growing of many garden flowers, such as Roses, Dahlias, and Irises.

WEEDS AND WATER

The cultivation of the surface soil is unaccountably neglected when one considers its value in aerating the soil, keeping down weeds, and conserving moisture. Far less expensive watering would be needed if continuous attention were given to this, and the value of each watering would be greatly increased if the soil were cultivated as soon after as its condition would permit. Everywhere cultivation is important, but in such a semi-arid country as California its unremitting practice cannot be too strongly insisted on.   In the small garden, cultivation should reduce the surface soil almost to powder, as this will best prevent evaporation by the sun.

In this connection the importance of early weeding should be emphasized, as weeds not only compete with one's plants for food and space but for water.   So large a proportion of our weeds are annuals and spring up with the first rains of the fall that a hoeing of the ground at that time will save an immense amount of work later on. Where there are large permanent plantings of Daffodils, Tulips, and other bulbs which do not appear above the ground until January, by lightly hoeing off the weeds once or twice in fall one can avoid all further weeding until after the bulbs have bloomed.

THE ALL-IMPORTANT MULCH

As some substitute for cultivation to retain the moisture in summer, gardeners should resort to mulching, that is, surfacing the ground with rotted leaves, straw, grass clippings, or strawy manure. This is more generally done where plants make many roots near the surface, as does the hardy Phlox, which would be injured by cultivation.

The fertilizing of established plants is often accomplished by giving them a heavy mulching or top-dressing of manure. The top-dressing is usually forked in, while in the case of mulching the plant foods are carried down into the ground by watering through the mulch. This last method is an excellent way to feed such plants as Dahlias, where it is undesirable to cause rank growth by early fertilizing but where the plants will appreciate more food when they begin to bloom.

IMMODERATE WATERING

Much damage is done and an immense amount of water wasted every summer by light and casual sprinkling in our gardens. About the only excuse for sprinkling is to wash the dust off the leaves of the plants or to get rid of aphis or other insect pests which feed on the stems and buds. It really does much harm, because a small amount of water encourages the production of surface roots, quite undesirable in gardens where the summers are as dry as on the Pacific coast. What one should do is to encourage deep rooting. Water, therefore, less frequently but more thoroughly.

In other words, if you water every morning or evening devote your attention to a small space each time and thoroughly soak it, even though you will not water this part of the garden again for a week or two. In some places flooding will be the best method. In others the procedure will be like irrigating. In this case shallow trenches are dug on each side of the row of plants and the hose is allowed to run long enough to soak the subsoil thoroughly. With individual plants, particularly shrubs, make a shallow basin around the crown and let the hose fill it up often enough to allow the water to permeate the subsoil.

Again it cannot be too strongly emphasized that the value of this irrigation will be greatly prolonged by cultivating as soon as the surface has sufficiently dried out. If the expense were not too great, an ideal system of supplying moisture would be to have irrigation pipes well under ground, so that the water would immediately reach the place where it is most needed. In a small way an approximation to this is reached where a careful gardener, to provide moisture for some cherished plant, will sink a can with perforated base in the ground near it and will occasionally fill this with water. Or drain pipes may be sunk at intervals through a bed and the hose allowed to run for a while in each one of these. It is to such careful watering that one Berkeley gardener largely attributes his great success in growing and flowering the difficult *Lilium Humboldti.*

Plants cannot grow well in wet, sour soil. Where drainage is poor something may be done by planting in raised beds, so arranging the paths that the run-off will be carried away. But this will not be effective in all cases, and the conditions must then be remedied by providing drainage, preferably with tile, but where this is not possible by using broken stone.

INCREASING AND MULTIPLYING

There are many ways of securing or increasing plants. These processes are generally referred to as plant propagation. Nature's commonest method is by seed, and we shall first consider this way, though we shall attempt to improve on natural conditions, for all gardening does that.

Propagation by seed is the accepted method for obtaining all annuals. It is also an excellent way to raise at small cost large numbers of hardy perennials, always keeping in mind that in some families, such as the Irises and the Chrysanthemums, it is not easy to get in this way seedlings equal to the fine named kinds which are the survivors of generations of garden selection. Species will, however, come true, and in addition fine plants in a wide range of color may be had from sowing seed of such garden plants as the long-spurred Columbines or the tall perennial Larkspurs. In such cases, on the quality of the seed a great deal depends.

Neither is it difficult to raise from seed many of the

popular bulbous plants, Freesias, Ranunculus, Anemones, Gladioli, and others less known. The several years generally required to bring Daffodils, Tulips, and Lilies to the flowering age from seed discourages any but the breeder. The present difficulty of getting many of the lesser bulbs from abroad suggests the possibility of using this method.

Shrubs and trees are not generally easy to start from seed, and they take so long to reach any size that he who needs only a few will be willing to pay the nurseryman to save him the time and trouble. In some cases, as with such berry-bearing shrubs as the Cotoneasters and Pyracanthas, or with the members of the Broom family, germination and early growth are so rapid that this is an easy and inexpensive way to get a stock of plants.

SEED SOWING

In nature all seeds are sown in the open ground, and those which do not happen to get the conditions necessary for germination and growth perish. Where we sow in the open ground we should note some of the factors which promote good germination. Most important of these are moisture in the soil and an absence of the cold or hot winds which dry out the soil or kill the young seedlings.

In California it is with the first fall rains that we find these conditions in nature, and it is then that our many beautiful native annuals come up. Where soft rains are followed by balmy, windless weather the germination is good, but we have all seen a blasting north wind and a long dry spell follow such a rain and quite prevent germination or destroy any precocious seedlings.

Following nature, in our climate fall is certainly the best time to sow hardy annuals in the open ground. In that way we may get large returns in spring flowers from comparatively little effort. There are also some annuals which transplant so poorly that they are far better sown where they are to flower —Eschscholtzias, Poppies, Candytuft, Centaurea, and Mignonette are instances. While there is always an element of risk in it, the gamble will be much more in our favor if before sowing we prepare the ground and after sowing by fine spraying insure adequate moisture even should the rains fail us. It is also possible somewhat to reduce the chances of the ground's drying out by spreading on the surface a very light covering of straw or grass, as is frequently done to assist the germination of grass seed, but care must be taken to remove this the moment the seedlings come through the ground. Burlap or muslin shades will answer the same purpose.

If the plants are not to be allowed to grow where they germinate, or if the seed sowing is to be done at any time during the year, it will be better carefully to prepare seed-beds in a shaded portion of the garden, providing the light sandy soil, shade, and moisture necessary to germination and early growth. These can be more easily given where the seed-raising processes are confined to a small space.

There is another way of starting seeds which is not only more economical in effort but more certain in its results, that is, sowing them in boxes. In this less prepared soil is required, moisture and shade can be more easily controlled, if the plants are to be pricked out into other boxes this can be done without the necessity of working on the ground, and, lastly, the boxes of young seedlings can be moved to wherever they are needed. The boxes need not be over three inches in depth, and should be of a size convenient to handle, say fifteen by twenty-four inches. The wooden boxes in which canned goods are generally packed will make excellent seed-flats if cut down to about three inches deep. Unless there are cracks in the bottom, half-a-dozen holes should be bored with an auger, and these should be covered with pieces of flower-pot or thin stones to prevent the escape of the soil. The soil should both be sandy and have considerable humus in it, so that it will both drain well and yet retain moisture. Either leaf-mold or very old rotted manure is a good source of humus. The soil should be just pleasantly damp when it is put in the boxes, enough so that it will not stick to the hands. If too dry it is impossible to wet it properly after sowing without washing out the seeds; if too wet it will certainly pack too tightly and cake. The two inches of soil at the bottom of the box may well be less finely pulverized than the layer on top, in which the seed will be sown. To remove stones and lumps use a small sieve, which can easily be made by knocking the bottom out of a small box and replacing it with wire screening. The soil should not reach the top of the box by about half an inch, and care should be taken to see that it is well packed around the edges of the box and quite level on top. For this purpose use a float, simply made from a piece of smooth board about an inch in thickness, say four inches by eight, nailing a smaller piece in the centre of the top for a handle. A perfect level is important because otherwise in watering the moisture will accumulate in one place.

In sowing the seed it is doubtful if there is any better way than scattering it direct from one end of the opened packet, though this requires a little skill. Above all things do not sow too thickly, as this makes the seedlings leggy and difficult to transplant later. If the seeds are very minute the chances of scattering them evenly will be greatly increased if they are thoroughly mixed with a greater quantity of dry sand. This gives greater bulk to scatter, and the light color of the sand gives some evidence of how well they are distributed. With seeds which are not too small, one can look over the flat and by the aid of a match or toothpick thin out where too thick into places where none have fallen. The general rule for covering is to have seeds from three to five times their own diameter under ground. Such rules cannot be actually adhered to in practice, and with some very fine seeds, such as those of the Petunia, only such a sprinkling of soil as is necessary to cover them will be given. After sowing and covering, firm the soil again with the float, and water gently with a pot

having a fine rose.   Should this not be handy, one may
with greater patience use a whisk broom.

All seed sowings should be marked with the name of
the variety and the date of sowing.   Where flats are
used, the seed packet may be tacked to the box to
indicate what has been sown, or, if several varieties are
in the same box, labels must be used.   It is desirable
to sow in the same box only seeds which require the
same conditions and the same length of time for germination.   With many annuals this will occur within
a week, but some take longer.   Many will germinate
more quickly if they have been soaked in tepid water
for several hours before planting.   This is, however,
more generally advisable with larger seeds, such as
Nasturtiums and Sweet Peas, which are generally
sown in the open ground.   Where several varieties of
Snapdragons, Zinnias, or other popular plants are sown
in the same box, wooden divisions an inch deep should
separate the surface soil, as otherwise seeds may wash
all over the box.   At an early stage there is no means of
telling varieties apart excepting that a few annuals
such as Snapdragons and Cosmos will have green seed-
leaves for pale-flowered forms and reddish ones for the
dark varieties.

SHADE AND WATER

The grower will have to learn by experience the
amount of shading and watering required for the best
germination of different species.   Some, such as Pansies, must never be allowed to become dry or germina-

tion will fail. On the other hand, Stocks are liable to perish by the fungus known as damping-off if the seed-boxes are kept too wet. It may, however, be taken as a rule that once germination has occurred the seed-boxes should gradually be exposed to sunlight so as to prevent the plants from becoming drawn and spindling. Watch out for this, as a single day's delay may be serious.

Germination with such easy annuals as Snapdragons, Pansies, and Salpiglossis will be great, hence the warning about thin sowing. If the plants are to be moved directly from the seed-boxes to the open ground, a good deal of thinning will be necessary to make the seedlings strong and stocky enough for this treatment. In most cases success, or a much greater measure of it, will follow if, instead of doing this, other flats are filled with fine soil and used as a halfway house for the seedlings, a specially favorable place where they may spend the first few critical weeks of their lives. This is called pricking out.

Scoop out a handful of soil filled with seedlings and loosen it up so that each one may be gently taken out of it with the least possible laceration of the little roots. With the aid of a peg or a plant-label make a hole in the soil of the newly prepared flat, and, holding the plantlet by its top, drop the roots into the hole, then complete the operation by pressing the soil together around it. In this transplanting each seedling should be an inch away from its neighbor. Where each seedling has been conserved by this method it is astonishing what a number of plants may be obtained from a single sowing; a flat twelve inches by twenty-four will produce two or three hundred Pansy plants, and with some of the finer seeds the number will be embarrassing.

An alternate method to pricking out into flats is potting up the young seedlings. The process is just the same, but the expense of the pots and the greater rapidity with which seedlings dry out in them makes it less desirable for annuals or perennials.

The flats of pricked-out plants should be watered and kept from too great sunlight until they have become established. In due time, when they have made sufficient growth, they may be transferred to where they are wanted to flower, and as each can then be moved with ample soil around the roots there should be practically no casualties whatever.

The seed of many of the common annuals will germinate even when it has been kept for two or three years, but the percentage declines rapidly with age. It is, however, handy to know that where a seed packet contains more than is needed in one season it is often worth while saving some for another year.

Hardy perennial plants are less quick and regular in their germination than annuals; even such easy subjects as Columbines and Delphiniums generally take three or four weeks to come up. But apart from this most of them present few difficulties. With shrub and tree seeds the time required is usually still longer; with some species a whole season elapsing before the plants ap-

A small house of desert type of architecture appropriately planted with Agaves, Yuccas, Cactus, and a few shrubs. Mesembryanthemum instead of grass as a ground-cover

Simple but appropriate planting of adjoining houses in beautiful St. Francis Wood, San Francisco. The plants of the parking have the effect of completing the framing of the small lawn.

pear. For this reason seeds of shrubs and trees are often sown outdoors in a protected place, sometimes in frames shaded with lath shutters.

PROPAGATION BY CUTTINGS

For the propagation of selected forms of herbaceous plants which do not come true from seed, or to raise more than can be secured by division of the plant, green cuttings are used. Among the many plants which may be increased in this way are the Geraniums, Chrysanthemums, Coleus, Begonias, Pinks, Heliotrope, Pentstemons, *Nepeta Mussini,* and Calceolaria. Such cuttings should always be taken from young, vigorous, short-jointed growth. The ends of unbloomed shoots are best, in particular those which spring up after the plant has been cut back. Old and tough or thin and sappy growth is unsuitable. A fair test is that when bent the shoot be brittle enough to break. The pieces selected should be severed from the plant with a sharp, clean cut below a joint. Length will vary from an inch and a half to about three inches, the plan generally being to have cuttings with two or three joints. Remove the leaves from the two lowest joints and shorten back those which come from the top one.

Green cuttings may be rooted either in a specially prepared cutting-bed, in boxes, or in pots. In all cases either pure sand or very sandy soil free of organic matter should be used. The cuttings may be placed quite close together, an inch or two apart, and the two lower joints buried in the soil. Do not force the cutting into it, but make a hole with a peg, drop the cutting into it, and press the soil around with the fingers. The ideal conditions for rooting green cuttings are only to be found in greenhouses, where the hot-water pipes under the cutting-bench keep the soil warm and induce root production, and where the close, humid atmosphere prevents drying out and wilting.

A carefully handled hotbed is also a great help, but as neither of these is commonly to be found in small gardens the average amateur must do the best he can without them. The desirable bottom heat cannot be supplied, but some degree of still, moist atmosphere will be assured if the gardener can have a frame for his cuttings. Surround a bed with a wooden frame about eight inches high and cover it with an old window, and it will do the work just as well as a more expensive frame. Where comparatively few cuttings are to be made, bell glasses or even large gem jars will serve. Without any of these aids one may get plants from cuttings of Geraniums and other easily rooting herbaceous plants. Try, however, to keep the cutting-bed moist and away from drying winds.

It is impossible to make positive statements as to the length of time required to make roots, for this is wholly dependent on conditions. When top growth shows that this has occurred, lift the cuttings by levering them from underneath. Do not pull them up by the tops and thus damage the very tender rootlets. Most herbaceous cuttings will be the better for being potted up or grown on in a well-prepared and protected bed before they are subjected to the bright sunshine and competition with other plants of the flower border.

HARD WOOD CUTTINGS

Certain shrubs, trees, and vines may be propagated by hard wood cuttings, taken in fall when the growth of the year has been finished. A few of those which can readily be rooted in this way are the Poplars, Willows (both very easy), Lilacs, Quinces, Hydrangeas, Fuchsias, and of course Roses. In this case somewhat longer cuttings, about eight or ten inches, are to be preferred, but, as with green cuttings, they should be severed just beneath a joint or, in the case of side branches, taken off with a heel from the main stem. Remove all leaves on the lower part of the stem and bury the cutting two thirds of its length in sandy soil in a shady place. Hard wood cuttings are generally made in late fall. Calluses will be formed by spring and in some cases sufficient roots to justify potting up, but in other cases it is just as well to leave the cuttings until the succeeding fall, when they will have made such root growth as will allow of moving them direct to the places where they are to be used.

THE LATH-HOUSE

Mention has been made of the assistance in plant propagation to be derived from greenhouses, cold-frames, and lath or muslin shades for seed-beds. Another contrivance which can be very helpful is the lath-house. It has many uses; the filtered sunlight which alone pen-

etrates it gives favorable conditions for the germination
of seeds, the recovery of small plants from pricking out or
potting, the rooting of green cuttings, and the starting
of tuberous Begonias, as well as an agreeable place in
which to grow Ferns and many shade-loving rock plants
and shrubs. The presence of benches on which all
such operations as seed sowing and potting may be
done is a great advantage over the tiresome practice
of kneeling on the ground or stooping over seed-beds.
In its simplest form the lath-house is rectangular, with
a roof which may be either flat or slightly peaked;
practically, a small shed but without its solid roof and
walls. The length may be as desired. Seven feet is a
good width, as that will allow for an aisle of three feet
with a bench of two feet on either side. The height
need not exceed seven or eight feet. Redwood is the
best material for the frame, using 2 x 4's for the supports. Both top and sides will be formed of laths set
their own width apart. It is important that those on
the roof run north and south, and those on the sides
run up and down, as with this arrangement any part
of the interior will get, through the day, a steady alter-
nation of sun and shade. The benches should be of
redwood boards an inch thick, with occasional auger
holes in them to provide drainage. Where the work is
to be done standing or seated on a stool the bench
should not be less than thirty-six inches from the ground.
By nailing a board across the front of the bench support, a bin will be formed beneath which may be used
for the storage of pots and prepared soil. The house

should be provided with a door, which also should be lathed, so as to keep out birds and animals.

SUCKERS, OFFSETS, AND LAYERS

Some shrubs have the habit of producing suckers and offsets. Such are *Kerria japonica, Viburnum tinus* (Laurustinus), and *Abelia grandiflora*. Others occasionally root where a branch rests on the ground, as happens when *Cotoneaster microphylla* or *Juniperus Sabina* is grown on a hillside. In all cases the rooted piece may be detached from the main plant, the top trimmed back somewhat, any broken roots removed, and the new shrub started out for itself. This operation is best done in fall and winter. It is often possible to induce such rooting as the latter by pegging down to the ground (technically "layering") branches, and assisting the rooting process by making a longitudinal cut part through the portion of the stem which is to be buried in the soil. This injury promotes root-making, but the cut should in no case sever the branch, as for a long time it will be dependent on the parent for life. This method is very successful with Azaleas and Rhododendrons.

A great many hardy herbaceous plants can be most easily increased by removing offsets, or, where many plants are desired, digging up a clump and carefully dividing it into as many pieces as have roots. It is thus that fine garden forms of Iris, Phlox, Geum, perennial Sunflowers, Hemerocallis, and Michaelmas Daisies, to name only a few, are increased. The process is so evidently simple that the only warning necessary is not to chop the clump to pieces with a spade but to shake off the soil and, with the aid of a sharp knife when necessary, to divide it carefully with as little damage as possible.

MULTIPLYING BULBS

The stock of bulbous plants is increased by detaching the little bulblets which will be found around the blooming bulbs when they are dug up after ripening. These will always come absolutely true to the parent. The gardener who is willing to give the time to growing them on to a flowering size should plant these little bulbs close together in some inconspicuous place where they may be left until they reach the adult stage. The time varies greatly in different species. With the Gladioli and all the South African bulbs small flowers are often produced the year the bulblets are planted. With small Tulips or Daffodils the time needed is longer but the ultimate result just as certain.

BUDDING AND GRAFTING

As a means of propagating, budding is largely confined to Rose bushes and their botanical allies the fruit trees. The advantages of the process are the quickness with which some particularly desirable variety may be perpetuated without variation on ready-made roots, or the greater vigor which may be added to some fine kind by putting it on a specially adapted wild stock. It is also used to replace with a more desirable variety one which is established but no longer wanted. The process is simple, but for the greatest success speed and dexterity are necessary. The operation must be performed when sap movement is active; spring or fall is best, but it is also possible in summer. On the stock plant make, to the depth of the bark only, two cuts, one lengthwise and the other across it, so that these cuts form an incision like a plus sign or the letter T. The bud should be cut by having a sharp knife enter the bark some distance below the bud, cutting gradually in under it and coming to the surface in a similar way above the bud. Thus, to avoid injuring the bud, a small piece of wood will have been left adhering beneath it. This must be carefully removed before the bud is inserted. With the handle of the budding-knife lift the bark where the incision has been made in the stock. If this cannot readily be done, the time chosen for the operation is unfavorable. When the bud has been gently inserted with as little friction as possible, the bark should be put back in place and the bud made secure by binding the stem above and below with muslin or soft cord. When by its evident growth it is seen that the bud has taken, the binding should be loosened and the stem of the stock should be cut back close above the bud so as to throw the energy of the plant into it.

SIZE AND FORM OF THE HOLE

There are certain other garden processes which deserve mention. The planting of annuals, perennials, and bulbs is a very simple matter, as they generally **go** into soil already prepared by digging and levelling. But even with herbaceous material it is highly desirable to make the hole ample in size, to bury the plant no deeper than it was previously, and to make the soil quite firm around the roots or the ball of earth which contains them. This last is quite important, as failure to connect the plant closely with the surrounding soil will often result in its drying out before spreading growth starts. Where the ground is very dry at planting time it is a good plan to turn the hose into the hole and soak the subsoil some time before planting. With trees and shrubs it is particularly worth while digging large, deep, square holes, and, in the case of those whose roots are bare, spreading them carefully before filling in with good soil. The advantage of a square hole over a round one is that the roots are less likely to confine themselves to the limits of the hole. For drainage it is better to have the bottom of the hole slightly convex. With potted material, crocks should be removed in planting and a slight loosening of some of the outside roots will be of assistance. It is best to remove cans before planting where plants are received in them; it is generally done by cutting the container, unfortunately not always an easy job. Owing to this difficulty, it is a consolation to know that if the plants are put in cans and all with a few holes punched in the bottom, the cans will soon disintegrate. With balled plants wrapped in burlap it is quite unnecessary and sometimes disastrous to remove the covering. It will soon rot. In transplanting from the open ground it should be recognized that there is considerable shock, and that shrubs and even herbaceous plants, if in growth, will be helped by removal of a good deal of the top and some shortening back of the longer roots.

After planting, if the weather is warm or drying, the small plants especially will appreciate some protection, even though it be only that of a strawberry-box, a flower-pot, or a shingle stuck into the ground on the sunny side. Where hard, cold winds make the starting of more delicate shrubs a matter of some difficulty, as, for example, near the seashore, they may be protected by driving in two stout stakes on the windward side and nailing burlap across them. Where planting is done in summer a light mulch of grass or hay is of great assistance in conserving the essential moisture.

STAKES AND LABELS

Staking should always be promptly attended to. The absence of summer rains spares us much labor in this respect, when dealing with tall herbaceous plants such as Delphiniums and Hollyhocks, but particularly in windy places there is danger of young trees and tall shrubs blowing over before well established. The staking of special plants will be mentioned in dealing with their culture. Here I would merely draw attention to the value of bamboo for this purpose, to the advisability of using soft material for tying, and to the necessity of so tying brittle plants to the stake that a heavy head will not be so left that it is apt to be snapped off.

Cheap but sightly and permanent labels for the open ground have yet to be invented. Embossed zinc or aluminum names may be obtained to order, at from two to three cents, but with these one must also have heavy wire stakes to which they may be attached. They are, however, unobtrusive and permanent. A simpler method is to use small strips of zinc, writing the names on the upper end with the special inks made for this purpose. These will remain legible for several years. Wooden labels are more obtrusive, less legible, and less permanent. Redwood lasts very much better in the ground than do most woods. Painting both retards decay and makes writing legible for a longer time, particularly when this is done before the paint is quite dry. There is much to be said for careful planting plans and diagrams, either to supplement labels or as a substitute for them, this being most true in the collector's garden, where there are many varieties of some special plant.

When once established, herbaceous plants need little further attention. It is important to recognize that their business in life is to propagate themselves, and that only by the prompt removal of seed-pods can one induce them to keep on producing flowers. A few minutes each day in the garden with a pair of scissors will not only keep many plants neater by the removal of the dying flower-heads but will also prolong the season of bloom by preventing the formation of seed. Most annuals if allowed their own way would soon go to seed; some, such as Poppies, Candytuft, and others which flower in spring, have short seasons which cannot be prolonged. Many herbaceous perennial plants if their stems are cut back almost to the ground after their first flowering will make new foliage and excellent secondary displays of bloom. Delphinium, *Anchusa italica*, Pinks, *Nepeta Mussini*, to mention only a few, will do this.

The pruning of shrubs is by no means a simple matter. This may help to explain the crass ignorance regarding its proper practice on the part of the day-laborers who so often sell their services as skilled gardeners, and whose custom it is simply to shear or cut back without regard to the nature of the plant, the object of the pruning, or the probable results. Most deciduous flowering trees and shrubs can be covered by a single rule. The object here is chiefly to induce strong new growth which will bear flowers the succeeding season, in the vast majority of cases the spring. The pruning with this class should always follow the flowering season and will consist mainly in cutting back those branches which have bloomed. If this pruning is done in fall, the spring show of Spiræas, Weigelas, Lilacs, and flowering fruits will be lost.

With evergreen shrubs the practice must be greatly varied because not only are the materials more diverse but the objects to be attained differ greatly. We have many vigorous, rather rampant evergreens of quick growth and somewhat soft wood. Such are the Escallonias, Lantanas, Veronicas, Iochromas, and *Plumbago capensis*, all shrubs which tend to become straggly in

growth.   With them, complete renovation is the object,
as this will not only bring them to the desired size and
shape but will produce an abundance of new shoots and
a consequent finer display of flowers.   Cut them to
within two or three feet of the ground in late winter,
not every year but at intervals as they seem to need it.

Most other evergreens are best handled by selective
thinning or by heading back.   The object of selective
thinning, that is, taking out stems which have already
flowered, is to stimulate the production of new growth
which will ultimately bear blossoms, to keep the plant
from growing too large, and to admit light and air to
the centre of the plant and so encourage new and fresh
foliage.   Shearing fails to accomplish this and moreover
changes the natural, often beautiful, shape of the plant.
This thinning out is a process similar to the pruning of
deciduous shrubs, and is likewise best done immediately
after the season of bloom.   *Abelia grandiflora* is a good
example of a shrub which should get this treatment.
This is also the best method for berry-bearing shrubs,
but the pruning can here be delayed until late winter,
thus making the fruits available for decoration.

Heading back is the term applied to the removal of
the ends of those stems which have bloomed.   It stim-
ulates the production of strong new shoots from the
remaining part of the stem, thus providing new flowering growth, thickening the foliage, and keeping the
plant compact.   Some of the shrubs which should
be so treated are the Brooms, Barberries, *Choisya
ternata*, Ericas, *Diosma ericoides*, and shrubs such as the

Hakeas, grown wholly for the beauty of their foliage.
Many of these have several periods of bloom, and the
cutting back may be done after any of them. In using
any of these methods, care should be taken to remove
dead wood, or that so weak as to be incapable of producing bloom.

The term pruning is not generally applied to that
shearing or clipping necessary to give the even surface
or desired shape to a hedge. This clipping process is
done with special tools, and for the best results hedges
should be gone over two or three times a year.

COMMON INSECTS AND DISEASES

It is not surprising that where the climate is so pleasing to plants and to man, insect life should also be very
abundant and certain rusts and mildews should worry
the gardener. The best preventive is to keep up vigorous growth, as strong, healthy plants resist blights and
more readily withstand the attacks of insects. Keeping the garden clean is also a great help; the prompt
removal and burning of parts of plants affected by rusts
or scale will prevent the spread of these, and the absence of weeds and vegetable refuse around the garden
will make it a less attractive and habitable place for
slugs and snails, which do not like the bright sunshine.
Our seedsmen offer both the apparatus and the insecticides and spraying mixture needed to combat the
pests most commonly found in our gardens. Therefore
only general advice will be given here.

Our commonest enemy is the aphis, the green

members of which family often cover the stems and buds of our Rose bushes and other plants. The use of the hose with a strong spray will often suffice to discourage both these plant lice and the red spider, but tobacco powder and nicotine solutions are used with great success.

Members of the caterpillar tribe are got rid of by hand picking or by dusting with Paris green. In the case of infested Oaks an expert should be called in to spray them in late winter.

Slugs and snails are a curse, particularly in old and shady gardens. They are difficult to get rid of. The large number of remedies suggested merely goes to show that we have here an unsolved problem. Certainly they can be reduced in numbers by trapping with leaves of lettuce or cabbage placed in the garden in the evening. In the morning the insects may be killed. They will also take refuge during the day under boards. When they attack some cherished plant, visit it at night with a light and destroy them at their work. Powdered lime strewn on the ground and around plants will destroy any slugs with which it comes in contact but our frequent winter rains greatly reduce its efficacy. Slugs will not crawl over rough surfaces, and a ring of rough coal-ashes around a plant will serve to protect it. They are particularly fond of Delphiniums, and in one badly infested neighborhood the only method which would keep them away from these plants proved to be putting a collar of wire netting around the base of each. With snails which have a protective shell, hand picking

is the best method. If we could only cultivate the
French appetite for them we might have more help in
collecting them.

GOPHERS, MOLES, AND GROUND-SQUIRRELS

Gophers, moles, and ground-squirrels do much
damage, especially in newer residential districts. Moles
are carnivorous only. The damage which they do is
incidental to their search for food, in that they make
tunnels and loosen up the soil under growing plants,
often leaving the roots suspended where they can get
no sustenance. It is sometimes possible to dig them
out as they are seen at work, but the best way is to get
a good mole-trap and go after them.

Ground-squirrels do not do a great deal of damage.
They are best destroyed by throwing poisoned grain
into their burrows during the dry season, or by the use
of gas bombs, which are most effective when the
ground is wet. Both these methods are also used with
the common pocket gopher, which is much more
destructive than any other garden rodent as he is a
vegetarian with a fine appetite and a taste for Tulips,
Spanish Iris, Dahlias, Pinks, and innumerable other
herbaceous things. He is also very apt to gnaw off the
roots of anything obstructing his underground way.
This is most distressing, and in a badly infested garden
it may well be worth while in planting Rose bushes and
small trees and shrubs to line the hole with chicken-
wire or put an underground collar of it around the
roots. Contrary to general belief, gophers are stupid,

animals, and no great skill is required to trap them. The essential is to discover the main run, open it up as one would a quarry, and place a trap in each of the two exposed tunnels, tying them together or to a stake so that they cannot be dragged away. A few lettuce leaves placed just back of the traps for bait, and a sack to cover the hole, will complete the preparation. It is a waste of time to put traps in the side passages which gophers so frequently make for the purpose of getting rid of soil. Disregard these, and, taking a strong stick, press it into the ground in the vicinity until by its sudden sinking the main passage is discovered.

(*Upper*) This pleasant little formal garden in Pasadena, designed by Miss Florence Yoch, has the qualities of flatness and simplicity desirable in a small place. Its Box-bordered beds provide place for flowers through the year.

(*Lower*) In the front planting of this house, slightly higher than the street, the always presentable evergreen shrubs are grown at the base of the house and patio walls, and to soften the lines of the low retaining wall.

(*Upper*) A flagged walk, softened by a border of the
Mexican Daisy, Erigeron mucronatus, accords with the
informal planting.

(*Lower*) Cement garden walls make good backgrounds
for evergreen shrubs, can be had at once, and never rob
the plants near by as do some hedges.

CHAPTER III

PLANNING THE SMALL GARDEN

THE rare person who has the temerity to begin the building of a house without making, or having made for him, a careful plan of the structure is generally considered highly irresponsible. Is not this criticism equally applicable to the casual individual who starts on his garden without the remotest idea of how he will finish it, often with no consideration of what he wants, or of what he can get out of his property? Before he realizes it his place becomes a conglomeration of casually acquired material, arranged with no law or order, not beautiful in itself, not pleasant to live in, and adding nothing as a setting for his house. He has, moreover, in all probability put trees or shrubs in places which they will outgrow, and perhaps put bulbs and flowers in situations to which they are not adapted, and his garden is in a continual state of being changed, always failing of the repose which comes with order, and never entirely satisfactory because every alteration is a compromise with existing conditions, due to his disinclination to give up the years of growth acquired by shrubs or plants wrongly placed to begin with.

Compare this sad picture with the prospects of the man who has had a plan in mind from the beginning, even locating his house on the lot with reference to the garden that is to be. Should the cost of his house exceed his expectations, as so frequently happens, he may not be able to carry out completely the plans which have been prepared for his garden, but with its future mapped out before him he will throw no obstacles in the path of its development, and each step he takes will be one toward the realization of his scheme. If he be wise, his first expenditures will be for those plant materials which take years to make the desired effect, for trees, vines, and shrubs, all of which will fall into their appointed places. His early work in the greater part of the garden may have to be crude and largely with the less costly materials, but his rough paths will be along the lines laid out, and his flower-beds, bright with inexpensive annuals, will be where he at some time hopes to have more interest- ing bulbs and perennials. Each year something can be added, as in furnishing a house, and the pleasure will be a continuous one in that he sees progress being made toward an ideal. Garden accessories are rather costly, and that summerhouse which would be the natural ter- minus of a main path may not be possible now—a simple bench may be all that can be afforded at present—but with a plan the path will be right and planting can be done so that when a summerhouse becomes a possibility it will soon fit into the place already prepared for it.

GETTING ADVICE IN TIME

It is not within the scope of this little book either to give at length the principles of landscape architecture, on which many books have been written, or to compete with the landscape architect in offering plans for gardens. The gardener should rather, after long and careful study of the principles involved and preferably also after having examined good gardens approximating his own in size, make a plan of his place for himself, or better, if he can afford it, call into consultation an expert who will at least start him right. There are so many spurious landscape gardeners, perhaps excellent workmen but without the knowledge, the training, or the necessary taste for this work, that I cannot too strongly urge that when advice or a plan is being purchased a person known to be an expert be employed. The satisfaction given by his plan will be remembered long after the slightly greater cost of his services has been forgotten.

Ready-made or stock plans can never be entirely satisfactory. Good ones may be very useful in showing how the principles of design may be carried out on a given plot; the study of them may be very helpful and suggestive, but it is inherent in them that they cannot have taken into consideration varying contours, different exposures, conditions of soil, prevailing winds, heat and cold, and other climatic factors. The principles of garden design are independent of country or climate, and for purposes of inspiration a good plan is valuable everywhere. If plant materials are suggested, however, their perfect applicability to any particular garden must be carefully questioned.

The landscape architect, no matter how small a place

he may be planning, will always prefer to visit it, to examine its contours, or even if it be perfectly level to give careful consideration to the other factors mentioned. Moreover, like a good architect, he will endeavor to acquaint himself with the interests and pursuits of his client, so as to provide him with a garden which will be adapted to his needs and will in some measure reflect his personality.

It is this careful consideration of individual preferences which has made it possible for some very interested amateurs to plan their own small gardens so successfully. The secret of their success was the intense preoccupation with their personal problem and the study of all matters which in any way affected it. For just as individuals have varying interests, so should their gardens express these interests. The purpose of one man may be merely to present as good a front to the street as possible. He will naturally be ready to give up much of his property to a front lawn and to spend considerable money for the purchase of fine trees and shrubs to set off his house. To him the space in the rear may be of no value except for drying clothes or other household purposes, and he will be unwilling to spend either time or money in its development.

Another man may look upon his garden as an outdoor living room, or if it be large enough as a series of these, each with its different interest or purpose. He will either so screen the plot in front of his house as to secure some privacy, or, much more probably, he will endeavor to reduce the size of this more public part so as to give him more ample room in the secluded rear garden. Where his property is large enough he may have a further and different garden to one side of his house but with such planting between it and the front of the place as to allow him great privacy. Such a man will build high walls, or will give much attention to the planting of boundaries. He will use more trees and shrubs than flowers, and may consider the trouble and cost of maintaining lawns as well paid for in the greater comfort of the place. To him garden furniture, summerhouses, pergolas, pools, or running water will especially appeal, as all these add to the pleasure of living in a garden.

The flower-lover gets his greatest satisfaction in flowers at all seasons of the year, lots of them, in many varieties and well taken care of. To satisfy this desire he may have to give practically all his space to them, and may eliminate lawns as a waste of room and trees because their shade or their roots would be a hindrance to the flowers. Sometimes the flower-lover becomes a specialist, centring his interests on a single flower and subordinating landscape effect to the exigencies of a collection.

Inasmuch as the excuse for a garden is the pleasure which it gives to the owner and his family, all of these aims are equally legitimate. Of course compromises and combinations of these purposes are often found, where conflicting claims have to be satisfied. In a small place it is generally quite impossible to do everything, and as simplicity of design should be the keynote in arrangement, simplicity of purpose will be one of the greatest elements of success.

Further, a site will often have an individuality of its own which merits first consideration, some unique feature which deserves development, or some seeming obstacle which may be turned into an asset. Where this is the case, if the owner is to have the best possible garden on the site he may have to modify his wishes to conform to the natural possibilities of the place. For this reason, before purchasing a property it is well to consider its garden possibilities. To illustrate, a friend of mine, a good amateur gardener, had a choice of three small properties offered him. Each was about one hundred feet square. One was in a tract which had originally been a grove of native evergreen Scrub Oaks, still preserved in subdividing. The soil was light and composed almost wholly of leaf-mold: the ground was strewn with boulders and occasionally there were out-croppings of rock, picturesque and covered with beautiful green moss through the colder months. The second property was on a rather steep side hill, sloping to the west and with a wonderful view its main attraction, quite bare of trees, and with a layer of sometimes only eighteen inches of clay loam over the hardpan. The third offered the easiest building site, a level lot with no striking features of any kind.

If he bought the first he would want of course to save that part containing the finest trees and most pictur-

esque rocks for his garden. He would perhaps put his
house to one side so as to allow as large a part as possible to retain its natural beauty. This beauty he would
develop by removing the weaker trees, allowing the
finest ones better growth and letting in some sunshine.
He would endeavor to learn what shrubs and flowers
were best adapted to such woodland conditions, aiming
to keep in all his gardening the note set by nature.
Ferns, Fuchsias, Azaleas, Foxgloves, Columbines,
Japanese Anemones, Primroses, Forget-me-Nots,
spring-flowering bulbs, and shade-loving rock plants
would be the material for his garden pictures.

If he chose the second, unless able to afford the construction of a series of expensive terraces, his best plan
would be an informal treatment, with shrubs and trees
around the edges to frame the property. The combination of slope and western aspect would furnish a serious problem in the selection of materials which would
withstand the inevitable summer drought. This would
be simplest with the trees and shrubs, whose roots
would naturally go deep, but even here sun-loving
plants such as the Brooms and Cistuses would be particularly happy. On the slopes, dwarf shrubbery and
drought-resistant creepers would be used instead of
grass. If he were willing to have his main display of
flowers in spring he would find his task very much
easier. Flowering fruit trees, spring bulbs, sun-loving
rock plants, and fall-sown annuals would be largely
used. Of all the hardy perennials he would find the tall
Bearded Iris much the most satisfactory. He would

restrict his summer flower display to a few spots where
the ground could be kept moist, but even on the dry
slopes Lavender, Salvias, and *Zauschneria californica*
would give him bright color. In fall, berry-bearing
shrubs and pompon Chrysanthemums could be had.

On the third, the perfectly level lot, he would have
almost complete freedom of choice, and there, after
having planted screens to insure privacy and the ob-
literation of unsightly objects, he could very well lay
out a formal garden, there being no difficulties of contour. This style would allow him equal opportunity
for development as an always sightly outdoor living
room or as a place where great numbers of flowers could
be effectively grown.

There has been much unnecessary argument about
the relative merits of the formal and the informal garden, a good deal of it due to confusion of terms. The
advocate of the first has in mind the advantages of
form or design in what he feels is distinctly an art. The
man who opposes him frequently does so because of
a fixed idea that the term formal garden means the
torturing of shrubs into artificial forms, the perfect bal-
ancing of all plant materials, and the use of character-
less bedding-plants arranged in geometrical designs in
the beds—a centre of pink Geraniums surrounded by
gaudy Coleus and edged with Hen-and-Chickens, what
William Robinson calls "an Italian pastry cook's idea of
beauty."

As a matter of fact, excepting in the most formal of
places, the advocate of design is willing to allow great

leeway in the selection and arrangement of plant material. He feels, however, that there are advantages in a certain formality and symmetry of lay-out, making paths go directly to destinations instead of describing meaningless curves, and having the flower-beds as an integral part of the design. He may feel that the part of a garden which is near the house should be regarded as an extension of it, and may not wish it to simulate a forest any more than he would want the house to be the replica of a cave. He will appreciate the esthetic and the practical advantages of having the main path or axis start from the natural entrance from house to garden and end at a seat or summerhouse, thus focussing the interest within the garden. The formal garden, he will claim, is both easier to design and to plant than one which at best can be merely an attempt to imitate nature, maintaining also that in the small garden, where its boundaries can never really be concealed, there should be a frank recognition that the garden is a work of art, therefore artificial.

Lots are usually rectangular in shape, therefore straight lines will harmonize with the boundaries and will be economical of space. Besides, a methodical arrangement is of great assistance in keeping the garden in order. It also particularly lends itself to the use of pergolas, summerhouses, pools, and other adjuncts which give delight to hours spent in the garden. The spirit of such a garden may be quite the reverse of formal. It may be through a large part of the year the social centre of the home.

In larger places where the gardens often extend far from the house, even out of its sight, there is every reason why the treatment may well melt into the informality of the landscape. As straight lines are not found in nature the plantings of trees and shrubs will assume an informal or picturesque character, and paths among them will follow the natural contours. The feeling of spaciousness contributes to the natural effect of the landscape as no narrow, rectangular city lot could do. In such gardens lawns should not be broken up by flower-beds, but color should be obtained by informal plantings among the shrubbery edging the lawn.

MAKING OUT A PLAN

If the amateur proposes to make his own plan he should first draw to scale the outline of his property, indicating the points of the compass, and putting in the house. Where irregularities of contour exist, these should be indicated. He can then draw in service ways and yard, automobile road and garage. Where these must be provided for it is best to confine them to one side, preferably the north, and to screen them either by trellises or by shrubs and trees. Where the lot is on a corner and access to a garage in the rear may be had from the side street, it simplifies the problem.

Having put down these features on his plan, the next step is to map out the areas to be devoted to lawns, borders, trees and shrubs, and flowers. All paths and beds should be drawn to scale, and all garden accessories should be properly located and indicated on the plan. On the areas to be planted, or preferably on separate enlarged drawings of them, detailed arrangements of all proposed plantings should be made, and lists of the kinds and quantities of materials should be prepared. The need of simplicity has already been emphasized. On a lot measuring fifty by not over a hundred and fifty feet, little more can be done in the front and on the garden side than to put in a lawn and frame it with suitable trees and shrubs. The base of the house should also be screened, preferably with evergreen shrubs of refined growth. The endeavor in these parts of the garden open to the public view should be to keep them always presentable. The use of large numbers of bulbous plants in the foundation beds may give a striking effect for a few weeks, but an unattractive spectacle follows. The real garden will here be behind the house, where privacy is more easily obtained. This side, which the English often call the garden front, can be made most attractive by good gardening. To keep it always presentable it will be well in planning to reserve a small portion at the rear, best shut off by a trellis which may be planted with vines, for garden processes such as raising new plants for use in the garden proper. Where the gardener has a specialty of limited seasonal beauty, such as the Gladiolus, the Iris, or the Dahlia, an alternative use of a screened-off portion would be to devote it wholly to the specialty.

Sometimes a small vegetable garden is to be found

in this relative position. In this last case, by planting a few flowers on each side of the main path, which is commonly visible from the house, a more pleasing vista will be made. The problem of having both a back garden always attractive and pleasant to live in and also a flower garden or a place in which to grow quantities of flowers for cutting is so common that I venture to suggest the solution worked out by a Pasadena amateur.

The house was built as near the street as the setback line permitted, thus allowing as much space as possible behind the house. Two thirds of this area was devoted to one of the most beautiful small formal gardens I have ever seen. Walls on either side were covered with climbing plants, fronted by occasional shrubs of attractive foliage and not too rampant growth. Around four sides ran a straight path edged with *Myrtus microphylla*, kept in bounds by clipping. Between the outer edge of the path and the walls there was room for a few choice flowers to add life and color. The main axis from the porch entrance ran through a small formal pool, surrounded by a beautiful lawn which extended to the side paths. In the corners were Italian Cypresses. Across the back a pergola extended, supporting many beautiful climbers and screening the remaining portion of the grounds. Through the centre of the pergola, on the main axis, was the entrance to the rear garden. Here it was frankly recognized that the growing of flowers for their own sake and for house decoration was the object, and this

could be freely indulged in without regard to the fact
that at certain seasons of the year this portion was very
evidently not at its best.   The impression conveyed by
the formal garden was one of perfection and finish,
of always being ready for the reception of garden
friends, yet the gardener did not have to do without the
many flowers, bulbous and herbaceous, not always
ornamental but very dear to her heart.

PLANNING ON A 100-FOOT LOT

On the lot of fifty-foot frontage the greatest simplicity
of design is essential.   When the frontage is twice as
great, more complexity is permissible, that is, the
garden space, while still planned as a unit, will have
parts more or less screened off for particular purposes
and to add to the interest of the whole.   On a lot a
hundred feet square, with the house set rather to the
front of the northern half and the automobile drive
along the northern boundary, by the informal framing
of the front lawn with trees and shrubs a place will be
provided on the south side of the house where leisure
hours may be pleasantly spent.   This space may be
informally hedged off from the rear garden, and should
be planted in lawn, shaded by an occasional tree or two,
and furnished with comfortable seats.   The wider area
across the rear may either be altogether given to a
flower garden or the smaller part directly behind the
house may be treated in a formal manner, with a sunken
garden, a pool, or a path ending in a summerhouse.
The remaining section of the rear will still be available

for a general flower garden or for a rose-garden or collection of any other specialty.

There are many sources from which the construction of roads and paths may be learned. In California much of the practice may be simplified because of the absence of hard freezing which necessitates thorough foundation work to avoid breaking up. The important thing is to have them properly laid out. Roads and service ways should be as inconspicuously located as possible, and when they do not come directly in front of the house their presence may well be disguised by plantings. In the small garden paths are of relatively greater importance. Having located them so that they have no meaningless meanderings, the question of material must be considered. Cement walks have the advantages of being clean, permanent, and inexpensive, but they have no others. They have no beauty, and their hard and smooth surfaces are inappropriate in the garden. In level gardens gravel is good, but on sloping ground it is liable to wash away. It should have a foundation of larger broken stone so as to provide drainage. In formal work particularly, brick walks are good. They are clean, they dry quickly, and they are of a pleasant warm color. They are less adapted to slopes. For all types of gardens, walks made from flagstones set in no regular pattern are very successful, but unfortunately their cost is practically prohibitive for most people. A substitute is to make similar walks from the large irregular pieces of cement sidewalk quite frequently obtainable, or such pieces may be made in molds on the job. There are places where it would be a pity to cut up a nice piece of lawn by a path, yet access across it during wet weather may be necessary. For such conditions, stepping-stones are the solution, sunk in the sod so that they are just above the surface.

THE LAWN

Fondness for making lawns is not by any means a universal accompaniment to a love of flower growing. Many excellent gardeners regard it as a loathsome task either to make or to take care of grass. Where they feel so and can afford it, it is far better that they employ a competent lawn-maker, for there can be no doubt that a fine lawn is in itself a great asset to any garden and its assistance in bringing out the beauties of trees, shrubs, and flowers can hardly be over-estimated. The making of a good lawn entails much preliminary hard work, and its maintenance continual attention, but the time necessary to get it started is astonishingly short in a country where there is no perennial sod and all lawns are raised from seed. An expert will get germination any time from early spring to late fall, but an amateur had better make his attempt either in spring, preferably March or early April, or else in fall, preferably October. Each season has its advocates, basing their claims on their own conditions or on certain inherent advantages of each season. The advantages of spring sowing are that the ground is then warm, germination and

growth are rapid, and there is no danger of cold
weather killing off the young plants. The drawback
is that the summer drought quickly follows, and before
the young plants have made deep root growth they
must depend wholly on artificial watering. The advantages of fall planting are that the ground is then
more moist, it is the natural season for grass germination in California, and considerable root growth will be
made during the winter in preparation for next summer's drought.

In preparation for a lawn the soil should be well and
thoroughly dug a month or so before it is proposed to
sow seed, and at this time well-rotted manure should be
spread on it and dug in. If this has been wetted
thoroughly and turned over occasionally so that the
weed seeds have germinated and the young plants
burned out, it will cause no trouble by producing
weeds.

After digging, the soil should be raked to a perfect
level, all stones removed, and clods broken up. Firm-
ness is essential, and may be secured by rolling or
thorough tamping. If by this time it has had a
thorough soaking from a rain, leave it until weeds have
germinated, when these should be hoed off. The same
results can be obtained when the weather is dry by a
thorough watering, and if time can be given to allowing
a second germination and hoeing it will save the maker
much future labor.

Before sowing, the surface of the soil should be
made quite fine. Choose a windless day, the early

morning or evening is most likely to be quiet. Scatter the seed as evenly as possible, standing on a board to do the work and withdrawing it as the operation progresses. Authorities differ as to the area of ground on which a pound of seed should be scattered, opinions varying from two hundred to three hundred square feet. Thick sowing is one way of preventing disappointment in the stand secured.

After the seed has been scattered and raked lightly, the greatest percentage of germination will result if a thin mulch of well-rotted manure is sifted over the area sown. Great care should be exercised in the first waterings, using the fine spray but thoroughly soaking the ground. There is great danger before germination of washing out the seeds. In later watering for the maintenance of the lawn the rule should be to so thoroughly soak the ground that the roots will find the moisture from below for some time, thus encouraging deep rooting. Frequent sprinklings merely encourage the formation of surface roots, a very undesirable growth where warm dry summers prevail. As soon as the young grass has made sufficient growth it should be mowed, but not too close to the ground. Rolling is also of great assistance in this early stage of its growth.

There can be no question but that the Kentucky blue grass will make the finest lawn. That it is not universally used is presumably due to its also demanding the finest care. Because it is slow to get established some gardeners believe that the seed should be mixed

with about half its bulk of white clover, as the latter
comes up very readily and shelters the young blue grass,
but gives way to it later. The sowing of lawns exclusively of white clover must be a matter of taste.
It is not to be generally recommended for beauty,
though in sandy soils and where less water can be
supplied it is easier to grow. For a quick, easy lawn
Australian rye is generally used. It has the advantage
of making rapid early growth and it will stand much
abuse, but it will always lack the perfection of a Kentucky
blue grass lawn and as it gets older it has a distressing
tendency to bunch and to make stems as well as grass-
blades in its attempt to bloom. Various mixtures of
grass seed are offered for unusual conditions or places,
such as very sandy soils or shady places.

GRASS SUBSTITUTES

The cost of making and maintaining lawns in a semi-
arid country has naturally resulted in attempting to
find substitutes. From the present writer's view-
point these are all much inferior in beauty and in garden
value to even a mediocre lawn, but they have advocates
even in the landscape profession who will claim that
lawns are not natural to California and that in our
brilliant sunshine the grayer effect of some of the
substitutes is more grateful to the eye. Their greatest
use is unquestionably for the covering of sloping ground,
where lawns are excessively difficult to maintain
through the summer.

It is particularly for situations such as this that

Lippia repens (syn. *L. canescens*) is to be commended, as it is very resistant to drought and spreads rapidly, rooting at every joint. The gray-green foliage is rather dull, and the light purple flowers which appear in summer are of a color not particularly appreciated but they may be easily kept down by mowing. Its drawback is that in winter the stems become rather bare and evident, its limitation that it will withstand very little frost. Seed cannot be obtained, and small plants must be put in, a foot apart, preferably in March.

Another substitute is the native sand-strawberry, *Fragaria chilensis*, also good for slopes. A warm sunny place is excellently adapted to the growing of the various trailing Mesembryanthemums. The large, coarse *M. edule* is fit only for rough places. The smaller-leaved, pink-flowered *M. roseum* spreads widely from its single root, making a thick cushiony cover, almost hidden by starry flowers during its season of bloom. The English Ivy has been much used in a few places as a ground-cover. Its greatest value is for planting in shady places, as for example under trees. It is very sombre in effect and will not endure being walked on.

It must be clearly understood that the planting of a ground-cover does not free the gardener from future responsibility for the appearance of that portion of the ground. The watering necessary to establish the plants or cuttings will inevitably bring up weeds, and until such time as the cover becomes so dense that they may no longer grow, continual attention will be needed to eliminate them.

PLANTING TO FIT THE HOME

The grouping and arrangement of trees and shrubs to frame the lawn, set off the house, give privacy to the property, or plant out undesirable views is a matter in which more can be learned by observation than by precept. To secure a restful and satisfying result, one must first give up all thoughts of growing a large number of species in a small garden, planning rather to select a few of those which are best adapted to one's purpose or to one's garden conditions, and making these groups serve as screen or background. Observation will soon show that some kinds consort well with others, and that some differing too greatly in form or texture of leaf do not blend. The gardener will further note that a broken skyline is beautiful in itself and opens up the possibility of distant vistas. Of course, walls and hedges will frequently take the place of informal boundary plantings, but the former, if beautiful and permanent, are expensive to build, and the latter entail much labor to maintain. They have, however, generally an advantage in taking less room from the garden proper.

Banks and slopes are often regarded by the unimaginative gardener as liabilities rather than assets, but if properly handled they may add great variety to the place. Where the area is not large it may well be used for a rock-garden, and many comparatively small subjects may be grown on it, but where there is more space to cover and a broader treatment becomes necessary there are dozens of low-growing evergreen shrubs which are at their best when so placed. Among these are the prostrate Cotoneasters; the prostrate Juniper; Cistuses, Thymes, and Brooms in variety; Rosemary, Lavender, and Germander (*Teucrium fruticans*); *Coprosma baueri; Sollya heterophylla;* Myrtles, and Barberries. Attractively grouped, these alone would make a bank a thing of beauty.

PROPER USE OF ACCESSORIES

The interest and livableness of a garden can be greatly enhanced by such accessories as bird baths, pools, pergolas, summerhouses, and benches, but there must be a reason for the placing of each one. Meaningless ornaments and superfluous furniture merely litter the garden. An appropriate place for a bird bath or pool is in the centre of the garden or on the axis of the paths. When a wall-fountain or a sundial is preferred, this, like a seat, may often form the terminus of a path. These objects form points of interest and they add animation to the garden by the play of the birds around their bath, the splash or the trickle of the water, and the movement of the sun on the dial. Where sunshine is so prevalent we have the same excuse as the Italians for the free use of the pergola, to provide shade on long walks. Incidentally, it offers the necessary support for beautiful climbing Roses, Wistarias, and other vines, and on either side of its walk are delightful half-shady places offering a refuge from our sometimes fierce sunlight to those plants which cannot perfectly endure it. It is strange that in small gardens the pergola is not more frequently used to secure privacy quickly. By surrounding the small garden on three sides with a pergola, its outer sides covered with wide wooden lattice and its inner ones left quite open to view from within, a delightful feeling of seclusion may at once be secured, a feeling which will increase as vines cover the trellis and ramble over the top. An excellent way to close a vista or end a path is to erect a summerhouse at that point. Careful study of proportions is necessary to make certain that it will be a thing of beauty, but as it will presumably be partly covered with growth, expensive construction and fine finish are not essentials. Every summerhouse should contain a comfortable seat, with which may often be combined a storage place for tools.

A simple bench placed in the shade at the end of a path will many times prove quite as acceptable as the more pretentious summerhouse. In the heat of the late afternoon, when in full sunlight the glare is still strong, what is more delightful than to sit in the shade and look out on a well-ordered garden, beautiful in design and glowing with color, a garden which would not have existed without the work of our head and hands?

CHAPTER IV

Color and Continuity in the Flower Garden

IF THE one wish is for a small garden which is to be pleasing twelve months of the year, this will be best satisfied in a plan where the boundaries will be of evergreen shrubs selected for their not too rampant growth and beauty of foliage rather than for flowers. The centre of such a garden will be of grass rather than flower-beds, for it can be kept green at all times and it is a practical impossibility to keep flower-beds in bloom continuously. In it, attention will not be focussed on a picture created by the adjacent planting of ephemeral flowers of harmonizing colors but again by a permanent feature such as a pool or bird bath. Such a garden may be a pleasant place in which to live, and its appearance will call forth no apologies at any time of the year. This type of garden will, however, fail to satisfy those who love flowers and who prefer the continual development and change whereby they add interest to the garden. Flower-lovers must recognize, however, that without the permanent framework of evergreens a garden would in winter look very bare indeed, and even in summer it would suffer for lack of backgrounds. It must therefore be seen that shrubs are essential to a continuously attractive garden.

But it is not for this purpose alone that one should

employ shrubs, trees, and climbers.   Many of them are
very beautiful when in flower, and are of great assistance
in providing color throughout the year.   For the winter
months we have the Acacias, *Choisya ternata*, the
Japanese Quince, *Berberis Darwini*, and in frostless
areas *Linum flavum* (syn. *L. trigynum*) and the wonderful orange *Bignonia venusta*.   Following them in early
spring come the flowering fruit trees, *Kerria japonica*,
Cestrum elegans, Laurustinus, *Streptosolon Jamesonii*, and
the white Broom.   By March the Wistarias, the white
and the pink *Clematis montana*, and the deep pink form of
the Cherokee Rose (this last in bloom since January) will
be at their best.   In late spring come *Pyrus floribunda*,
most of the deciduous flowering shrubs, and the finest
Roses of the year, *Ceanothus thyrsiflorus*, the Rock
Roses (Cistus), and such Brooms as *Cytisus Scoparius*
and its variety *Andreanus*.   Where they thrive, early
summer is the season of the Rhododendrons and Azaleas.
For midsummer color from shrubs there is nothing
better than Fuchsias and Hydrangeas for cool gardens.
The climbing Lantana, beginning in summer, blooms
for months, and in warm gardens in southern California the bush forms do likewise.   Summer is also the
time of the flowering of Escallonias and Veronicas, and,
among climbers, of the red-purple Bougainvillea and
the scarlet Trumpet-vine.   There are few flowering
shrubs in fall, but *Pyrus angustifolia* and all the Cotoneasters give by their orange or red fruits an effect as
brilliant as that of many flowers.

Most gardeners will be unwilling to restrict themselves to flowers produced by shrubs or climbers, but will want the interest and variety given by bulbs and herbaceous plants, annual or perennial. Here is where selection is all-important, and for this purpose the notes on these plants, their habit, size, and season of bloom, should be studied.

It is easy for any one in California to have a garden full of flowers in spring, and particularly in late April and early May. The Bearded Irises and Columbines are examples of flowers we must have then or never, but the gardener with foresight will realize that if his whole available space is given up to spring-flowering bulbs and perennials the garden will be very dull for the rest of the year in so far as herbaceous flowers are concerned.

To be sure of continuity it is a good plan to pick out certain bulbs and herbaceous plants which in themselves form a sequence, choosing those most effective in the garden and giving each a sufficient opportunity to display its charms. Among bulbs, Daffodils, Tulips, Spanish Iris, Gladioli, and Montbretias would form a sequence, with the tuberous-rooted Cannas and Dahlias to help out in summer. Among biennials and perennials, Wallflowers, Bearded Iris, Delphiniums, Pentstemons, Michaelmas Daisies, Japanese Anemones, and Chrysanthemums would cover the year. The season of annuals may be made to vary by the time of sowing. In southern California, Beauty of Nice Stocks, small-flowering Petunias, Candytuft, Nemesias, Calendulas, and numerous other hardy annuals may be flowered in winter from seed sown in early fall. With

the exception of the Stocks and Calendulas they will
not bloom in the colder parts of California at that time.
In spring, among many we can have Pansies, Verbenas,
Eschscholtzias, and Poppies. In early summer, Lark-
spurs, Clarkias, Godetias; in midsummer, Zinnias,
Salpiglossis, Snapdragons, and in fall China Asters,
Cosmos, and Marigolds.

GETTING MUCH INTO LITTLE SPACE

Devices of various kinds will enable one to have
many flowers in a small space. Keeping the seed from
setting on annuals, cutting back some perennials to
encourage new growth, and the use of the same ground
for succeeding crops of annuals, are some possibilities.
As an example of this last, one may have a winter border
of the Tom Thumb Sweet Alyssum from a fall sowing
in the open ground, and before it goes to seed replace it
with young plants of bedding Lobelias, grown in boxes
or in a reserve garden for this purpose. As suggested
in the planning of a garden, a space set aside for the
raising of plants is practically essential to gardening
of this character. The same ground can also be used
for other successions. A bed which in winter and early
spring is filled with Wallflowers or Stocks can be cleared
in May and replanted with pompon Chrysanthemums
taken from the old stock plants, which may have been
heeled in in any out-of-the-way place since their
blooming the previous fall. Again, the corner which is
gay with Tulips in May can be planted to Dahlias after
the ripened Tulips have been taken out. Where Gladioli

are not to be planted until late April or May there is no reason why a fall sowing of Linaria, the Scarlet Flax, or indeed any early-flowering annual, may not occupy the ground during the winter and give interest in spring.

When it comes to the question of bulbs enthusiasm must be curbed by the sad fact that their season of bloom is comparatively short, and in this type of garden their subsequent appearance is a detriment. There are two alternatives—digging up the bulbs after they have bloomed and ripening them in trenches elsewhere, or interplanting them with light-rooting flowers. I have had good results from different combinations of this kind, for example, in groups of Daffodils, deep-rooting bulbs, I have interplanted Spanish Irises or Ixias, which are more shallow-rooting, while in Tulip beds I find that by cultivating the ground in March and sowing a summer-flowering annual between the already evident leaves of the Tulips I can have a summer crop of flowers without harming the bulbs. There seems no basis of fact in the popular impression that Daffodil or Tulip bulbs are harmed by occasionally watering the ground in summer. One great lesson has to be learned, that if a flower-border is to be kept in even fairly good bloom through many months of the year it should not be restricted to any one class of plants, but should embrace in a catholic manner shrub, perennial, bulb, and annual alike.

MAKING PICTURE GARDENS

One of the most delightful occupations of the present-day gardener is the planning and execution of garden pictures. This involves careful study of the forms and colors of his plant materials and of their seasons of bloom, so that he may group together those which will add to each other's beauty when combined. There have been whole books written on the color arrangement of flower gardens, some indication of the impossibility of adequately treating this subject in the few pages which could be spared in a general book. I have chosen, therefore, rather to make a few suggestions which may stimulate the reader to plan pictures for himself. I have also given the list of plant materials which could be effectively combined in the arrangement of a dry bank to give a cool harmony of lavender, blue, gray, and pink, and in detail a plan for a brilliant red-and-yellow border.

In a large garden there can be flower-borders for the different seasons and for various color schemes. In many small places the whole garden can be seen at a glance, and this naturally imposes certain restrictions. This does not mean that it is necessary to limit the flowers in it at any one season to a single color or to a very narrow range, thus depriving it of much variety, life, and interest, but that large, complicated plans will be far less successful than where a simple programme is adopted. We are less afraid of color to-day. Artists and decorators have shown us that almost any colors of an equal degree of intensity may be attractively combined, providing that one of them is used in sufficient quantity to be clearly dominant. In practice it is astonishing what a medley of color can be pleasingly

used in even a small garden. Certain Geranium reds,
bluish pinks, and red-violets are almost the only
makers of trouble, and in skillful hands any one of
these can be successfully used for simple combinations.
As the aim in the small garden should always be toward
simplicity and restfulness, striped, blotched, and bizarre
flowers are to be shunned, for they do not combine well
with others and they are distracting in themselves.

In a fine old garden far enough north to be favorable
for the scarlet Japanese Quince and the dainty white
Spiræa Thunbergi I saw these two together, the Spiræa
with its tiny flowers and slender growth bringing out the
strength and vividness of its more gorgeous companion.
Rather easier, and even more effective against the
background of an evergreen Oak is an early red-flowering Peach near which has grown a large clump of the
double-flowered *Spiræa prunifolia*, which in California
is often called Bridal Wreath. This semi-double red
Peach, the best in color of the flowering fruit trees,
makes a beautiful picture sheltering under its branches
the fine white Daffodil Seagull, and if one of the early-
flowering forms of the wild Ceanothus is near by its
misty blue will add to the picture; this last is less
essential where the Peach tree is planted so that the
blue sky comes into the composition. The possibility
of naturalizing under our various flowering fruit trees
drifts of spring-flowering bulbs should always be borne
in mind, for not only are delightful combinations of
color to be made, where, for example, the pale pink-
flowering Almond rises over a planting of blue Grape

Hyacinths, but in such arrangements the bulbs may be allowed to remain for years, as in summer the ground is too shaded to be of use. A suggestion of somewhat similar character is to put pink Tulips among plantings of the white Portugal Broom. They flower together, and, as is best in such combinations, the flowers are very different in size and shape. Character will be added to this rather simple combination by a foreground of purple Aubrietias. The beauty of large border plantings of Daffodils will be increased by the use of white and yellow Primroses as an edging in close harmony, or Forget-me-Nots in contrast.

Tulips are more easily handled in groupings than are Daffodils. Try the cottage Tulip Inglescombe Pink, a fine vigorous variety, grouped in front of the lavender *Ceanothus thyrsiflorus*, or, if you prefer combinations with a herbaceous plant, grow the purple Darwin, Mrs. Potter Palmer, behind creamy yellow Wallflowers or the Darwins, Rev. Ewbank and Clara Butt, with the deep garnet Wallflower Miss Willmott. Sometimes pink Tulips of the cottage or Darwin classes will bloom at the same time as the blue and purple *Iris germanica* or the white *Iris albicans*. Where these Irises are in clumps in a border it is worth while trying this grouping, as it is so attractive when it works out.

Countless pictures may be made by grouping other plants with the tall Bearded Irises, available in so many lovely colors. One unpremeditated combination which repeats itself from year to year was due to a clump of *Iris pallida dalmatica* Princess Beatrice happening to find a place in front of a specimen of Bechtel's double-flowering Crab, a very dwarf tree which is covered with pale blossoms of a beautiful pink in spring. For a closer harmony, plant a dark red-purple Iris such as Edouard Michel where it will be seen with the rosy-lilac *Tamarix parviflora*. Some day I hope to plant a number of clumps of *Iris Kochii* with space between them for deep orange Wallflowers. It has been done, with striking results. A somewhat more varied grouping which I have used included the lavender Iris Albert Victor, Petunia Rosy Morn, the white annual *Omphalodes linifolia*, and the lavender *Nepeta Mussini*.

The last mentioned is a Catmint with fine grayish foliage and small lavender flowers on stems which tend to droop. It is a wonderful harmonizer, equally valuable to combine with blues and purples or with rose and pink, an invaluable plant for informal edging, drought-resistant, and giving a secondary crop of flowers if cut back quite hard after its first spring bloom. It is astonishing that gardeners on the Pacific coast make so little use of a plant which is so pleasing in itself and adds so much to the beauty of others.

Of summer groupings I shall mention only two which have been pleasing in my garden: pink Pentstemons grown beside well-established bushes of Lavender, and perennial Larkspurs bordered with Shasta Daisies.

In all these groupings it will be noticed that these are not merely combinations of colors but that an attempt has been made to associate those plants which in their growth, stature, leaf form, and shape and size of flower are sufficiently different to provide that contrast necessary in a successful group. Shasta Daisies and *Coreopsis lanceolata* are excellent in color combination, but both have Daisy-like flowers and a rounded character of growth in the plant. If orange or yellow and white are to be grouped together it is far better to plant the yellow Coreopsis in front of the tall, spiry, white Watsonias, or the white Shasta Daisies in front of the orange *Leonotus leonurus,* whose flowers are carried in whorls up their tall stems.

A COOL COLOR SCHEME

Gardens along the coast are not infrequently on uneven ground, with slopes which get warm and dry in summer. For clothing such a place a cool color scheme of lavender, pink, blue, and gray is suggested. The materials would be equally satisfactory whatever the direction of the slope, but the season of flowers would be later if it were north or east, and such shade- and moisture-loving plants as Forget-me-Nots and Violas would last longer into summer. On irregular ground groupings must be made to fit the location, and I therefore give no planting plan but rather indicate materials which may well be used. Several plants of a kind should be in drifts or irregular groups, due attention being given to variety of outline. Few large plants of upright or spiry growth are included as their lines unfit them for any place but the top of the slope. A bold group of one or more subjects should be repeated throughout the planting to hold it together and give it a certain unity. Trailers making strong summer growth will be best just above winter-flowering bulbs or annuals, so that they will cover the ground left bare in summer.

In the planting of a dry slope the first consideration must be to make use of those shrubs and perennials which are very resistant to drought. The proportion of evergreens, whether shrubs or herbs, should also be quite large, as otherwise the bank will be quite bare between fall and spring. Bulbs and annuals may be used to a minor extent, chiefly those which make their growth during the rains, for to keep such a place moist enough for annuals in summer is a practical impossibility. In planning a color scheme of lavender, pink, gray, and blue for such a situation, selection may be made from the following:

Of shrubs, we have the white Portugal Broom, of aspiring growth but submitting to hard pruning when young; the Rock Roses, of which *Cistus maculata* is a good and not too rampant white variety; *C. salvifolius* having better foliage but less attractive white flowers; *Erica melanthera* for winter and *E. persoluta alba* for spring; the white *Diosma ericoides;* dwarf forms of our native Ceanothus; seedlings of *Leptospermum Nicholsii*, or even *L. laevigatum* where there is space for so vigorous a grower; Rosemary; *Teucrium fruticans;* and for their beautiful coral berries in autumn *Berberis Wilsoni* and *B. subcauliolata.*

More prostrate shrubs to clothe the ground include *Juniperus Sabina, Cotoneaster microphylla, Sollya hetero-*

phylla, *Veronica chathamica*, and *Plumbago capensis*.
Invaluable for this kind of planting are the many kinds
of Thyme, as they are dwarf, drought-resistant, spreading in habit, evergreen, and soft in color.   Real trailers
but of evergreen foliage and therefore of great value
would include *Convolvulus mauritanicus*, for its violet
flowers; *Felicia rosea*, a winter bloomer; the single white
Ivy Geranium; *Arenaria montana*, and Helianthemums.   The small pink trailing Mesembryanthemum
would be used only if the slope were a very sunny one.
In any case, care would be necessary to prevent its
overrunning and smothering other things.   Other
somewhat trailing plants, not always evergreen, are the
perennial white Silene, *Erigeron mucronatus*, the rock
Pinks, Kenilworth Ivy for a shady situation, the Campanulas, the indispensable Aubrietias, and for summer
the blue trailing Lobelias.

The gray note to the planting is furnished by the
foliage of such plants as Santolina, *Nepeta Mussini*,
Dianthus plumarius, *Arabis albida*, *Cerastium tomentosum* and the larger *C. Biebersteini*.

Among the sub-shrubby perennials with blue flowers
will be found *Statice latifolia*, *Felicia celestis*, *Linum
narbonnense*, *Salvia azurea*, and Lavender, and in
colors other than blue we have the pale pink *Gaura
lindheimeri*, white *Linum monogynum*, white and
purple *Salvia leucantha*, pink *Aethionema grandiflora*,
white *Iberis sempervirens*, the lavender-pink *Iberis
gibraltarica*, and the salmon-pink *Diascia Barberi*.   Of
perennials which die down completely we have *Thalic-*

trum diptocarpum, the dwarf steely-blue Eryngiums, the native Pentstemon Blue Bedder, *Cheiranthus linifolia*, and *Gypsophila paniculata*. Of the bulbs for fall planting we can use *Scilla campanulata*, Freesias, Muscari, Triteleias, Brodaeas, and Daffodil Mrs. Langtry. The bulbs should be planted closely, in small drifts. On a large bank Agapanthus gives a fine blue note in summer, but here an occasional single specimen will be sufficient.

It would be possible to add a great many annuals or plants which can be treated as such, but this is hardly advisable, as it would leave too many bare spaces in summer, when they had gone to seed. A few should be sown, either because they are specially attractive in such a position, as in the case of the Forget-me-Nots and Violas (both of them in the shadiest place possible), or because they are long, continuous bloomers, such as the Verbenas and small Petunias like Rosy Morn. There are many dainty little spring annuals which under these conditions would become naturalized; some of them are natives of California. Instances are the pink and lavender Linarias, the white *Omphalodes linifolia*, Clarkias, Godetias, *Gilia capitata*, *Platystemon californicus*, *Nemophila insignis*, and Nigella Miss Jekyll.

·PLANTING FOR BRILLIANCY

The planting scheme for a brilliant border, mainly strong reds and yellows, grew out of a sentimental regard for our Spanish heritage, these colors always being associated with it. In my own sunny garden what came to be called the Spanish border proved so popular with visitors that it seemed possible other gardeners might find suggestions of interest in its scheme.

As given, the planting would cover a long, wide border having at the rear shrubs of considerable size and even a few trees, but if the space were narrow the background of shrubs could be eliminated and only the sub-shrubby, herbaceous, and bulbous plants used. The whole plan is intended to be suggestive, rather than a literal planting scheme, for doubtless not all the plants will be available in any one garden, and for some excellent substitutes may be found. I have made no effort to mention all the possible materials. Some were omitted because too vigorous or spreading; such are the Acacias, the perennial Sunflowers, and the Verbascums. Spanish Irises, Ixias, and the rarer bulbous flowers (which cannot now be imported because of Quarantine No. 37) I have little used, as the supplies in this country are still small. Many annuals might have been added, as Nasturtiums, Annual Chrysanthemums, Stocks, Sweet William, Celsias, and such natives as *Layia elegans* and *Leptosyne Stillmannii*.

A planting of the type suggested would be best facing south. In that position not only would all the one-sided flowers such as Gladiolus face the path, but the border would have practically continual sunshine, a necessary factor to bring out the warm coloring and give the brilliant effect sought. For that reason such

A Spanish Border for California Gardens

The gardener who loves brilliancy of effect will appreciate the possibilities of this vivid,
Old-World color combination.

shade lovers as Lilies and Primroses have not been included in the scheme. The planting would be best on level ground, because the effects are planned to extend through the garden year and on a slope it is hard to have a good summer show because the ground dries out in spite of irrigation.

It will be noted that I have not restricted myself to crude combinations of red and yellow only. White, cream, apricot, scarlet, bronze, yellow, and brown are used in the scheme and the wider range greatly softens and improves the effect.

THE SHRUBBERY BACKGROUND

In the shrubbery background the high points are given by *Eucalyptus ficifolia,* a species quite different from most in that it is dwarfer and slow growing. In August the best forms are a blaze of orange-scarlet. The shrubs are selected for their resistance to drought, varied texture of evergreen foliage, and conspicuous flowers or berries in the color range desired. The taller ones are in most cases the rearmost, and the somewhat shorter and less vigorous ones are used as facers. Between them they furnish some color all year. For example, *Choisya ternata, Kerria japonica, Berberis Darwinii,* and *Chorizema ilicifolia* are in flower from late January through February; *Leptospermum, Cytisus Andreanus, Cytisus albus* (white Broom), *Streptosolon,* the Cistuses, and *Diosma ericoides* through the spring; *Carpenteria californica, Lupinus arborea,* and *Fremontia californica* in early summer. For midsummer Spanish

Broom, Escallonias, *Cestrum aurantiacum*, and the Lantanas must be depended on, while through the fall we have the orange berries of *Pyracantha angustifolia*, which are generally retained for months. For none of these is any special culture required. Planting should all be done during the rainy season. The *Streptosolon,* Lantanas, and *Linum trigynum* should only be used where there is little frost.

The front would be best edged informally with rather flat stones over which the rock plants could clamber. Most of those listed are hardy perennials able to stand our dry summers. *Cheiranthus Allioni* is a beautiful orange relative of the Wallflower, best sown in summer and treated as a biennial, that is, allowed to bloom itself to death next spring. With good drainage the Verbenas and the Indian Pink Vesuvius are perennials, albeit requiring occasional replacing. A few spring-flowering Cape bulbs such as Freesias and Sparaxis have been added. They require fall planting and may be left in the ground throughout the year. To keep up the procession Violas (planted in fall) and certain summer-flowering annuals such as the dwarfer Eschscholtzias, Dimorphotheca hybrids, dwarf Marigolds, and Coreopsis are necessary. They may be sown in early spring where they are to bloom, and will require to be watered in summer and kept from going to seed.

Between the edging and the shrubby background will be found the hardy perennials, annuals, and bulbous plants which are depended on to give the strong color effects. In the early months of the year Daffodils

and Tulips are the chief contributors. The bare spaces
they leave when planted alone are a grave problem anywhere, but especially so here. With care and thought
the spaces can, however, be eliminated. Daffodils,
flowering in February or March, may be interplanted
with Ixias blooming in April or May, and among them
a summer-flowering annual may be sown in spring. So
Spanish Iris may follow Tulips, and similarly an annual
follow them. In both cases the later flowering bulb is
planted only two or three inches deep, between the
Daffodils or Tulips which will be five or six inches under
ground. To this middle planting the chief character
all through the spring will be given by the long-blooming Wallflowers. Fire King is a particularly brilliant
variety, the others are good for contrast and diversity.

To the April and May effect the tall Bearded Irises,
Oriental Poppies, Columbines, Hemerocallis, Geums,
and Linarias contribute. *Iris Monnieri* and *I. ochroleuca* are taller, later-blooming varieties of the Spuria
section, with fine stiff foliage.

In early summer are added Coreopsis, Gaillardias,
Alstromerias, and for later summer display we have the
various annuals, Gladioli, Montbretias, Tritomas, and
the members of the Sunflower family. A particularly
strong color note at this season is *Leonotus leonurus*, a
tall sub-shrubby plant with striking orange flowers in
whorls.

The main dependence in autumn is on pompon Chrysanthemums, which for this purpose are far better than
the large-flowered ones, as they need no staking. They

can, if desired, be treated as hardy perennials and simply cut back in April and June to keep them dwarf. This is the easiest way, but if the ground is needed for something else in spring the clumps can be planted out of the way after blooming and offsets put into the border again in May.

Perhaps the most pleasing effect in this border is the softening down given to the larger flowers in spring by the annual Linarias which bloom for months among the other plants. Seeds of the annual white, yellow, and yellow-and-red varieties sow themselves and have been so crossed by the bees that there are now dozens of delightful blends which in the sunshine glisten like jewels.

In this arrangement no attempt has been made to restrict the border to hardy herbaceous perennials. Under California conditions such restriction would be quite inadvisable even if possible, for with a season extending almost twelve months one must take advantage of all available materials. In any case, distinctions are to some extent done away with in a climate where Calceolarias, Cannas, and Montbretias can be left outdoors through the year, Eschscholtzias and Wallflowers are perennials, and Salpiglossis and Indian Pinks at least biennials.

CHAPTER V

What Are Best in Trees and Shrubs

IN A modest book which has as its purpose to help chiefly those with small gardens, hardly more than a mention can be made of trees, though even the smallest place may be the better or the more distinguished by the addition of one or two fine specimens. The diligence with which home seekers will search for a lot having a fine tree on it and the pride which they will feel when its protecting branches shelter their newly built house give some indication of the value of even a single tree. In planting a tree oneself there is also the satisfaction of watching its growth through many years and of feeling that it will go on even when one is no longer there to see it.

TREES

In the north, and particularly away from the coast where the winters are cold, a deciduous tree will be preferred, but even in southern gardens should the only suitable place be on the south side of the house, it may well be worth while considering the advantages in this situation of a tree which lets in the sun when you want it and provides shade in long summer days. Such a one is *Quercus lobata*, the Valley Oak, a fine spreading tree with deeply lobed deciduous leaves, one of the most beautiful and charactcristic of the native trees of the Sacramento, San Joaquin, and coast valleys.

Another fine native is *Juglans californica*, the California black Walnut, a symmetrical tree with handsome pinnate leaves, a tree of spreading habit, which in time reaches a large size. Others which may well be given early consideration in selecting a few deciduous trees are—*Gleditschia triacanthus*, the Honey Locust; the interesting *Ginkgo biloba*, with foliage shaped like the Maidenhair Fern; *Paulownia imperialis*, the Empress tree; the Liquidambar; the oriental Sycamore; the Huntington Elm; and the white Mulberry. There are places where a small group of Lombardy Poplars will give the ascending note desired, and others where three or four white European Birches will add the distinctive picture which only these graceful trees can give. Even when leafless their white bark renders them beautiful.

Even where space cannot be afforded for a large tree there will be room for one or more of the beautiful deciduous flowering trees, for they nearly all bloom in early spring when color is so much needed in the garden and if given a good background a single specimen will be an object of beauty for some time. Many of those best liked are forms of fruit trees of value only for their particularly beautiful flowers. The earliest is *Prunus Pissardii*, the purple-leaved Plum; a small tree with pinkish-white blossoms covering the branches before the purplish leaves appear. These last become much greener as the season advances.

The double-flowering Almond, *Prunus amygdalus*, another harbinger of spring, is covered with double flowers of pale pink, rather resembling little Roses. There are also several beautiful flowering Peaches, white, rose, and red. The semi-double form known as Early Red is the most favored. It makes a wonderful patch of glowing color in March. No one can fail to admire the flowering Cherries, the double forms of which are to be preferred, as their white or pink flowers last longer. These are especially at home in a Japanese garden.

The best of the flowering Apples is *Pyrus floribunda*, a small tree with most attractive pale pink and rose flowers appearing in late spring with the leaves. Much dwarfer is *Pyrus ionensis*, Bechtel's double-flowering Crabapple, a beautiful sight in the spring garden when its branches are covered with double pink flowers.

Other flowering trees which should be considered are *Cercis siliquastrum*, the European Judas-tree or Red-Bud; *Crataegus Oxyacantha*, and *C. monogyna*, the white English Hawthorn and Paul's double scarlet Thorn, medium-sized trees of attractive foliage and beautiful flowers, but requiring to be sprayed as they are very subject to scale.

For late spring bloom *Laburnum vulgare*, the common Laburnum or Golden Chain, is desirable.

While few large evergreen trees are to be recommended for growing in small gardens, they deserve more planting in the south, where the winters are comparatively dry and sunny, than in the colder and much wetter north. Their shade is moreover very grateful in warm southern gardens. When the house is on a plot of half an acre or more, they may be largely used for planting the boundaries of the property, shutting out undesirable vistas, giving seclusion to the garden, and forming a beautiful and permanent frame for a lawn.

Among the best of the large coniferous evergreens will be found the native *Sequoia sempervirens*, the well-known Redwood, which appears at its best near the coast. Two other good natives are the Monterey Cypress (*Cupressus macrocarpa*) and the Monterey Pine (*Pinus radiata*), both quick-growing and excellent as specimens. Other desirable Pines are *P. pinea* (the Stone Pine) and *P. Laricio austriaca*. Grand trees but requiring much room because of the spread of their lower branches are the Deodar (*Cedrus deodara*), the Lawson Cypress (*Cupressus Lawsoniana*), and *Araucaria Bidwilli* (the Chili Pine). *Araucaria excelsa*, the Norfolk Island Pine, is also excellent in a large place, but I can see no excuse for growing *A. imbricata*, the Monkey Puzzle, a monstrosity too often disfiguring our lawns.

The evergreens which I have mentioned are all coniferous, with the characteristic pyramidal growth of the conifer. The effect of planting a number of these together is always a colder and more rugged scene. Even in a garden of half an acre or so it would be un-

desirable to use many of them, planting rather the comparatively round-topped, broad-leaved evergreens so
characteristic of warmer countries. The largest of
these, *Ficus microphylla* (the Moreton Bay Fig), *Magnolia grandiflora*, and the larger Eucalypts, are fine trees
but best kept for parks and large places. If one large
evergreen is to be given place, do not overlook the
claims of the Live Oaks, which, contrary to popular
opinion, are by no means slow growers when properly
fed and watered. In Santa Barbara there are fine
impressive Oaks only ten years from the acorn. *Quercus agrifolia* is our California Live Oak; *Q. suber*, the
Cork Oak, is also very fine in California.

For the smaller garden choose rather such a smaller
tree as *Ceratonia siliqua* (the Carob), *Sterculia diversi-
folia, Camphora officinalis* (the Camphor tree), *Arbutus
Menziesi* (the native Madrone), or its much smaller rela-
tion, *Arbutus unedo* (the Strawberry tree). Not all the
Eucalypts need be put down as too big or too voracious
for the small place. *E. polyanthema* is a small, graceful
tree, with beautiful kidney-shaped leaves of gray green.
If a small evergreen of fine and graceful growth is what
you need, *Maytenus boaria*, the Mayten tree, from
Chili, is a good choice. Better known and of very similar habit is the Pepper tree (*Schinus molle*), which is so
beautiful in such places as Redlands, where the summers
are warm. Both the male and the female of this
species should be planted in order to get the beautiful
coral berries which hang in clusters from the female
tree.

In a garden where space is valued preference may be given to those evergreens which in addition to their good foliage add interest and color by their striking flowers. Such are—*Jacaranda ovalifolia*, too tender for places having much frost, but where it will thrive, a fine sight when covered with its panicles of tubular violet-blue flowers; *Grevillea robusta*, the Silk Oak of Australia, also rather tender, but a drought-resistant tree of rapid growth, crowned in its season with gorgeous orange flowers; *Eucalyptus ficifolia*, differing from most of this family in being rather a slow grower, not very hardy, but worth growing for its bunches of wonderful flowers of varying shades of red, sometimes a glorious orange-scarlet.

Of the great family of Acacias several are commonly grown in California, chiefly by those who crave quick results. They are exceedingly rapid growers, but of less permanent value, as they break or blow over in storms or become straggly in growth. *A. baileyana* is much planted, particularly in southern California, presumably because it blooms as early as January, for the combination of greenish-yellow flowers and gray-green feathery foliage is not specially happy. *A. dealbata* (syn. *mollissima*) is more popular, as in February its darker feathery foliage is almost hidden in the profusion of very fragrant clearer yellow blossoms. *A. pycnantha*, the Golden Wattle, has undivided leaves and large flower-heads of better, deeper yellow, also quite fragrant. Where flowers produced intermittently through the year are preferred to one big show, a good choice is *A. neriifolia* (syn. *floribunda*). *A. melanoxylon*, the Black Acacia, is of little value for its flowers, which are whitish and not showy; for shade or a dark background it is better than any of those mentioned, and it is more permanent.

The California State Board of Forestry has issued a large and profusely illustrated book, Shade and Ornamental Trees of California, by Merritt B. Pratt, which should be consulted by those interested in the trees most grown here, treating as it does not only of natives but also of trees introduced from other countries.

In the small place shrubs are of far greater moment than trees, as they have a number of important functions, in particular those with good evergreen foliage. For tying a house to the ground, that is, for blotting out the sharp line where the foundations of the house meet the ground, evergreen shrubs are more desirable than any other plant materials. The characteristic most wanted in this position is as good an appearance as possible twelve months of the year. They are also most excellent for boundary plantings and hedges, to define the limits of lawns, and to divide off different parts of the garden. The foliage of evergreen shrubs affords good background for flowering plants. Some of them have fine flowers, others beautiful berries.

DECIDUOUS SHRUBS

In the parts of California where the finest gardening is done, that is, along the coast, where the winter temperature is never very low, the evergreens have quite

Where space will permit, an open lawn, bounded by trees and shrubs and a few plantings of flowers will give a beautiful and restful prospect from the loggia.

Interesting use of pergola to shade a hill-side walk. Pansies are best when massed as they are above this pool.

A pleasant ending to a path, the circular sitting-place so shaded as to need no summerhouse. In their season Iris will add beauty to the walk.

properly so great a preponderance over deciduous
shrubs that one almost comes to think of shrubs as
evergreen. In Washington, Oregon, and those parts
of California where the winters are cold, few broad-
leaved evergreens can be used, deciduous shrubs being
used in their place. The larger rainfall and the shorter
summer drought are more agreeable to deciduous
shrubs than are the climatic conditions of southern
California. Everywhere deciduous shrubs have the
drawback that their foliage is not usually interesting,
and that after flowering many of them look somewhat
shabby. When one adds that most of them look rather
stiff and naked in winter by contrast with evergreens,
and that their flowering is of short duration and by
no means always effective in southern California, it is
not surprising that their wide use is not advocated
where many evergreens do so well. I shall, however,
mention a few, of varying value for our gardens.

Very early in the year, often before the close of the
previous one, the flowering Currants come into bloom.
Ribes sanguineum, a native, with fragrant deep pink
flowers, is undoubtedly the most popular, and though
rather shabby in summer is often found in gardens because of its very early blooming. The Japanese Quince
(*Cydonia japonica* syn. *Chaenomeles japonica*) also begins to bloom in January, and in central California and
northward it is largely grown as an informal, impenetrable hedge, for groups, and as single specimens. When
in full bloom the typical scarlet variety is a glorious
sight; the pink and white varieties are less striking

Beginning to bloom at about the same time and there-fore good to group with the latter are the Spiræas, particularly the double form of *S. prunifolia*, the Bridal Wreath, so called from the purity of its white flowers, borne before the leaves appear. Other Spiræas may also be grown, but in California the gardener who has seen *S. van Houttei* in its glory in colder climes need not expect the same avalanche of snowy flowers. Similarly the Forsythias are a disappointment in that they open a few blossoms at a time and their greenish-yellow flowers, at no time in great abundance, have to compete in their season with the far more showy Acacias. *Kerria japonica*, on the other hand, has a distinct garden value. The very deep yellow rosettes of the double form, the one most worth growing, last for several weeks in spring-time. The foliage is unimportant but the green stems are beautiful.

Blooming about the same time you may have the Pearl Bush (*Exochorda grandiflora*), a larger shrub than the Spiræas and one more generally satisfactory. Like them, it is not decorative when out of flower. Another white-flowered deciduous shrub of great beauty in spring is Magnolia stellata.

It is regrettable that it is now so difficult to buy the many beautiful Tree Pæonies, forms of *Pæonia Mou-tan*, with huge flowers, pink, white, or red, far finer than the type, which is a rosy purple. The Tree Pæonies, un-like the herbaceous ones, do very well in California when planted somewhat in the shade. As shrubs they have no garden value, but when in bloom they are very striking.

On the Atlantic coast the mainstays of early summer among the shrubs are the Deutzias, Weigelas (Diervillas), Syringas, Snowballs, and above all the Lilacs. None of these are anything like as satisfactory in California. In central California many of them are grown fairly successfully by those who plant them for auld lang syne. As one gets into colder sections with more rainfall, all of these shrubs greatly improve. In the south they should be tried very sparingly, and even in the San Francisco Bay region they should not be given the prominence they justly receive in Eastern gardens.

For a color effect not unlike some of the Lilacs plant *Tamarix parviflora*, a tall, upright shrub of slender branches, feathery foliage, and, in spring, long racemes of pinkish lilac flowers.

Among our deciduous shrubs which we value chiefly for their summer flowering are several plants which are grown only in greenhouses in colder climates. Most important are the Fuchsias, which along the coast of California rarely suffer enough from frost to be killed. In favored places close to the ocean, where summer fogs abound, many varieties grow into huge bushes eight or ten feet in height, blooming freely from early summer until cold winter rains discourage them. They vary greatly in growth, in foliage, and in size and color of flowers, the most vigorous ones generally bearing the smaller, single flowers. As they like the shade, they are admirable for banking around the base of a house to the east or north, and also for growing under trees.

their graceful growth fitting them particularly for association with the native Oaks.

Fuchsias are not yet planted nearly as much as they
should be, especially in gardens near the coast. They
are very easy to grow, submitting cheerfully to transplanting and to cutting back in winter whenever it is
desirable to keep them from getting straggly or to
improve the flowering by inducing new growth. Give
them plenty of water during the summer. As many
excellent kinds cannot be procured from nurseries but
may be found in the gardens of friends or neighbors,
it is well to know that Fuchsias root readily from
cuttings of the ripened wood, taken about December
and planted preferably in light soil mixed with leaf-
mold. Where the foliage suffers from the work of the
tiny thrips who work on the under side of the leaf, spray
with a solution of whale-oil soap.

The best Hydrangeas for California are the varieties
of *H. hortensis*, which have been so greatly improved by
French hybridizers and now give huge rounded panicles of white, pink, or rose flowers, heavily tinged with
blue where iron is present in the soil, naturally or by
design. Not only are these plants of great value for
growing in tubs, but in the localities where frosts are
light they do beautifully in the open ground in partial
shade. Do not expose them to long periods of hot
summer sunshine.

In such balmy climates as that of San Diego or Santa
Barbara, the Hibiscus is a fine summer shrub, sometimes attaining great size. There is a tropical beauty

about its brilliant flowers, but it is very susceptible to
frost. The Pomegranate (*Punica granatum*) has bright
scarlet flowers in summer. *Lagerstromia indica,* the
pink Crape Myrtle, especially thrives in the hot interior
valleys; in the foggy coast districts it is too much
affected by mildew.

The Buddleias are rather weedy, rangy summer-
flowering shrubs of rapid growth. *B. variabilis,* occasionally called Summer Lilac, will be recognized by
its Willow-shaped leaves and long drooping spikes of
lilac or purple flowers, which last for many weeks. This
is best cut back severely in early spring. *B. asiatica,*
a still finer form, is rather tender, but can be grown in
favored places.

From the many available the above have been selected as the most worthy of consideration for the small
garden.

The evergreen shrubs vary greatly in their size,
character, appearance, and use. From the very large
number which can be grown in California I have made
a selection of the more desirable, with short notes in
reference to their characteristics and use.

ABELIA.—A barely evergreen shrub is *A. grandiflora*
with its stems four or five feet high. It has small,
glossy leaves and pinkish white tubular flowers in late
summer, with bronzy-red sepals which persist through
the fall and add to its beauty. Good to grow with

Fuchsias, as it also does well in the shade. It can be increased by cuttings or by dividing the plants. Cut out the old wood occasionally to induce new growth.

ABUTILON.—These loose-growing shrubs with leaves like the Maple are also semi-evergreen. They are chiefly valued for their drooping, bell-shaped flowers, generally either red or yellow.

ACACIA.—There are several shrubby Acacias, excellent plants for growing where plants must stand neglect, as on the boundaries of a large place. *A. armata*, the Kangaroo Thorn, is of very graceful habit, its long, slender drooping branches covered with small green leaves, each armed with a sharp thorn so that a bush becomes impenetrable. The flowers are light yellow, profuse in spring. *A. cultriformis* is of somewhat similar growth, but the leaves are very glaucous, so that the general effect is a rather gray green. The flowers are a deep yellow, and come freely in early spring. *A. verticillata* is a taller shrub, reaching a height of from ten to fifteen feet; the dark green needle-like leaves about three quarters of an inch long are very distinct. The pale yellow flowers are borne in spikes about an inch long. *A. longifolia* (syn. *latifolia*) is a still larger spreading shrub, of very quick growth and thus useful for boundaries, or informal hedges. It has long narrow leaves, and bears many spikes of greenish-yellow flowers in spring. It can be trimmed to tree form.

AUCUBA.—A rather low-growing shrub with large shiny leaves. To secure its red berries, male and female plants must be grown together. One form is variegated with yellow, hence the name Gold Dust Plant. Aucubas grow very well under trees.

AZALEA.—The evergreen Azaleas, being small and compact, and of neat growth with brilliant flowers, add greatly to the beauty of the more shaded rock-garden and thrive under trees, if these are not too dense. They dislike a bright sunny place, and for soil prefer one which is light and rich in leaf-mold. *A. indica*, the well-known Azaleas forced by florists for the Easter season, can be grown outdoors in California. Also successful and now being offered in many beautiful colors are the Japanese Azaleas of the Kurume class; at present the best known of these is *A. hinodegiri*, of showy magenta color.

AZARA.—Quite tall and erect in growth is *A. microphylla*, so called from its very small glossy leaves, of graceful growth and of particular value for growing in a shady place.

BERBERIS (Barberry).—The Barberries grown in the eastern United States, the varieties of *B. vulgaris* and the superior *B. Thunbergi*, all deciduous, are of far less value in California than the semi-deciduous *B. Wilsoni*, the similar but more persistent-leaved *B. subcauliolata*, and the quite evergreen *B. Darwini* and *B. stenophylla*.

Both *B. Wilsoni* and *B. subcauliolata*, from their dwarf,
twiggy growth and beautiful waxy coral berries, are
great additions to our rock-gardens. The latter has the
advantage of being slightly taller. The narrow little
leaves of both tend to turn red in fall, but again *B.
subcauliolata* has the advantage, in that its leaves are
far more persistent. *B. Darwini* is older and more
familiar, and is readily distinguished by its pendent
racemes of orange flowers, which appear as early as
February. Its blue berries are not conspicuous. Its
glossy foliage, suggestive of Holly in shape, has recommended it for use as a hedge plant, but in this capacity
it is not wholly satisfactory as it does not lend itself
perfectly to pruning and plants occasionally die out.
B. stenophylla has very narrow needle-like leaves and
paler yellow flowers. Several plants should be grown
together to obtain the graceful effect of which a group
is capable.

BUXUS (Box).—There are many good varieties of the
familiar long-lived Box. *B. sempervirens* is the one
most planted, and in its different forms gives us the
very dwarf varieties used to edge beds in formal gardens
and the much taller form which will make in time a fine
permanent hedge. Boxes submit so well to pruning
that they are greatly used for formal work, as specimen
plants both in the open ground and in tubs.

CALLISTEMON.—The common and very descriptive
name of these Australian shrubs is Bottle-brush, as their

flowers are of exactly that shape. Their bright color, generally red but occasionally varying to pink, is very striking and their shape decidedly unusual. They are very drought-resistant, and are best planted in full sun.

CAMELLIA.—The once very popular greenhouse plant, *C. japonica*, grows very well outdoors in California, being at its best in cool gardens near the coast, planted in partial shade. Plant Camellias where they may readily be watered through the summer, and where rough winter winds will not destroy the blossoms. There are both single and double-flowered Camellias, the former more graceful, the latter with a certain old-time formal charm.

CARPENTERIA CALIFORNICA.—This fine native shrub resembles a large Syringa or Mock Orange with evergreen foliage, and when well grown is much superior in California to the *Philadelphus*.

CEANOTHUS.—Everyone knows the Wild Lilac which grows among the chaparral and covers the California hillsides with misty blue in the springtime. Here is a substitute for the real Lilac where the latter does not thrive. Though it is scentless and its range of color not so great, it has the advantage of being evergreen. The narrow-leaved *C. thyrsiflorus* will grow up to twenty feet in height, and when covered with large panicles of pale blue flowers it will be appreciated in any garden. *C. arborea* is more tree-like, and its leaves are larger and broader.   It is excellent in southern California, where it blooms in midwinter.   There are hybrid varieties, of which C. Gloire de Versailles is the best known.   It should be planted, as it blooms all through the summer.

CESTRUM.—Erect and quick-growing shrubs, with leaves about the size of the Lilac; not fine plants, but distinct in their clusters of tubular flowers.   *C. aurantiacum*, of a pale orange-yellow, blooms in winter and frequently again in summer.   *C. elegans* gives its purplish-red flowers in winter and early spring.

CHOISYA TERNATA (Mexican Orange-flower).—This handsome glossy-leaved shrub of bushy habit is not only one of our earliest winter bloomers, but, where it is cared for, it will make a second crop of its fragrant white flowers in summer.   It is one of the most desirable shrubs for small places, and is hardy in western Oregon and Washington.

CHORIZEMA ILICIFOLIA.—This almost prostrate little shrub of elegant habit with small Holly-like leaves is not very hardy, but in warm gardens it deserves a place where it will be protected from cold north winds and encouraged to produce, from November through the winter, its dainty spikes of pea-shaped flowers, in a beautiful combination of orange and rose, an unusual but interesting and attractive color scheme.

CISTUS (Rock Rose).—The Rock Rose family is so thoroughly at home on the dry sunny banks so often left bare in our gardens that it is regrettable that it is not better known and that so few of the many species can be supplied by our nurseries. The dwarfest in growth and finest in flower is *C. ladaniferus maculatus,* its large white flowers with deep crimson blotches at the base of each petal. *C. laurifolius* is larger and more vigorous in growth, but the pure white flowers are smaller. Another species, with innumerable small white flowers carried above its small, wrinkled, but attractive foliage is *C. salvifolius,* a very desirable shrub. *C. albidus* gets its name from the white down on the leaves; the flowers are of a deep lilac-pink, of good size but of a color difficult to harmonize with others. While the flowers of these Mediterranean plants last only a day, the succession makes this of no importance, and the resistance of the plants to drought is a great asset.

COPROSMA.—The variety grown, *C. Baueri,* is a New Zealand shrub of almost prostrate habit and so may either be used as a ground-cover, especially on a slope, or to lean against the base of a house. Its rounded, very glossy leaves are fine for a background, as they do not get dusty. It should not be planted where more than a few degrees of frost are usual. Very desirable for southern California.

CORONILLA.—This little shrub, though not of prime importance, is sometimes planted for its deep yellow flowers which are very freely produced in winter and spring. The varieties grown are *C. Emerus* and *C. glauca.*

COTONEASTER.—Among the Cotoneasters are found some of our best berried shrubs. A few are deciduous, but the ones chiefly grown in California are not. They vary greatly in habit. *C. horizontalis* is almost prostrate, deciduous in the north, where its leaves turn red in fall, but nearly evergreen in the south; a beautiful sight when covered in fall with bright red berries. *C. microphylla* has the advantage of being evergreen, and as it roots wherever its branches touch the ground it makes a fine ground-cover, particularly for a bank. Its little pinkish-white flowers are agreeable, but its pinkish berries are less bright than those of *C. horizontalis.* Of the taller varieties, *C. pannosa* is the best in general cultivation, a shrub of five or six feet in height, with graceful, arching branches and small green foliage, white beneath. Its chief beauty comes from the many bright red berries which it bears the whole length of its branches. These persist from fall into late winter, as the birds do not care for them. *C. Francheti* is of dwarfer and more spreading habit, desirable for planting in front of *C. pannosa.* Its orange berries are less conspicuous and are usually eaten by the birds in early winter. *C. acuminata* is less desirable, being large and stiff, though it has fine orange-red berries. In California, where we so lack color in the garden in fall and winter, these Cotoneasters and the related Pyracanthas should be far more planted, for the brilliance of their fruits. The beautiful shrub formerly listed as *Cotoneaster angustifolia* is now considered a Pyracantha.

CYTISUS (Broom).—The Brooms, in their many varieties, are most useful shrubs for covering dry banks and planting where the soil is poor and no water can be given. Some have small leaves on the long branches, but on others leaves are almost wholly absent, yet they are ornamental, as the stems are always green. The two points to note in their culture are, first, that they are very difficult to transplant and should be put in their permanent places when very young or out of pots; second, that if fine bushy specimens are wanted they should be pruned back to some extent each year after blooming. Their tendency is to become tall and leggy. Propagation is by seed, in fact, many of the species sow themselves where they like the conditions. Visitors entering the harbor of Victoria, B. C., in June will have noticed how yellow are the low surrounding hills on which the Scotch Broom (*C. Scoparius*) has become naturalized. This very hardy variety is not one of the finest, being indeed exceeded in beauty by its own red-and-yellow variety, *Andreanus*. *C. albus*, the Portugal Broom, is a dainty, early-flowering species with very small white blossoms. When young it may be used in the rock-garden, but it is hard to keep it dwarf. *C. prae-cox* is a much more compact, cream-colored hybrid Broom, unfortunately seldom listed in this country. Among the Brooms with foliage, sometimes called

Genistas, will be found *C. racemosus*, a bushy yellow Broom which blooms long and profusely. One of less importance is *C. canariensis*, a rather straggly and very rapid grower, with yellow fragrant flowers, its green leaves having a downy white reverse. *C. monosperma*, a tall almost leafless shrub, earns its name of Bridal Veil from the small white flowers which clothe its drooping, silvery branches.

The Spanish Broom (*Spartium junceum*) will be considered under its own name.

DAPHNE.—Of the very fragrant Sweet Daphnes, *D. odora*, there are two forms generally grown, the normal green-leaved type with white flowers and *D. odora marginata*, which has leaves edged with creamy white, the flowers being pink. They are good small shrubs for semi-shaded places.

DIOSMA.—As its name indicates, *D. ericoides* has feathery foliage like that of the Heaths. Its growth is more spreading, its flowers are small and white, and the foliage is of a pleasant pungent odor. These qualities make it a desirable rock-garden shrub, or it may be used in the front of any shrubbery planting.

DURANTA.—A South American shrub reaching ten or twelve feet, with lilac-blue flowers followed by deep yellow berries, *D. plumieri* is well worth growing in such almost frostless places as Santa Barbara, but around San Francisco Bay it usually fails to fruit and suffers from cold snaps.

ERICA (Heath).—There are many fine Ericas, some with large white, pink, or scarlet flowers, but these large-flowered kinds require special culture and the peaty soil with absence of lime which all Ericas prefer. Choose rather from among the more vigorous small-flowered species, and if only one or two kinds are to be grown give preference to *E. melanthera* for its beautiful winter bloom of rosy lilac with prominent black stamens. This South African species will be found thriving in coast gardens from Berkeley to Pasadena. It is far superior to *E. Mediterranea*, as the flowers of the latter do not come all at once and it is often marred when blooming by the presence of dead flowers. For second choice, the April-flowering *E. persoluta alba*, a smaller erect-growing white Heather, is desirable, because it extends the season. The Ericas do well in partial shade, and after flowering should be pruned to keep them from getting straggly. Failure is generally due to heavy soil or to excessive lime in soil or water.

ESCALLONIA.—Where quick-growing, erect shrubs of clean glossy foliage are needed the Escallonias may fill the bill. The nomenclature in nurseries is very badly confused. In choosing a white-flowered kind, *E. montevidensis* (syn. *floribunda*), distinguished by the notch at the apex of the leaves, is to be preferred to *E. berteriana*. The pink *E. rosea* has rougher, somewhat sticky leaves. All these grow from ten to twelve feet high, but *E. rubra* does not generally exceed five. It has very dark leaves and red flowers. These South

American shrubs are of the easiest growth, and are excellent for boundary planting. Where shapely specimens are sought, they will need a good deal of pruning.

EUGENIA.—The handsome pyramidal growth of *E. myrtifolia* and its glossy green foliage, bronzed on the new growth, fit it peculiarly for avenues and other formal uses. It should be planted with due consideration to the fact that it is readily damaged by frost and cold winds. It can be grown in tubs for use in courts and patios.

EUONYMUS.—The evergreen Euonymus are forms of *E. japonicus* and are grown for their attractive foliage, which is often variegated with yellow or white. They are good shrubs for foundation planting, and make good backgrounds for other plants.

FATSIA.—The Fatsias, or Aralias, are grown for their large palmated leaves, good for tropical effects and for planting near water. *F. japonica* and its variegated variety grow as high as eight feet. *F. papyrifera* will attain more than twice that height.

FREMONTIA.—*F. californica* is a beautiful native evergreen with large yellow flowers in late spring.

GARRYA.—Another native evergreen with good dark green leaves and beautiful drooping catkins of pale green is *Garrya elliptica*, which flowers in winter, and is then very distinct and attractive.

Looking from the house into Mr. Myron Hunt's small but beautifully secluded garden in Pasadena—a garden to live in.

A Pepper tree shading a bench at the end of a broad walk planted with Snapdragons and edged with little English Daisies. What could be more simple or more satisfying?

GREVILLEA.—The shrubby *G. Thelemanniana* is a small plant with very distinct feathery pointed leaflets and small clusters of curious spidery crimson flowers. Its pleasing foliage and continuous flowering habit fit it for planting along a driveway, but only in a section where there are no hard frosts.

HAKEA.—A genus of very drought-resistant Australian shrubs, mainly grown for their interesting foliage, though they have red or white flowers. *H. laurina* is the largest. *H. saligna*, with its Willow-shaped leaves, is hardly half as tall. *H. suaveolens* is very different in appearance, its leaves being needle-shaped.

HYPERICUM.—The most commonly grown is the hybrid St. John's wort, *H. Moserianum*, a dwarf shrub with deep yellow flowers like large Buttercups, a useful plant for partial shade. *H. calycinum* is of less value for its flowers, but is a good ground-cover under trees.

ILEX (Holly).—Nowhere does the English Holly, *I. aquifolium*, grow more wonderfully than on the north Pacific coast, indeed in Oregon growing it for its beautiful berries is a commercial possibility. For success it needs abundant moisture, and consequently as one comes down to central California it does not do as well, and it is not recommended at all for southern California.

IOCHROMA.—These shrubs are of rather rangy growth and coarse leaves, but are worth having because they flower in late summer and autumn. *I. lanceolata pur-*

purea, bearing large clusters of purple-blue flowers, is the best known.

JUNIPERUS (Juniper).—There are many Junipers, the one singled out for mention here being *J. Sabina*, because it is a dwarf spreading shrub which roots along its branches and makes a very clean and tidy ground-cover on slopes of the poorest soil.

LANTANA.—In central California only the climbing Lantanas are really satisfactory, but from Santa Barbara south the bush forms thrive and are used for hedges or for brightening the garden through the long summer with their heads of Verbena-like flowers in white, yellow, bronze, scarlet, and shades of pink. Drought-resistant, but sensitive to frost and requiring warm summers. Mention of the climbing and trailing Lantanas will be made in the chapter on Vines and trailing plants.

LAUREL—English, See *Prunus lauro-cerasus*.

LAURUSTINUS—See *Viburnum tinus*.

LEPTOSPERMUM.—An Australian shrub, drought-resistant and of easy growth in California, is *L. laeviga-tum*. Allowed free growth it becomes a large, spreading shrub, almost a small tree. Its small gray-green leaves and somewhat pendulous habit render it always attractive, but in spring when covered with small white flowers it is particularly so. It will submit to pruning and may be kept quite dwarf and compact, but not formal. The introduction of *L. Nicholsii*, a small, upright shrub with ruby flowers, gives us a very different plant, fine enough for a small garden.

LIGUSTRUM (Privet).—The Privets, of which there are many kinds besides the very familiar *L. ovalifolium* (California Privet), are quick-growing vigorous shrubs adapted to hedge-making. The Chinese and Japanese Privets have quite large glossy leaves, and would make good specimen plants were it not that the odor of their white flowers is so distasteful to many people. The California Privet roots so readily from cuttings that hedges may be started in that way. It is, however, such a robber that in a small place it is not very desirable, as no fine plant will grow well near it.

LINUM.—The shrubby Flax with golden-yellow flowers borne in midwinter which is listed by the nurserymen of southern California as *Linum flavum* should not be confused with the herbaceous species of the same name. This attractive shrub should really be called *Linum trigynum*, or, even better, *Reinwardtia trigyna*. It is only satisfactory in southern California.

LONICERA (Honeysuckle).—The dwarf shrubby *L. nitida* was heralded a few years ago as a fine addition to the garden, a shrub which would so submit to shearing that it might be used in place of the slow-growing Box for edges. While it is useful, it has probably been overrated, for its natural habit is not always graceful, and in colder sections it loses many of its small shiny leaves in winter. It roots so easily from small cuttings half buried in sandy soil that a quantity may quickly be obtained without expense.

MAHONIA.—The Oregon Grape, *M. aquifolium*, is also native to northern California. Its large dark green leaves with serrated edges turn a bronzy purple in winter. Its chief value is as a ground-cover in partially shaded places.

MELALEUCA.—Where a smaller shrub than the drought-resistant Callistemon is needed for the same dry situation and garden effect, try one of the many species of Melaleucas. Most of them have flower-spikes like diminutive Bottle-brushes, and the shrubs are graceful in growth.

MYRTUS (Myrtle).—The Myrtles are very old shrubs and were largely used in Roman and Italian gardens, chiefly on account of their neat habit and small, fragrant foliage. It is the common Myrtle, *M. communis*, which we chiefly grow and which, either in the typical form or in the small-leaved *M. communis microphylla*, is an excellent choice for planting in front of other shrubbery or even as a hedge plant. While quite slow in growth, it presents no difficulties. To maintain a low bushy habit it needs pruning, for if allowed free growth for many years it is capable of becoming a small tree. *M. luma* and *M. ugni*, sometimes classed with the Eugenias, are Chilean forms of the Myrtle, of similar use but different shape of leaf. The former especially is very dark in color.

NANDINA.—*N. domestica* is a graceful Japanese shrub, somewhat suggesting a small Bamboo in appearance, but with large light green leaflets which turn a beautiful red in winter. It also has bright red berries following its small white flowers. It prefers a moist, semi-shady situation, and is particularly appropriate in a Japanese garden or on the banks of an informal pool. In a dry sunny place it makes almost no growth.

NERIUM (Oleander).—There are many garden varieties of the fragrant Oleander, a tall shrub sometimes growing to be a small tree. This is not a good shrub for cold, foggy coast gardens, as it rarely flowers there, but in warm sunny places it is a free and gorgeous bloomer all summer. The double pink kind is particularly bright and fragrant.

PHOTINIA.—The native shrub variously called Toyon, Christmas Berry, Redberry, and California Holly is *P. arbutifolia* (syn. *Heteromeles arbutifolia*). As our canyons tend to become denuded of it gardeners should take advantage of the fact that it can readily be domesticated and should raise quantities of plants from seed (sown in fall) to supply the yearly demand for bunches of berries for decoration. With a little attention to pruning it can be kept at all times a shapely and ornamental shrub.

PIMELEA.—The only Pimelea widely distributed in California is the Australian *P. feruginea,* a small tidy shrub suggestive in growth and foliage of the shrubby Veronicas. Its pink flowers appear in early spring at the ends of the branches.

PITTOSPORUM.—Though these Australian and New Zealand shrubs and small trees are best known in California as hedge plants, many of them make beautiful single specimens. The varieties most used for clipped hedges are: *P. eugenioides,* with yellowish-green wavy-edged leaves and inconspicuous yellow flowers; *P. nigricans* (syn. *tenuifolium*) of similar growth, but with smaller, darker leaves, black stems, and small almost black fragrant flowers. *P. undulatum,* the Victorian Box, is a handsomer shrub which can be used for a very broad hedge, but it is a pity not to grow it in a more naturalistic way so as to take advantage of its white and very fragrant flowers and of the orange berries which follow them. It has beautiful green leaves, large and with waved margins. *P. crassifolium* is different in that its leathery dark green leaves are white on the under side. This strong-growing shrub is very resistant to wind, and may with advantage be used in exposed places as an informal hedge or windbreak. The Japanese Pittosporum, *P. Tobira,* is not adapted to hedge-making, but its broad, dwarf, spreading growth fits it for planting at the base of a house where its very fragrant flowers, more conspicuous than those of most Pittosporums, may be admired.

POLYGALA.—At almost any time of the year the magenta, pea-shaped flowers of *P. Dalmaisiana* may be seen in California. It prefers cool summers and warm winters.

PRUNUS.—From the many evergreen species of Prunus we get three at least which have a decided garden value. *P. ilicifolia*, the California evergreen Cherry and its variety *integrifolia*, the Catalina Cherry, are not only attractive as specimens but they make fine, clean hedges. The former has the smaller leaves with serrated edges, more glossy than those of the Catalina Cherry. The latter is a more rapid grower.

The English Laurel (*P. laurocerasus*) has large, broad, dark-green leaves, and when one is looking for good evergreens to grow under trees it should be considered.

The Portugal Laurel (*P. lusitanica*) is also a handsome evergreen shrub, which can be used for backgrounds or even grown in tubs for formal work.

PYRACANTHA.—Though very much stiffer in growth than the related Cotoneasters, when they are in full fruit they are far more showy. *P. coccinea* is an old inhabitant of our gardens which has earned the name of Fire Thorn from its bright red berries. The variety *Lalandi*, with its deep orange berries, is better than the type, but when raised from seed it unfortunately varies a good deal. Plants from cuttings taken from a good specimen are best. *P. angustifolia* is a newer shrub from China, which is rapidly displacing *P. coccinea* as it is a strong, vigorous grower, fruits most abundantly, and retains its wonderful masses of orange berries through the whole winter. In southern California it has an unfortunate tendency to die suddenly, probably from the attacks of a borer. It is hardy as far north as Victoria, B. C. *P. crenulata* is more compact and pleasing in growth, and can be used for beds or informal hedges. It produces many small red berries, but they are not as decorative nor as persistent as the ones just mentioned. All the Pyracanthas can readily be grown from seed, and so should be more largely used to brighten our winter gardens.

RAPHIOLEPIS.—Where a low, compact evergreen shrub is needed, *R. ovata* (syn. *japonica*) will give the gardener no trouble by overrunning its bounds. It is a very slow grower, in some places a good characteristic. Its dark leathery leaves give it distinction.

RHODODENDRON.—Were it not for their outstanding beauty of flower and their always presentable foliage it would hardly be worth while mentioning the Rhododendrons in a book on small gardens, for the plants are rather expensive and they are exacting in their demands. In the San Francisco Bay region there are places, notably Golden Gate Park, where the Rhododendrons in early June are glorious to behold. Such displays may fire the small amateur with enthusiasm, and if he can provide the proper conditions he may succeed. Should his garden be on the north California coast or in Oregon, his chances will be good. Their requirements are for a light, sandy soil, shade and water in summer, and absence of lime and alkali. The garden hybrids, such as the wonderful Pink Pearl, are gorgeous indeed, but the large white Himalayan Rhododendron is being more widely grown as its habit is less formal and its culture less difficult.

ROSEMARINUS (Rosemary).—The Rosemary (*R. officinalis*) is a shrub of somewhat straggly growth, its best use being for covering dry banks, as it is very drought-resistant. The very narrow leaflets give a gray-green effect, to which its modest gray-blue flowers are added in winter. The foliage is aromatic.

RUSCUS (Butcher's Broom).—Only because it can be grown in the shade and drip of trees is any mention made of the Butcher's Broom, *R. aculeatus*. Its rather dull foliage is sometimes brightened by red berries.

SPARTIUM JUNCEUM (Spanish Broom).—This is by far the most valuable of the Brooms for California, for unlike most of the others it is in flower almost continuously from spring to late fall, and its yellow flowers are quite fragrant. It is easily raised from seed, and after being established requires no artificial watering. It is difficult to transplant excepting when very young. Though it can be used to cover sunny slopes it is more satisfactory where it is behind other shrubs, as its natural tendency is to grow quite tall and to flower on top. If a shapely plant is to be obtained prune back long growths each year: it is very difficult to restore a tall, leggy old plant to shapeliness.

TEUCRIUM (Germander).—*T. fruticans* is a grayish-leaved shrubby plant of straggling habit with pale blue flowers in early spring. Though of less compact growth, it can be associated with Rosemary and Lavender in a dry, sunny corner of the garden.

VERONICA.—The shrubby Veronicas, natives of New Zealand, are much happier in the cool summers of the San Francisco Bay region than in the interior or the southern part of the state. In a hot, dry climate they are rather subject to scale. They are nearly all rather formal in shape, making compact, round-headed bushes varying in height from the twelve-inch *V. pimeloides* through *V. buxifolia* (two feet), *V. traversi* (three feet), to *V. imperialis*, which grows to four or five feet. Visitors to the gardens of the New Zealand building at the Panama-Pacific Exposition may remember the many interesting little varieties suitable for edgings and for rock-gardens. These dwarfs are grown for their foliage value, but some of the larger ones for their spikes of white, blue, or red-purple flowers. Though the varieties of *V. speciosa* are the most showy, without question when it is in flower *V. hulkeana*, with its large spikes of porcelain-blue blossoms, is the most beautiful. As nurserymen do not offer long lists of shrubby Veronicas it will be useful for the amateur to know that all these shrubs come very easily from cuttings, making these from the ends of the new shoots.

VIBURNUM.—The evergreen Viburnums are more successful in California than the deciduous Snowballs. They are more commonly referred to as Laurustinus, though *Viburnum tinus* is the more authoritative name, While their foliage is coarse and uninteresting, shrubs which produce in midwinter broad heads of whitish flowers, pink in the bud stage, are valued. Like the Myrtles they are very old garden plants, from Italy, and consequently there are forms differing in worth to be seen in our gardens. Whenever it is possible to do so, get the freer-growing variety, *V. tinus var. lucidum*, which has not only finer foliage but larger flowers. They are useful for large plantings, where fine quality is not essential, and also as fillers for the intermediate portions of a shrub border. They will stand being brushed against, therefore they are good to use in public grounds.

SHRUBS FOR SPECIAL PURPOSES

HEDGES

Acacia longifolia	Buxus
Atriplex Breweri	Cupressus macrocarpa
Berberis Darwini	(Monterey Cypress)
Berberis stenophylla	Escallonia

Euonymus japonicus
Hakea saligna
Lantana
Leptospermum laevigatum
Ligustrum
Lonicera nitida

Myrtus
Pittosporum
Prunus ilicifolia
Pyracantha crenulata
Veronica
Viburnum tinus
    (Laurustinus)

SHADE-LOVING

Abelia
Azalea
Azara
Berberis Darwini
Camellia
Daphne odora
Erica
Fuchsia

Hydrangea
Hypericum calycinum
Mahonia
Nandina domestica
Prunus laurocerasus
Rhododendron
Rhus aculeatus
Sollya heterophylla
Veronica

BERRY-BEARING SHRUBS

Arbutus unedo
Aucuba japonica
Berberis Wilsoni
Berberis subcauliolata
Cotoneasters
Duranta Plumieri
Madrone
    (Arbutus menziesi)

Nandina domestica
Photinia arbutifolia
Pittosporum undulatum
Pyracantha angustifolia
Pyracantha coccinea
Pyracantha crenulata
Sambucus glauca
Solanum pseudo-capsicum

SHRUBS ENDURING DROUGHT AND NEGLECT; GOOD FOR DRY, SUNNY SLOPES

Acacia armata
Acacia cultriformis
Acacia verticillata
Buddleia
Callistemon
Carpenteria californica
Ceanothus
Cistus
Coprosma
Coronilla glauca
Cotoneaster
   (prostrate forms)
Cydonia japonica

Cytisus
Hakea
Hypericum calycinum
Jasminum primulinum
Juniperus sabina
Leptospermum laevigatum
Ligustrum
Melaleuca
Pittosporum
Punica granatum
Rosemarinus
Spartium junceum
Tamarix

Teucrium fruticans

CHAPTER VI

Vines and Trailers and Their Uses

THE ways in which climbing and trailing plants may contribute to the beauty and comfort of the garden are many and varied. They may first of all be grown on buildings, in some cases for the beauty of their foliage or the interest of its tracery. It is for this reason that the Boston Ivy (*Ampelopsis Veitchi*) is used on large wall spaces, breaking their monotony by the delicate pattern of its stems and foliage, pleasing the eye by its fine greenery in summer and adding warmth and color by the autumn tints of its falling leaves. With many climbers the chief beauty is the flowers, and when these cover the wall of the house their attractiveness will to a notable degree depend on the background, that is the wall itself. Thus, the brilliant magenta Bougainvillea makes a picture of extraordinary color beauty against a creamy white background, but planted as it sometimes is against a house of rusty red the effect is deplorable.

Again, a vine such as *Clematis montana*, with white flowers which appear before the foliage, is singularly appealing on a building of dark brown shingles, but against a white plaster background it makes little or no

effect. With others—the orange, red, and yellow
Lantana is an example—growing on a building covered
with weathered redwood shakes the color of the flower
harmonizes successfully with the background, but yet
on a creamy plaster wall there will be an equally attractive contrast between flower and background. With
vines used in this decorative way it is most important
to plant only those in proximity which will harmonize
in color and growth, and throughout their life to keep
them under reasonable control. In fact, we must use
discretion in the selection, trying to visualize the house
as it will appear a few years after planting. In one's
enthusiastic desire to have the beautiful climbers one
sees or reads of it is easy to plant too many, thus
eventually obscuring the architectural lines of the
house and creating a tangle which can only suggest
neglect.

In many cases vines are planted on houses and even
more on outbuildings for purposes of concealment, to
disguise the architectural lines which do not appeal to
the owner of the house, or in the case of smaller buildings to obliterate them as much as possible from the
landscape. For this secondary use rapid and vigorous
growth and good and persistent foliage are the most
acceptable qualities. Fineness of form or beauty of
flower become of minor importance.

There are also many instances where vines are used
on houses to give shade, where the summers are long

and warm and there are verandas to be screened. But
this use for shade extends beyond the house to the
covering of summerhouses, pergolas, and arches.
Pergolas not only provide pleasant shady walks but
they frequently offer opportunity to use certain climbers
in a more attractive way than is possible against a
flat surface, as is instanced by the added beauty of
Wistaria when its low drooping racemes are seen over-
head.

When gardens are small, every inch of room is needed,
and broad boundary plantings of shrubs or hungry
hedges would not be welcome, privacy and an attractive
green background for the flower border are often secured
by a lattice or wire fence over which evergreen vines
are grown. Ivy has been used in this way, and though
it takes some time to cover the fence, it will do so completely. It is, of course, rather sombre in effect. The
Muehlenbeckia, by careful and constant trimming,
will make a solid wall of greenery, quite formal in effect.
The Jasmines are excellent also for purposes of screening.

Plants which trail rather than climb are often used
to cover rough slopes or banks, or unattractive rocks
or stumps. Of the many available for such purposes,
Plumbago capensis, *Lantana Sellowiana*, *Lonicera Halliana*, and *Sollya heterophylla* are examples.

While the aim should be to have a few fine permanent vines, there are times and places where an immediate
screen is wanted. In such cases use will be made of the

rapid-growing herbaceous climbers. Among these are the annual Morning Glories or their close relatives the perennial Ipomeas. While one is waiting for Roses, Jasmines, and other permanent vines to grow up, a quick effect may be had with these. *Cobæa scandens*, from Mexico, is one of the quickest of vines, with large leaves and bell-shaped purple or white flowers. *Dolichos lignosus*, the Australian Pea Vine, small-leaved and with pink or, better, white flowers, is good for a low screen. For the quickest possible effects one may use the Hop Vine for shade or shelter. Other possibilities are the Gourds, with their many peculiar fruits, and the Scarlet Runner Bean.

In making a selection of vines the question of frost must always be taken into consideration. Many beautiful climbing plants are of tropical origin, and some should not be planted indiscriminately even in southern California. Aspect and shelter of walls are of importance where somewhat tender subjects are to be tried. Occasional freezes have taught us not to depend too much on tender vines, but to use those adapted to our conditions.

Vines vary greatly in their manner of growing and of climbing. A few support themselves by pads or feet; examples are *Ampelopsis Veitchi* and *Ficus repens*. Others climb by means of tendrils, and still others pull themselves up by hooking on to other plants. A very large group is made up of those which twine. Thus it may be seen that the support to be provided for them should vary according to the character of the growth. For vines which twine, lattices or very large-meshed wire are best. For those with tendrils a fine-meshed wire such as is used for chicken fences is more acceptable. It has been found by experience that vines suffer if allowed to sprawl at an early stage. They should be urged from the beginning to climb. Each stem should be trained horizontally for a short distance at first, rather than taking them straight up from the leader.

The characteristics, uses, and limitations of a selection of the more permanent vines follow:

AKEBIA.—Rather delicate, slender-growing vines, evergreen in southern California. *A. quinata* has purplish-rose flowers. It will make a low screen.

AMPELOPSIS.—The variety known as the Boston Ivy, *A. Veitchi* properly *A. tricuspidata*, a native of Japan, is the beautiful deciduous vine which is so great an addition to brick, stone, or cement walls, on which it supports itself by disks. It is less satisfactory on wood. As it does not need help it is a good vine for very high walls. *A. quinquefolia*, the Virginia Creeper, will readily be distinguished from the former by its large leaves divided into five leaflets. It is deciduous, the leaves turning bright scarlet in fall. The newer *A. Engelmanni* is very desirable.

BIGNONIA.—Beautiful evergreen climbers, generally with yellow, orange, or red tubular flowers. *B. tweediana* is the hardiest; it has clinging tendrils but ap-

preciates support. It withstands drought and heat.
The flowers are single, sulphur-yellow, blooming at one
time in spring. *B. buccinatoria* (syn. *B. cherere*) is a
very handsome variety with large blood-red flowers
and rich green foliage; a very vigorous grower but
rather tender, though it does well as far north as
Berkeley. It blooms all through the warm weather.
B. speciosa has flowers of mauve with a lighter colored
throat, borne in large clusters. Somewhat tender and
less rank in growth, it generally prefers a shady place.
It is a free bloomer. Perhaps the most gorgeous but
unfortunately the tenderest of the Bignonias, not
satisfactory in a cool section, is *B. venusta*. Its flaming
orange clusters of finger-shaped flowers are glorious
in midwinter in such places as Santa Barbara. It does
best against a warm surface, as on the top of a sunny
wall, flat roof, or pergola.

BOUGAINVILLEA.—These climbers from South
America make a wonderful display, not from their
inconspicuous flowers but from the beautiful bracts
surrounding them. *B. spectabilis*, a bright magenta,
is the hardiest and thrives in a protected position as
far north as the San Francisco Bay district. Its form
lateritia, a wonderful brick red, needs the sun upon it to
bring out its color. It is unfortunately rather tender,
and is only really satisfactory in warm, nearly frostless
places such as Santa Barbara.

CLEMATIS.—These deciduous climbers should be
more used. The large-flowered forms, however, such

as *C. Jackmanni* (violet-purple), are slow-growing and demand good culture and proper training. The soil must be well drained, and preferably cool and moist. Of smaller forms, *C. montana* (white) and its variety *rubens* (pale pink) are most vigorous, easily grown, and beautiful when they flower in early spring. *C. paniculata* has very small white flowers in late summer. Prune the Clematis after blooming.

CLIANTHUS.—The Parrot's Bill, *C. puniceus*, an evergreen leaning plant from New Zealand, with pinnate leaves and extraordinary bright red curving blooms, should be planted against a latticed fence or on a low trellis. It is very distinct in appearance.

FICUS.—The climbing Fig, *F. repens*, is a very useful small evergreen for covering low walls or clothing the foundations of a house. It clings as does the Boston Ivy, and requires no support. It is always presentable, but as it gets older is apt to make larger, coarser leaves, a condition often brought on by too rich feeding.

HARDENBERGIA.—These Australian twiners, with their racemes of small pea-shaped flowers, white, pink, or purple, bloom profusely in late winter and early spring, but they are rather tender and therefore best fitted for southern California.

HEDERA.—The Ivy, *H. Helix*, is generally used as a ground-cover in California but is equally good as a climber. Its advantages are that it is not rampant,

supports itself, and stands shade. It is readily propagated from half-ripe cuttings almost buried in the
soil. These make little growth the first year. There
are some beautiful varieties of more delicate shape and
lighter color, little disseminated as yet in California.

JASMINUM.—The Jasmines, twiners with sweet-
scented flowers either white or yellow, are best adapted
to southern California, though the hardier ones, such
as the old white fragrant *J. officinale*, are everywhere
easy to grow. *J. grandiflorum* is a much better white in
every way, but is unfortunately not hardy enough for
the cold of the interior valleys. *J. primulinum* has
much larger yellow flowers, and its double form is
especially good. It is a very rapid grower, evergreen,
and makes an excellent ground-cover. It is fairly
hardy.

LANTANA.—In addition to the shrubby Lantanas
grown in southern California there are scandent or
climbing kinds, very vigorous in growth and more able
to resist frost. They are distinctly unsuited to a cold
location, and should be sheltered from the north wind.
Though they can be trained high on a house, they are
more generally useful for foundation planting, where
their evergreen foliage and long season of bloom (from
early summer to very late fall) are decided assets.
There are creamy-white, pink, and other soft shades,
but the most effective is unquestionably the more
common red-and-yellow form. *L. Sellowiana* is almost
invariably used as a ground-cover, for which its trailing

growth fits it.   Its lilac-pink flowers are not particularly pleasing in color.

LONICERA (Honeysuckle).—The greatest attraction of the Honeysuckles is the fragrance of their comparatively inconspicuous flowers.   Their growth is very strong and dense, and the old wood generally loses its leaves, so that when cut back bare brown stems are left for a long time.   Trained on a wire fence, they make a thick screen, but spread out in growth at the top so that they occupy too much space in a small garden.   Their best use is to cover old outbuildings, stumps, or slopes to which little care can be given. *L. Halliana*, the Japanese Honeysuckle, with white and yellow flowers and bright green leaves, is the usual form.   The less common Chinese Honeysuckle will be distinguished from it by the reddish-purple tinge on the backs of the new leaves and by its white and purple flowers.

MANDEVILLA.—This sweet-scented summer-flowering deciduous vine is of slender growth, which makes it very suitable for growing with a sturdier plant of whose support it can take advantage.   It is sometimes grown on Oaks, and will make its way to the top of the tree, there spreading out its clusters of large white flowers which have earned it the name of the Chili Jasmine.   A good vine for southern California.

MUEHLENBECKIA.—The evergreen twining vine with black wire-like stems and tiny round leaves, variously known as the Maidenhair Vine, Mattress Vine, Wire Vine, and Tasmanian Ivy, is *Muehlenbeckia complexa.* It is grown wholly for its fine foliage, which will ultimately take possession of any surface which it can reach. It has a certain value when grown on chicken-wire and kept clipped, or used to cover unsightly objects, but its rampant, persistent, and penetrating stems so readily get out of control that it should never be planted in any choice position.

PASSIFLORA (Passion Vine).—The term Passion Vine is applied to two groups of very rapid-growing climbers, the Passifloras and the Tacsonias. The latter, distinguished by their longer tubes, are quite tender. The rank, untidy growth of both families, the necessity of cutting them down occasionally, and their extreme attraction for caterpillars have so reduced their popularity that in spite of their bright and curious flowers they are now being little grown.

PLUMBAGO.—While of no value for high climbing, *P. capensis* can be very satisfactorily employed trailing down a slope or covering any low unsightly object. Though rather a strong grower, with a little attention it will be quite good treated as a shrub, planted at the base of the house, or wherever its pale blue flowers are wanted all through the long summer.

ROSES.—The culture of Roses is considered elsewhere in this book. Here we shall merely emphasize the great garden value of the climbing kinds. As early

as January the Cherokees are often blooming freely in
sunny locations, and their season extends until April.
They are not rampant, and are best used on fences and
low supports.   In April and May we may have the very
high-growing white and yellow Banksias, the floriferous
Noisettes, and the climbing forms of many bush Roses,
as different in size and manner of growth as Caroline
Testout and Cecile Brunner. The season may be
further extended by adding those of the Rambler type,
chiefly Wichuraiana hybrids, Tausendschön and Lady
Gay being good examples. With this last class it is
very desirable to learn before planting how well any
variety is adapted to the location, for some, such as
Dorothy Perkins, are so subject to mildew in some
places as to be worthless.

SOLANUM.—There are many members of the family
of the Potato Vines, but being tropical in origin few will
stand the occasional frosts of even warm sections of the
state. *S. jasminoides*, a free-blooming white-flowered
variety, is the only one which will stand much cold.
S. Rantonneti, so low as to be almost a shrub, has
clusters of small violet-blue flowers and is occasionally
seen in our gardens.   It is not hardy, yet in a protected
place it will grow as far north as Berkeley and will make
a good color effect as late as Christmas.   It is regrettable that the really beautiful *S. Wendlandii*, with its
fine trusses of large pale blue flowers, is so tender as to
be permanent only in sheltered gardens in such favored
spots as Santa Barbara.

SOLANDRA.—Another tropical climber, only to be used in the warmest and most protected situations, is *S. grandiflora*, which has been given the name of· Copa de Oro for its really gigantic cupped flowers of golden yellow. This vine is a wonderful sight when in bloom in late spring. Its best use is on a pergola.

SOLLYA (Australian Blue-bell).—Of less rampant growth than *Plumbago capensis*, with better foliage and with small flowers of more intense blue, *Sollya heterophylla* is generally grown for the same purpose, as a trailing ground-cover. It is rather a fine thing.

TACSONIA.—See under *Passiflora*.

TECOMA.—These close allies of the Bignonias are strong, tall-growing vines, climbing to the tops of houses if they have some support on which to twist their way. *T. radicans* and *T. grandiflora* are both deciduous and have large orange-red flowers. As *T. radicans* gets very woody and in some gardens has suckered to such an extent as to become a menace, *T. grandiflora* will be generally preferred. Of the evergreen Tecomas, we have *T. jasminoides*, with small dark green leaves and white and carmine flowers; its white form, *T. jasminoides alba*; and *T. australis*, more valued for its bronzed foliage than for its small creamy flowers. *T. capensis* and *T. Smithii* are generally grown as shrubs.

VITIS.—The evergreen Grape, *V. capensis*, is a very beautiful vine which has become extremely popular because of its clean, beautifully formed foliage and fine

clusters of ornamental fruit. It is good for pergolas
and arches, but not very hardy.

WISTARIA.—Where these beautiful deciduous climbers are grown the development of their long pendent
clusters of blue or white flowers is eagerly awaited each
year in early spring.   While they are often attractively
grown on the sides of houses, they are at their best on
pergolas, or along the edge of a porch, where the racemes
may be seen from beneath. Two forms are grown—
the commoner one the Chinese Wistaria, more compact
in growth, with shorter racemes of large, sweet-scented
flowers, occasionally white but more generally blue. The
Japanese Wistaria is more vigorous in growth, the
flowers are smaller, and the racemes much longer and
looser, giving a more graceful effect.   Of this species it
is usually the white form which is grown.

CHAPTER VII

The Problem of the Perennial

THE gardener in California is, in regard to hardy perennial plants, both better and worse off than if he were in a colder, wetter climate. He is better off in that he may consider as in that class plants which elsewhere in America are used only in greenhouses or for summer bedding, such, for example, as the Geraniums, Pelargoniums, and Heliotrope. Others somewhat tender in many places but always quite hardy with him are *Anchusa italica*, Chrysanthemums, Pentstemons, and Tritomas. Some families, such as the Bearded Irises, Flaxes, Sages, and Valerians, whose country of origin is around the Mediterranean, are particularly happy in his dry summers. It is rarely that he ever loses a hardy perennial plant because of winter cold; summer drought is more likely to weaken if not kill them. On the other hand, he will find that certain very popular perennials of colder climates, in particular the wonderful herbaceous Pæonies and the colorful hardy Phlox, should not be depended on in California for the fine garden effects they will give in the East or on the Pacific coast from Oregon north. The careful gardener may achieve a measure of success with them, but, as in the case of the Lilacs, they do not attain perfection. With the careless gardener they are very poor.

If the Eastern gardener finds it his most difficult problem to keep in bloom for five or six months a flower border restricted to hardy perennial plants, the Californian with a twelve-months period to cover will acknowledge the impossibility of so doing. He will do well to cast aside all distinctions between flowering plants, and in his flower border use anything which will bloom—shrubs (preferably at the back), true perennials, spring- and summer-flowering bulbs, and annuals. In his climate some plants commonly grown as annuals, such as Scabious, Snapdragons, and Salpiglossis, often become short-lived perennials in favorable places, and others generally biennial, Sweet Williams and Hollyhocks for example, if well placed live over for two or more years. In the flower border he will have to give careful consideration to size, height, season of bloom, and color to achieve a pleasing and satisfying whole, and will recognize that striking effects are given by grouping, not by the scattered planting of single plants. In the chapter on considerations of color and continuity in the flower garden more is said on the subject of arrangement, but in the notes on separate species which follow, suggestions for particular use are frequently made.

There is no need to restrict these plants to flower borders. Many of the dwarfer ones are indispensable in a rock-garden, where they are more effective because the scale is smaller; others may be planted around pools. Some of the most continuous bloomers are good bedding plants, and some are at their best in groups by themselves, Japanese Anemones near Ferns or where they are in the partial shade of Oak trees, Hollyhocks along a divisional fence, Primroses in thin woods, Pentstemons in groups between shrubs, Irises or Chrysanthemums in special gardens by themselves.

In their cultivation it will be quickly seen that plants which are to remain undisturbed for years should be put in soil which has been really deeply dug and well fertilized. Fall planting and dividing are best in a country where the summers are dry, as it gives the plants a few months of cool wet weather in which to become established. Where this is impracticable, as in a new garden, most perennials may be moved in spring, preferably early, but the best results should not then be expected until next season.

For increase of stock, division is very often the simplest method and a perfectly satisfactory one, though there are some exceptions, such as Aquilegias and Delphiniums, where raising from seed is preferable. Excepting in the case of named garden varieties of Phlox, Iris, and similar highly developed families, hardy perennials may be very easily acquired by sowing seed. Some, such as the Pentstemons, will bloom profusely the same season if the seed is sown early in the spring, but most will not flower until the second year, therefore when an immediate effect is wanted plants must be purchased, but where the gardener is willing to wait he can get large numbers of perennial

plants from a small expenditure for seed. It cannot
be too strongly emphasized that the best possible seed
should always be bought, regardless of cost, and this is
particularly true of plants which are to be so permanent
as perennials. When fifty or a hundred Aquilegias,
Delphiniums, or Oriental Poppies come from a single
packet of seed it will at once be evident that the extra
cost of seed per plant will be negligible, and yet it will
make all the difference in the quality.

ACANTHUS.—The chief value of the Acanthus is in its
large, beautifully shaped, glossy leaves, which come up
with the first rains and die away in midsummer. The
spikes of peculiar white and lilac flowers, three or four
feet high, though rather sombre, have a certain architectural effect and add dignity to the planting. It is
best planted in fall, being readily increased from the
many offshoots it makes.

ACHILLEA (Milfoil, Yarrow).—Of the various Achilleas
the one best known, particularly to those who have
gardened in the East, is *A. Ptarmica*, in its forms The
Pearl and Perry's White. This is everywhere a rather
weedy and spreading plant yet is still grown for its
multitude of small double white flowers on stems two or
three feet high. It does not do particularly well in
California, and we can get along very well without it.
A. millefolium roseum, quite a different plant, with
flat panicles of rose-colored flowers surmounting two-
foot stems draped in feathery foliage, is rather to be

recommended as it will endure drought and neglect. *A. tomentosa* is one of several very dwarf species whose growth and many flat panicles of bright yellow flowers fit it for the sunny rock-garden. Increase by division in fall or spring.

AETHIONEMA.—A dwarf evergreen perennial allied to the Candytufts is *A. grandiflorum*, which in the spring-time produces many racemes of bright pink and lilac flowers. A Mediterranean plant, it enjoys the sun and is at its best in a well-drained place in the rock-garden. It is most readily raised from seed.

AGAVE.—For a sub-tropical or desert effect, the Agaves with their fine clumps of thick fleshy foliage are most useful. The variety most grown is *A. americana*, the well-known Century Plant, so called from its slowness in flowering. It may be used in a formal manner, or a number of plants may be grouped together for big effects. From the time the plants are started from offsets until they send up their tall, picturesque branched flower-stems at about fifteen years of age, they are ornaments requiring no care. After blooming the plants die.

ALOE.—In sunny situations where winters are warm, from Christmas through to spring, it is possible to brighten up the landscape with the long-branched red or yellow flower-spikes of these great succulents. Visitors to Westlake Park, Los Angeles, or to the botanical garden of the University of California at

Berkeley will have seen them and noted how effective
they are in large gardens. The nomenclature is much
confused, and it is best therefore to get offsets or cuttings
of known plants, allowing cuttings to dry out for two or
three days before setting them in sandy soil. Aloes
are quite successful in dry rocky soils, but most varieties require a lot of room. The smaller ones are good
rock-garden plants.

ALTHEA.—See HOLLYHOCK.

ALYSSUM.—During the winter months in my sunny
hillside garden I can always depend on masses of bright
yellow flowers from *A. saxatile*, one of the best permanent border-plants for California and equally adapted to
sunny rock-gardens. It is, moreover, very drought-
resistant, and when out of flower in summer its gray
foliage is always presentable. Besides the type, which
is quite rampant, there is one of similar color but
dwarfer growth, *A. saxatile compactum*, and also a
similar form, *A. saxatile citrinum*, with very pale yellow
flowers. All may readily be raised from seed, indeed
they often self-sow. They may also be increased by
dividing the clumps in fall, when even pieces with
little or no root will grow.

ANCHUSA.—The form of outstanding value in California is *A. italica*, a very hardy and vigorous plant
with large hairy leaves and spikes three or four feet
high of beautiful blue flowers, in form like Forget-me-
Nots. Its ease of culture, its indifference to drought,

and the need of blue in the garden all combine to make it popular. It is almost terribly permanent, and should be planted only where one is sure it will be wanted always. Bits of the root left a foot or eighteen inches under ground will crop up cheerfully again. Propagate either by seed or by a division of the thick roots. My experience is that practically any piece will grow. The Dropmore variety is most grown, but the paler Opal is sometimes seen.

ANEMONE (Windflower).—Of all the late-blooming perennials none is more satisfactory than the Japanese Windflower, *A. japonica*. In the warmer parts of California it should be given a rather shaded position, and anywhere it will appreciate a cool location, such as one would give Fuchsias or Ferns. So treated, its tall, graceful habit and beauty of blossom and foliage entitle it to a large and prominent use. Plant preferably in groups, and choose the location advisedly, as this Anemone is much better if not frequently moved. Increased by suckers, the new plants may be put in any time from the fall rains until April. The semi-double white Whirlwind and the pink Queen Charlotte are particularly liked, the latter being a much better color than the type, which is a rather unpleasant shade of deep pink. *A. sylvestris*, a smaller, dwarfer single white flower, is rarely seen, but is quite attractive in early spring in a half-shaded place.

ANTHEMIS (Rock Camomile).—*A. tinctoria*, the variety grown, is a yellow, Daisy-like flower, of the simplest cultivation, enduring poor soil and drought. It is rather coarse, and its habit of turning down its petals when out of the sun relegates it, in the better gardens, to a position of secondary importance.

AQUILEGIA (Columbine).—The Columbines are among the most valuable of the larger families of perennials, and many of them seem particularly adapted to California. Though the more vigorous ones will stand considerable sunshine and drought, they are all better where they have only morning sun and plenty of water. This is particularly true of *A. caerulea*, which is in any case never really perennial. Better adapted to our conditions are *A. chrysantha* (yellow, three feet high, and grows like a weed), its pure white form, and also *A. Skinneri*, a form from Central America, which is red and yellow. Various strains of long-spurred hybrids have been developed by crossing these, and the variation is so great that there is more interest in these hybrids than in the types. Of the short-spurred Columbines, the native Californian *A. truncata* is a good orange and red, and in the seedling forms of *A. vulgaris* one can obtain a wide range of colors though some of them are rather dull. A fine white variety of this type, which comes true from seed, is Munstead White.

They may be readily raised from seed sown at any time in boxes and kept moist until germination occurs. It is very hard to get them true to any color, and it is practically useless to gather seed from a particular plant with the idea of perpetuating its color. Propagation by division of the root is possible, but will generally be found to weaken the stock.

ARABIS (Rock Cress).—In a rock-garden not exposed to continual sun, or for an edging to a cool border, *A. albida* is most desirable, for its gray-green foliage is pretty and permanent and in early spring it is covered with short spikes of snowy flowers. It does not enjoy summer heat and drought, and if used where those conditions exist a few rocks under which its roots will be protected and an occasional soaking are advisable. There is a double form with finer flowers which lasts longer, but unfortunately it is rarely offered, and unlike the single one cannot be obtained from seed, but must be propagated by cuttings.

ARENARIA (Sandwort).—As its name indicates, this family is fond of a light, sandy soil. With me it is much better in semi-shade and with considerable moisture. *A. balearica* is so dwarf as to seem almost a moss, but its bright green is starred with many little white flowers. It spreads rapidly, and should be used both in rock-gardens and for planting between stepping-stones in shady walks. *A. montana* is a larger trailer, with more striking white flowers. It is best in a semi-shaded rock-garden or trailing over a wall which faces north or east. Propagate by seed or division.

ARMERIA (Thrift, Sea-Pink).—The common Thrift, *A. vulgaris*, is frequently used for edging, as its little tufts of green grassy foliage are always neat, though the flower-heads of the form generally used are of a magenta pink which many dislike. It stands considerable neglect and makes no demands for care. *A. caespitosa* is rarely offered, but the lover of rock-plants should raise it from seed as it is altogether a much larger and finer thing, with flowers of a pleasing shade of pink. All varieties may be propagated by division.

ASTER (Michaelmas Daisy).—This group of plants, the true Asters, should have a far greater use. Not only do they make pleasing groups of narrow green foliage, but they are literally covered in their season, midsummer to fall, with thousands of starry single Daisies, white, lavender, blue to violet, and lilac-pink to purple, in the different varieties. The cloud-like masses, going as high as three or four feet in such varieties as Climax and White Queen, have a great garden value, while for smaller and daintier effects and for cutting, varieties of the *ericoides* and *cordifolius* sections are preferred. Their culture is very simple, not dissimilar to the garden growing of Chrysanthemums. For the best effects the tall, strong-growing kinds should be planted each spring a foot apart, though they will still be pretty satisfactory if left for two years; beyond that they get too crowded. The absence of summer rain makes staking practically unnecessary where good culture is given and the growth is consequently strong. They enjoy a rich, well-worked soil, frequent watering through the summer, and a good mulch of rotted manure or leaves to retain the moisture. If they are prevented from going to seed by cutting the stems to the ground after flowering they will produce secondary growth which will greatly prolong the flowering season. The *Amellus* varieties, with their larger single flowers and lower growth, are better used for bordering, while *A. subcaeruleus* is most satisfactory in the rock-garden, as it forms merely a tuft of low foliage from which the blue flowers rise to a height of about eight inches in spring.

AUBRIETIA (Purple Rock Cress).—Through the late winter and the spring months there is no more effective rock-plant than the Aubrietia, which is then entirely covered by small flowers varying in color from lavender of the palest to violet, and including lilac-pinks and rosy purples. Another excellent use of it is to plant it where it will trail over a rock wall, for under favorable conditions it will make tremendous growth. It is perfectly hardy and also resistant to drought, but it certainly makes better growth where it is not so baked during the summer that it is practically dried up. Though it does not come perfectly true from seed, that is still much the best way to raise a stock of plants, starting them in boxes whenever desired. To increase a particular variety, remove rooted portions in the early fall, or make cuttings of the green shoots. It seems practically useless to try these latter methods at other times of the year.

BEGONIA.—The culture of tuberous-rooted Begonias will be found in the chapter on bulbs and tuberous-rooted plants. The section with which we are here concerned is that of the fibrous-rooted bedding plants which in the warm coastal regions are hardy perennials most valuable for summer beds and borders. In their culture avoid frost, windy places, and hot sun. Give them rather sheltered places in partial shade, with light, rich soil to which leaf-mold or peat has been added, and through the long dry summer see that they do not suffer for water. They are particularly satisfactory on the east side of the house, and if combined with Ferns they will add the desired color to the bed. The beautiful, tall Tree Begonias form excellent back-row plants, while the free-flowering bedding varieties, the *semperflorens* types, can be kept compact and neat as is desired for the front of the bed. The latter are easy doers, will flower from seed the same season if it is started in February in boxes, and can be increased by cuttings.

BELLIS.—The English Daisy, *B. perennis*, is almost a weed in some California lawns, where, however, it is very pretty in early spring. Its chief value is as an edging plant. It is easily increased by dividing the plants in spring or fall. Very large-flowered forms may be raised from seed, but they are less floriferous and rather overfed in appearance.

BOLTONIA.—Aster-like plants resembling the Michaelmas Daisies but inferior to them for general garden use and less permanent in southern California. *B.*

asteroides, white, grows about six feet high. *B. latis-quama* is rosy-lavender. Propagate by division of the roots, from fall to spring. They enjoy moisture.

CACTUS.—This large family of greatly differing suc-culents is of less interest to the general gardener than to the specialist who collects them to grow in pots or on a dry sunny slope. For the most part they are easy doers in light, sandy soil not deficient in lime. They are propagated by cuttings, which should be put in sand after the places where they were cut have become dry.

CALCEOLARIA.—Though the large Calceolarias are even in California only greenhouse annuals, the related *C. rugosa* is quite reasonably hardy along the coast, and does particularly well around San Francisco Bay. It is a long-blooming semi-shrub, valued for foundation plant-ing. The two colors chiefly seen are yellow and reddish brown. In almost any situation it will flower pro-fusely in late spring, but if given good soil and kept in active growth by watering it will continue into mid-summer. It is most easily propagated by winter cut-tings made under glass, but may of course be raised more slowly from seed.

CAMPANULA (Bellflower).—From this large family only a few of the more commonly grown species will be selected for mention, though a book might be written on them. *C. Medium,* the Canterbury Bell, is only a biennial, and one which does not bloom from seed until the second year. The simple, single-flowered forms are best, and all the colors combine well, an unusual and interesting result being obtained where the dark blue-purple and the pale pink ones are grouped together. Seed should be sown in boxes or seed-bed in the spring, and the plants grown on and put in the fall where they are wanted to bloom the following spring. The most popular of the larger perennial forms is *C. persicifolia*, the Peach-leaved Bellflower, which if planted in good soil and allowed to become established will develop into fine clumps with tall erect stems of cup-shaped flowers in blue or white. As with all Campanulas, the single forms are much more graceful and attractive. The more ambitious gardener may like to try *C. pyramidalis*, the Chimney Bellflower, which attains a height of from five to eight feet. In California it seems to be a short-lived perennial, with the peculiarity of often not blooming for the first two or three years and not infrequently dying after its wonderful inflorescence is over. It is a practically impossible plant in hot, dry sections, and even in cooler ones prefers a northern exposure and considerable moisture.

Very different are the dwarf-growing and trailing Campanulas, which are best adapted to rock-gardening and growing at the top of cool walls. *C. Portenschlagiana* (syn. *muralis*) is a very dwarf, tufted plant, covered in summer with small blue flowers. This increases rapidly by underground stems, and may also be propagated by cuttings. A beautiful variety to trail over a wall, particularly one facing east, is *C. isophylla alba*, with rounded grayish foliage and flat white flowers about an inch and a half across.

CENTAUREA.—The Dusty Miller, *C. candidissima* or *ragusina*, is valued for its silvery-white foliage which can be used for bordering formal flower-beds or for grouping with foliage-plants. It is a perennial most readily increased by rooting stem cuttings. Its flowers are no addition to its beauty.

CENTRANTHUS (Valerian).—The Garden Heliotrope of Eastern gardens, *C. officinalis*, is rarely grown in California but its relative, *C. ruber*, a Spanish Valerian, possesses the utmost vigor and very readily becomes a weed, as it spreads both by roots and seed. The only one with any merit is the deep red form, for the lilac-pink variety is a color difficult to combine and not attractive in itself, while the white form is rather dirty in effect. For their ease of growth they will be useful to careless gardeners; the careful ones will want if any only the red form, which should be obtained by division of the roots, kept from seeding, and not allowed to encroach on more delicate plants.

CERASTIUM (Mouse-ear).—These gray-leaved, dwarf creeping plants, neat at all times and quite pretty in spring when covered with their white flowers, should be used in sunny rock-gardens, over walls, and as edgings. *C. tomentosum* is the commonest form, but *C.*

Biebersteini, with its larger leaves and flowers, is quite worth while. Propagate by tufts of the creeping roots, which tend to overrun bounds.

CHAENOSTOMA.—*C. hispidum*, a sub-shrubby perennial which grows scarcely a foot high, is worth having in gardens comparatively free from frost. Its twiggy green foliage is always sightly, and from spring to fall it bears successive crops of tiny porcelain blossoms. Propagate by cuttings at any time.

CHEIRANTHUS (Wallflower).—From British Columbia south to central California the Wallflowers are among the most desirable of early spring plants. For beds in full sunlight and for bright, warm borders they are unexcelled. Seed of separate colors is obtainable, and the results are more satisfactory than where mixtures are used. Nothing can exceed the brilliance of the orange-red Fire King, but where such color is not wanted one may have the deep velvety red of Vulcan, the buff and salmon-pink of Eastern Queen, the pure ruby of Ellen Willmott, the pale yellow of Primrose Dame, or any of the deeper golden yellows. Wallflowers are not true perennials, and more exacting gardeners raise new plants from seed sown in August and planted out to bloom next spring. Such plants will, however, do very well for another year, when they will be taller and larger, but after that they should be discarded. For southern California the early-flowering or Parisian Wallflowers are best, and should be treated as annuals. A beautiful wild Wallflower, greatly surpassing even the garden Wallflowers in fragrance, is the brilliant orange *C. allioni,* whose best use is as a biennial in a sunny rock-garden. *C. linifolius,* sometimes called *Erysimum linifolium,* is a Spanish variety with lilac-mauve flowers which may be treated as a biennial or even as an annual.

CHRYSANTHEMUM.—For all the florists' Chrysanthemums see the chapter on Specialties. There are, however, groups of large white Daisies, hardy perennials and forms of *C. maximum.* These are little grown in California, their place being taken by the closely allied Shasta Daisies, important plants for summer gardening. Raised originally from seed, there are now so many forms that care should be taken to obtain plants of the most graceful type, which has a small centre and very long white petals. Shasta Daisies grow so readily that they are generally neglected; for the finest results the ground should be properly prepared by digging and fertilizing and the plants divided and reset in single pieces every second year. After blooming, the flower-stems should be cut well back, and the plants watered to induce continued bloom. Shasta Daisies are of great value for edging wide paths. In grouping they are most effective when used as a foreground to large plantings of perennial Larkspurs.

C. frutescens, the Marguerite or Paris Daisy, causes astonishment to visitors to California by the immense size which the bushy plants attain. Both the single white and yellow forms are useful for foundation planting and for bordering driveways, for they are almost continually in bloom. Though less graceful, the double white Mrs. Sanders is preferred by some, as its blooms are larger. The Marguerites are of the easiest possible growth, and root readily in sandy soil from green cuttings.

CINERARIA.—Even in the favored districts where they are generally grown outdoors, an exceptionally cold winter may kill off or seriously damage a border of Cinerarias. Where this happens only occasionally, the value of this plant for growing on the north side of the house or even under trees is such that many gardeners will take the sporting chance. We have nothing else like them in the flower garden, and when they bloom through the spring the profusion of their large panicles of bright flowers lightens up parts of the garden where few things would do well. The magenta shades found in some mixtures have caused criticisms of their color range, but by selection it has become possible to have beds exclusively made up of harmonizing shades of blue, rose, and pink. Where the large show type seems heavy and formal the taller, more graceful, but smaller-flowered Stellata strains should be used. Propagate by seed sown in spring or summer in shade, and plant out by fall. The plants do not last indefinitely, but they so frequently self-sow that they perpetuate themselves.

CONVOLVULUS.—A good many plants of the Bindweed family, either annual or perennial, tend to become serious weeds. Do not, however, fear to introduce *C. mauritanicus* into your garden. As a ground-cover on a dry sunny bank, or falling over a wall, it will through the summer be covered with beautiful little blue flowers of Morning Glory shape but without the habit of closing when the sun is on them. After it has become established it needs no watering. Propagate by divisions or cuttings.

COREOPSIS.—The perennial Coreopsis is *C. lanceolata* or *grandiflora*, an easily grown plant which produces during the summer from its compact clumps dozens of bright yellow flowers larger than any annual variety and on longer stems. Seed sown in the fall will give fine plants for next summer's flowering, or the stock may be increased by division of the roots during the rainy season. While generally a biennial in the East, it is perennial in California, but better when frequently renewed from seed.

CUPHEA.—Of this family the member most generally grown in California is *C. platycentra*, whose vermilion tubular flowers with ash-gray tips have caused it to be called the Cigar-plant. Its evergreen foliage and dwarf shrubby growth make it suitable for the rock-garden in places where there are no heavy frosts. All summer it is covered with flowers. Propagate by cuttings or by seed if necessary. Usually one will find many seedling plants springing up around the parent.

DAHLIA.—See chapter on Specialties.

Delphinium (Larkspur).—The tall perennial **Lark-spurs** are distinctly garden plants which have been brought to their present perfection by hybridization and high cultivation. In their height, their wonderful shades of lavender, blue, mauve to violet, and their profusion of bloom, they have no competitors. In large groups by themselves, in the foreground of shrubbery borders, banked against white or gray house walls, they are worth the trouble involved in their culture.

In California this means giving them deep, rich soil, a summer mulch of old manure, occasional thorough drenching, and cultivation to prevent the soil drying out. Snails and slugs are excessively fond of them, and where these are to be found protection must be provided. Among the methods used is to put rough coal-ashes around the crown in the fall, or to surround the plant with a protective ring of something over which slugs will not crawl. In badly infested gardens any damage can be prevented by putting a collar of half-inch wire around each plant. Where sparrows and linnets abound and eat off the young growth in spring, chicken-wire or other protection will be necessary.

Delphiniums are very easily raised from seed sown either in early fall or in spring in boxes, from which the plants should be moved out not less than two feet apart. The very best seed should be bought, as fine strains will give plants equal to named varieties and far outstripping them in vigor. If it is desired to make a selection from the seedlings, do this while the plants are still young, as they then move much better than when they have become large clumps. While it is true that any variety may be increased by division of the roots, there seems always to be decreased vigor as a result, and in California at least it is best to consider these plants as not very long-lived perennials which should better be renewed every few years from seed. Under good cultivation, after the spring crop of flowers is over the old spikes, before they go to seed, should be cut to the ground, and this process if continued will sometimes give three or four crops. This continual blooming doubtless exhausts the plants, and is one of the factors requiring their renewal.

Less striking than the tall hybrids are those of the *Belladonna* section, which have deeply cut leaves, more branching spikes, and flowers of a celestial blue. The native *D. cardinale* is a beautiful tall scarlet wildflower, but it is so difficult either to raise from seed or to transplant from the wild that only the most ambitious gardener should attempt it.

DIANTHUS (Pink).—The Pheasant-eyed Pink, *D. plumarius,* is an excellent perennial and on account of its evergreen foliage of grayish tint it is one of the very best plants for edging walks. From a packet of good mixed seed a range of color from pure white to deep carmine may be had, all the flowers having darker eyes. They are easily raised from seed, but care should be taken when transplanting the little plants from the seed-box to put them at least eighteen inches apart in their permanent places, as they spread very greatly.

Some of the seedlings in growth or in color will be more attractive than others, and if additional plants of them are required cuttings should be made from the new unbloomed shoots which come up when the plants are cut back after blooming. A box or bed of sandy soil is the best place to root them. While the main crop of flowers appears in April, by cutting back and watering the plants considerable bloom can be had throughout the year. They are fine for cutting. These Pinks are rather too rampant for a rock-garden; for that purpose grow rather the Wild Rock Pinks such as *D. deltoides*, the Maiden Pink, or *D. caesius*, the Cheddar Pink. Some seedsmen offer mixed packets of these dainty little alpines. *D. barbatus*, Sweet William, is best considered as a biennial, though under favorable conditions it will often drag along for several years. Sow seed in midsummer for blooming the following spring. For harmonious effects it is better to use groups of self colors such as a good salmon-pink or scarlet, instead of growing mixtures. The auricula-eyed varieties should in any case be kept apart as they are rather bizarre in effect.

DICTAMNUS (*Fraxinella*).—The Gas Plant of old gardens is *D. Fraxinella*, a quite attractive perennial with spikes of reddish-purple flowers throwing off on warm summer evenings a volatile oil which can be ignited with a match. This is a very slow-growing plant, and should be left undisturbed as it is only at its best when long established. The easiest method of propagation is by division of the fleshy roots.

DIGITALIS (Foxglove).—The Foxglove prefers a half-shady place, and is therefore particularly adapted to planting among the native oaks which have been left in many of our most attractive residential neighborhoods, but to insure success the soil should be thoroughly dug and enriched before planting, and watering should not be neglected. The Foxglove is not a true perennial. Seed should be sown in summer and the plants set out where they will bloom the following season. They generally die after flowering, but where they find congenial surroundings they become naturalized and so perpetuate themselves. They are also excellent at the back of the border or planted among Ferns or Fuchsias on the cooler side of the house. They are best by themselves, as their lilac-pink and rosy-purple shades do not combine readily with many other flowers.

DORONICUM.—Though the light yellow, Daisy-like flowers of *D. Clusi* are of large size and good shape, were it not that this plant blooms so early in spring it would not attract particular attention. As it is also good for cutting, and will stand neglect, it is worth growing in the larger garden. The foliage is quite dwarf, but the stems run up to two feet and it is therefore better away from the front of the flower border. Propagate by division.

ERIGERON.—This family is not of first importance, though it possesses one or two species quite worth

growing and some native forms, including *E. salsuginosus*, the Beach Aster, which is a typical Erigeron in
having single lavender-blue flowers borne on branching
stalks. *E. grandiflorus* and *E. speciosus* are attractive
species in this range of coloring. Entirely different is
E. mucronatus (syn. *Vittadenia triloba*), the so-called
Mexican Daisy, a trailer which is covered from spring
to fall with hundreds of pinkish-white single Daisies,
and in sections where there is little frost can be used
to cover banks. To keep it in bloom occasional waterings and cutting back should be given. It may be
used also for edging paths, and, though rather a rampant grower, a single plant in a pocket in a half-shady
rock-garden will long remain attractive. It sows itself,
and it also may be readily increased by division.

ERYNGIUM (Sea Holly).—Quite unusual and too rarely
grown, these plants possess a strange beauty from their
steel-blue stems and beautifully cut flowers. They
remain in fine color for a long while in the garden, and,
like many Everlastings, are useful for house decoration.
There are many kinds, varying in leaf form and in
shape and shade of the involucre. *E. amethystinum*
and *E. Oliverianum* are two good forms, the latter being
much taller in growth. The many varieties are best
raised from seed.

ERYSIMUM.—For *E. Allioni* and *E. linifolium*, see
CHEIRANTHUS.

FELICIA (syn. *Agathea*).—Two varieties are grown, the evergreen shrubby *F. celestis*, with its pale blue Daisy-like flowers, and the rampant, trailing *F. rosea* which has similar pale pink blossoms. The former, because of its neat habit, is an excellent plant with which to border beds or paths. It seems to prefer a cool situation rather than a very warm sunny one. It blooms most profusely in April and May. Propagate by seed or cuttings.

The trailing Felicia is to be recommended for covering sunny slopes, where its habit of rooting as it grows is a great advantage. It will give scattering flowers through the year but in midwinter it blooms best and is then a pleasing sight. Keep it from overrunning other plants. New plants can be secured from the rooted runners.

FRANCOA (Maiden's Wreath).—The Maiden's Wreath, *F. ramosa*, around San Francisco Bay where the winters are warm and the summers cool, is a wonderfully decorative plant, as its thick, shapely leaves are nearly always attractive and in midsummer they are surmounted by many beautiful sprays of the pure white flowers which have suggested its popular name. It seems to do best in well-cultivated ground where it can be well watered, somewhat out of the strong afternoon sun. Plants of it should be grown in large flower-pots, as Miss Gertrude Jekyll uses them in England, as in a partially shaded court or patio they will add greatly to the variety and attractiveness of the place. They may be raised from seed, or the almost evergreen plants may be pulled apart and reset.

GAILLARDIA (Blanket Flower).—There cannot be any hardy perennial which is easier to grow in California than the Gaillardia, which thoroughly enjoys a warm sunny place in the garden and makes no demands of any kind. It is not a fine thing, but is gay and cheerful, and its red and yellow flowers are borne continuously throughout the year. It appears at its best when used in combination with white flowers, such as Shasta Daisies. It is very easily raised from seed, indeed often so renews itself. Additional plants may also be had by division.

GAURA.—*G. Lindheimeri* is a most excellent summer-blooming plant for a dry, sunny place, as when established it will flower for months without watering or any other attention. It is not showy, but as its leafy flower-stems, three or four feet high, are set with numerous white and rose flowers swaying gracefully in the breeze, it is a pretty sight. Increase by seed or division.

GAZANIA.—*G. splendens* is one of our very best perennials for covering sunny slopes or edging hot, dry paths. It should always be planted in full sun as the flowers open only in such a position. The commonest form, a dark orange, is rather hard to combine with other colors in the garden. There is, however, a larger light yellow variety which is less brilliant but more adaptable. It never seems to sow itself, and I have had poor results from trying to raise new varieties by seed. However, old plants may be torn apart in fall or spring and any piece seems then capable of forming a plant.

GERANIUM.—This name properly belongs to a family of comparatively inconspicuous hardy perennials of which *G. sanguineum* (Herb Robert), an attractive rock-plant, is the best known in California. Custom, however, has given the name to the zonal Pelargoniums, the most widely used bedding-plants in existence. Where killing frosts occur these cannot be left in the open ground but must be handled as they are on the Atlantic coast. But in the almost frostless belt of the California coast they may be considered as hardy perennials, as in the open ground without protection they will live for years. While it is true that they are extensively used for hedge-plants and parkings, little discrimination has been shown in the colors and types most used. If instead of so many of the hard crimson shades more plantings were made of better colors, such, for example, as the scarlet Paul Crampbel, the rose-pink Gertrude Pearson, the beautiful salmon-pink Crabbe, or Fred Bean, and the white to scarlet Alice of Vincennes, the Geranium would have a landscape and color value quite equal to that of the hardy Phlox in Eastern gardens.

In the selection of varieties it should further be noted that singles are preferable, as the dead flowers of these

drop off to a considerable extent, while the doubles dry
up on the trusses and mar the appearance of the plants.
While this is one of the plants which will furnish some
color when shaded by Oak trees, its best situation is in
full sun and in a soil that is not too rich. Much
manuring will produce foliage rather than flowers.
They will do very well without any great amount of
watering. These are also most excellent pot-plants, and
in this way should be more used for the adornment of
courts and patios. Plants are most readily secured by
cuttings, which root readily almost any time, though fall
is the time when most propagating is done. To
promote a good stocky growth, while the plants are
still young the centres should be pinched out.

The Ivy-leaved Geraniums have their greatest worth
to cover ground, particularly on sunny slopes, and to
drape and clothe unpleasingly hard concrete walls with
their long, trailing growth, the deep pink Charles
Turner being chiefly used in this way. Doubleness of
flowers in the Ivy-leaved Geraniums is not a drawback,
as they clean themselves, but there are places where the
single white or single lilac-pink is more appropriate.

The Lady Washington section of the Pelargoniums
has acquired almost exclusive use of the name Pelar-
gonium. It is less hardy and not as satisfactory for
bedding as the zonal Pelargoniums, but the interesting
and often brilliant combinations of color have endeared
it to fanciers. Give it a very sunny situation, as for

example at the base of a wall facing south, and as a corrective to its straggling growth, during the late summer and fall pinch back any shoots which become too long, but discontinue this long before the blooming season, which begins about the end of April. This is a plant particularly happy in sandy soil near the seashore.

GERBERA.—The Transvaal Daisy, *G. Jamesoni*, may be considered a hardy perennial on the Pacific coast, though not one of easy culture. Both the type and the beautiful hybrids are, however, worth trying; they are particularly fine for cutting. It prefers a sunny position and a rich, light soil, in which considerable leaf-mold has been incorporated. The painstaking gardener may raise it from seed sown in boxes or increase it by division, but much the simplest way is to buy plants from a professional grower. In planting, be sure to have the crown of the plant level with the surrounding soil. If planted deeper, soil will collect on it and cause decay. Note this point in sowing seed: do not let them lie on their sides but push them vertically into the soil.

GEUM.—Though there are many species in this family, only too often the California garden will have only the small typical form of *G. coccineum*. This is quite unnecessary, as the semi-double scarlet Mrs. Bradshaw comes true from seed and is in every way larger and finer. Under good cultivation, in size and shape it is almost the equal of a Carnation. Yellow forms exist, but must be raised from seed as they are not offered by plant-growers. Stock of any variety may be increased by division in the fall. This plant enjoys a good rich soil and will give successive crops of bloom if the flower-stems are kept cut back and the plants watered and cultivated.

GYNERIUM (Pampas Grass).—This fine foliage plant with its beautiful white plumes can hardly be given space in a small garden, but where there is room for a good clump of it, it is unquestionably most striking and effective. It is propagated by division of the root in early spring, and for the best results it should be given good, deeply dug soil and plenty of water in summer.

GYPSOPHILA.—The best of the perennial forms is the double-flowering *G. paniculata*, which when established will make a mound of fine green foliage two feet high and spreading widely, covered once during the early summer with thousands of little white flowers—a most attractive sight. The single form is also very good, and rather more readily obtainable. It is best raised from seed, but young plants are generally purchasable. Division or moving of large established plants is hardly worth while, as the heavy roots do not easily recover from the shock. One way to use this plant is to put it to the north of a bed of spring-flowering bulbs, as when it makes its spreading summer growth it will cover up the empty space. *G. repens* is a dainty little rock-plant with rather larger flowers, quite different, and best adapted to the rock-garden, where it enjoys a rather cool place.

HELENIUM (Sneeze-weed).—A family of yellow Composites blooming for the most part in late summer, and much less successful in southern California than farther north. The best forms are those of *H. autumnale,* a rather misleading name as they do not bloom so late with us. The typical yellow form is less valuable than Riverton Gem, which is deep yellow shaded red like many Wallflowers. Growing to four feet, it is a plant for the rear of the border and should be allowed to make good clumps. It may be raised by seed, though where plants are available, division in fall or early spring is the easiest method of increasing them.

HELIANTHEMUM (Sun Rose).—These are not really herbaceous plants but dwarf, spreading evergreens, mentioned here because they are generally used for rock-gardens or for edging herbaceous borders. They have a preference for sandy, but not poor, soil and a dry sunny place, where in late spring and early summer they are very delightful when covered with innumerable little flowers like single Roses, white, yellow, copper, red, pink, and rose. Even when out of bloom their neat evergreen foliage is pleasing. They may be raised from seed, but any particular variety is best increased by cuttings, which, after being rooted in sand, should be potted up and later planted in their permanent places. Established plants can rarely be moved with success.

HELIANTHUS (Sunflower).—The perennial Sunflowers are valuable for their tall growth and abundance of bright yellow flowers in late summer, flowers which are considerably smaller and of better shape than most of the annual forms. Their drawbacks are that they are not in bloom for any great length of time and that most of them, all of the forms of *H. rigidus*, spread only too rapidly by underground stolons and can hardly be kept within bounds. If carefully watched they may be used at the back of a north border, but they are rather safer in some unkept part of the garden where they may be allowed free range. The single forms are more graceful than the double ones. Propagate by removing offshoots in fall or spring. They will all bloom in the succeeding summer.

HELIOTROPIUM (Cherry Pie).—In comparatively frostless places the Heliotrope may be treated as a hardy perennial, either bedded out or grown against a wall, preferably one facing south or west. In such a location it will grow to a large size and bloom almost continuously, even in the winter months. Both for its fragrance and its color it is desirable. Heliotropes may be raised from seed sown in boxes in early spring and will bloom the same year, but an easier method is to propagate by cuttings under glass in the fall. Its preferences are for a sunny situation, rich and light soil, and plenty of water in summer.

HEMEROCALLIS (Day Lily).—These hardy and easily grown perennials of grass-like foliage and Lily-shaped flowers thrive throughout the Pacific coast, but in the more southern parts require attention as to summer watering and therefore are best planted about pools or where the overflow from fountains will keep the ground moist. By growing a number of kinds one may have flowers from April to July, beginning with the dwarf *H. Middendorfiana* (golden yellow), continuing with *H. flava* (the Lemon Lily), *H. fulva* (the somewhat common but striking Indian-red variety), to *Florham* (a fine late-flowering yellow form). Propagate by removing offsets any time between the fall rains and April, but as these plants bloom much better when well established only divide the clumps when by decreasing bloom they show that they have become crowded.

HEUCHERA (Alum Root).—The   dwarf,   prettily marked, and practically evergreen leaves of *H. sanguinea* (Coral Bells) make this a particularly good plant for edging paths. Moreover, it is quite hardy, drought-resistant, and most readily increased in the fall by tearing apart the old plants and resetting portions of the newer growth, even where they possess no roots. Where they have some shade or are kept watered through the summer the wiry spikes of bright coral flowers will continue for months after the chief display in May. As the value of the flowers is chiefly from their attractive color, it is not worth growing the white form of *H. sanguinea*. All the Heucheras are excellent plants for the somewhat shaded or cool rock-garden, though the flowers of some of the natives and their hybrids are not very conspicuous.

HOLLYHOCK (Althaea).—Except in the drier and warmer parts of California, there is no easier plant to grow than the Hollyhock. It is true that it is not generally a real perennial and often dies after blooming, but it is so easily raised from seed sown from October on where the plants are to bloom and is so indifferent to culture that it should be largely used for planting along fences, in front of tall shrubs, at the back of borders, and even in the waste places in the garden. Try a pink Hollyhock in front of a gray or white house, and if possible grow near it some pale blue Delphiniums, and you will get a very satisfying picture. Double forms can be obtained, but the single ones are on the whole more graceful. A good compromise is the semi-double fringed or Allegheny type, whose individual flowers last longer than the single ones. Hollyhocks cross very readily, so that self-sown plants or seed collected where several colors are close together will vary greatly as to color.

HUNNEMANNIA.—*H. fumaerifolia*, the yellow Mexican Poppy, is not unlike a taller Eschscholtzia. Though a short-lived perennial, it is commonly considered as an annual, and will bloom from seed the first year. It prefers a sunny situation. Good for cutting.

IBERIS (Candytuft).—The perennial Candytufts, as they are evergreen in foliage and drought-resistant, should be appreciated in California, where they are best adapted to sunny rock-gardens. The pure white *I. sempervirens* is in full bloom in January and February, and is quite perennial in character. This is readily propagated by cuttings taken in early summer and rooted in sand. *I. gibraltarica*, which flowers in April and May, has larger and more attractive flowers, varying in shades of rosy-lavender. It seems to have a general tendency to die out after blooming, but produces seed so freely that new plants may easily be obtained, indeed where conditions are favorable it will often renew itself by self-sowing.

IRIS.—See chapter on Specialties.

KNIPHOFIA.—See TRITOMA.

LAVANDULA (Lavender).—Though really shrubby in character, the common Lavender is so generally associated with perennial plants that it is included here. Apparently perfectly adapted to Pacific coast conditions, it enjoys our dry summers and its large gray clumps topped in July by innumerable spikes of sweet lavender flowers should be seen in every sunny garden and used for clothing dry banks and bordering wide paths. If cuttings of the new growth are taken in late fall and rooted in a sandy bed, this will be found the easiest way to increase one's plants. The full-blown flowers may be cut, dried, and used for scenting linen. An attractive way of planting Lavender is to make a

group of a few plants, associating with them either pale
pink Pentstemons or Snapdragons.

LEONOTUS (Lion's-tail).—*L. leonurus,* though shrubby
in growth, is often cut to the ground to prevent its
getting straggly, and is therefore grouped with the
herbaceous perennials. In August its tall growth,
often six feet, and successive whorls of ruddy-orange
flowers of almost felt-like texture make it very conspicuous and useful where a strong note of color is
desired. The best places for it are in the planting
around a house, preferably one built of dark shingles,
at the back of wide borders, or in shrubberies. Increase by cuttings in fall. Self-sown seedlings will
often be found around an old plant.

LIBONIA.—For the almost continuous production of
its tubular scarlet, yellow-tipped flowers, the Libonia
most common in California has earned the name
floribunda. Though sub-shrubby in habit, it is best associated with herbaceous plants or used for bordering.

LINARIA (Toadflax).—In growth the perennial members of this family differ greatly from one another.
It includes *L. cymbalaria,* the Kenilworth Ivy, a dainty
shade-loving creeper which once established will cover
a north or east slope with its miniature Ivy-shaped
leaves dotted with mauve flowers. This is fine for
trailing over a shady wall. Other small Linarias
suitable for rock-garden work and with more attractive
flowers than the Kenilworth Ivy are the forms of

L. Alpina, also easily raised from seed. Quite different in every respect but the shape of its flowers is *L. dalmatica,* a gray-leaved herbaceous plant with stems of sulphur-yellow flowers two feet high, somewhat awkward in appearance but interesting for the variety of its Snapdragon-shaped flowers, and easily raised from seed or increased by division of the clumps.

LINUM (Flax).—The Flaxes are generally very happy in California, and it is a pity that the better kinds are not more often grown. Rarely is *L. narbonnense* offered, though it is incomparably finer than *L. perenne* or any other blue form. Like all Linums, it should be planted in full sun, as the flowers do not remain open in shade. Nothing could be more beautiful than a large clump of this drought-resistant perennial, with its myriads of light sky-blue blossoms surmounting the dark, narrow, wiry foliage. The best white Linum is the New Zealand Flax, *L. monogynum,* a somewhat shrubby plant, drought-resistant, and of the easiest growth, readily raised from seed or increased by dividing. A good large but not too spreading plant for a rock-garden. The herbaceous *L. flavum* is less important, but because of its dwarf growth and good yellow color it is a useful plant for a sunny rock-garden. Southern California nurseries sell under this name a beautiful winter-flowering shrub, rather tender and only worth trying in warm sections. Its right name is *L. trigynum,* or perhaps better still, *Reinwardtia trigyna.*

LIPPIA.—See Lawns and Ground-Covers.

LOBELIA.—The brilliant perennial *L. cardinalis* requires a rich soil, sunny exposure, and much watering. If these conditions can be provided, treat the plants much like Chrysanthemums or Michaelmas Daisies, dividing the clumps to single shoots very early each spring.   It may be raised from seed, which if sown early under glass will produce flowers the same year.   There are hybrids, giving a wider range of red and purple shades.

LOPEZIA.—The dainty little sub-shrubby *L. alba* is not very hardy and can never have any wide use outside the sections where there is little frost.   Its very dwarf foliage fits it as a ground-cover for bulbous plants, and in addition, for months, even in January, it will furnish its small red-budded white flowers, appreciated both in the front of the flower-border and to mix with larger cut flowers.

LUPINUS (Lupine).—In its home, the north Pacific coast, *L. polyphyllus* is a wonderfully effective hardy herbaceous plant, and in such moist sections the many fine new hybrids raised in England and obtainable from seed should be grown.   This species does not seem to be satisfactory in warmer and drier California, and the annual Lupines (which see), along with the sub-shrubby yellow *L. arboreus* and the blue *L. chamissonis*, should be substituted.   *L. arboreus* grows with the greatest ease in dry sandy places, and though a coarse plant is suitable for rough gardening. Its numerous spikes of flowers, mostly shades of yellow, are at their best in late May and early June. Hybrids between this and *L. polyphyllus* are fairly successful in California. Raise all Lupines from seed; they come with the greatest ease, and are best sown where the plants are to bloom.

LYCHNIS.—The perennial forms of Lychnis differ so greatly that only the botanist would recognize them as of the same family. They are not plants of first importance, but for variety a few species are worth growing. *L. chalcedonica* in early summer produces flower-stems two or three feet high, each ending in a scarlet head of flowers in shape something like Verbenas. Less striking is *L. Flos-cuculi* (Ragged Robin), which grows about eighteen inches high and bears through the summer light rose flowers somewhat suggesting double Pinks.

MESEMBRYANTHEMUM.—Owners of dry sunny gardens should grow more of these gay succulents. The only difficult thing about them is their name. These relatives of the common Ice-plant prefer warm dry locations and must have sun to open their flowers, but they are indifferent as to soil and root readily from cuttings inserted in sandy places after they have been dried in the sun for a day or two. Their nomenclature is so badly mixed that the easiest way to get what you want is to secure cuttings or plants from known stock.

Their variety is great. *M. edule*, the Hottentot Fig, is a coarse grower with three-sided leaves, and is only fit for covering dry slopes. Quite different is *M. rosea*, the mossy trailer often seen on banks or hanging over walls, the leaves almost concealed by the bright lavender-pink flowers. This was the plant grown in wired boxes to drape the inside walls of the Panama-Pacific Exposition at San Francisco. It is so rampant that it needs constant cutting back to prevent its smothering choicer plants. The shrubby varieties are less grown and more deserving of a place in the small garden, where they may be kept at the size desired. *M. aureum* has wonderfully bright glistening orange-yellow flowers two inches across, and there is a similar sulphur-yellow form, both flowering in March and April. In May the small-flowered types hide their clumps of fine dark foliage in a cushion of bronzy buff, coppery red, or magenta-colored flowers, wonderful sights at midday.

MIMULUS GLUTINOSUS (syn. *Diplacus glutinosus*) (Monkey Flower).—This perennial form, a native of California, is the species by far the best adapted to our dry conditions. The tubular flowers ranging from cream to orange are borne on leafy stalks two feet high. It is at its best in late May. Plants may be raised from seed or increased by cuttings, which will root outdoors in sandy soil in half shade. In southern California there are wild forms much superior to those found in the central part of the state. Though not truly perennial,

the many beautifully colored and spotted varieties of
M. luteus are particularly appreciated by any one
having the conditions they prefer, a moist, half-shady
pocket of rich soil such as one sometimes finds around
a pool.   These are readily raised from seed sown in
boxes in early spring.   They flower the first year and
are best then discarded.

Myosotis (Forget-me-Not).—Though some of the
forms of the Forget-me-Not are real perennials, all are
best considered in California as biennials, to be raised
from seed sown in a shady place in late summer for the
next spring's bloom.   Where the conditions are favorable, on moist, half-shaded slopes, they will bloom for
months and continue to renew themselves.   While
they are perhaps at their best when sown in shady
dells like wild-flowers, they should also be more used
for carpeting beds and borders in which such spring-
flowering bulbs as Daffodils, Tulips, and Hyacinths are
grown, as they continue the effect and to some extent
cover up the maturing bulb foliage.   Though there are
pink and white forms, both sentiment and garden effect will always give the typical blue first choice.

Nepeta (Cat Mint).—*N. Mussini* is a plant little
known and grown where it could be of the greatest value,
for plants as drought-resistant and as continually presentable are not common.   The best form cannot be
raised from seed, but cuttings of the new growth will
root most readily in sandy soil at any time of year, and

old clumps may be torn apart and divided into dozens of small plants. In a few months these will grow into nice clumps of finely divided gray aromatic foliage. In May the first and best crop of the lavender flowers, borne in long spikes, appears, and if the plants are cut back immediately after this flowering, a second crop will follow. There are few better plants for edging wide walks, where its spreading, informal habit of growth is most effective. It may also be used in full sunshine on slopes and to trail over walls. It is too rampant to be trusted among the cherished plants in a fine rock-garden. Its color is particularly effective in combination with bright pink.

NIEREMBERGIA.—The form of *Nierembergia* best adapted to the dry summers of the Pacific coast is *N. linariaefolia*, a sub-shrubby species which in central California is worth growing in the rock-garden. It has graceful wiry stems about eighteen inches high, on which sway modest porcelain-colored flowers of trumpet shape, about an inch across. It blooms continuously during the summer with no attention.

OENOTHERA (Evening Primrose).—These western, often California, herbaceous perennials should be more frequently grown because of their ease of culture, their fragrance, and beauty. Their preference is for light, warm soils, and they require little water to bring out their numerous flowers. Most of them open at night, and they last longest in dull weather. They are readily raised from seed, which may be sown in the open ground in fall, or they may be increased by division. Nurserymen offer many species, among them *Oe. brachycarpa*, *fruticosa*, and *Lamarckiana* (various shades of yellow) *Oe. cæspitosa* (white), and *Oe. Childsi* (pink).

PÆONIA (Peony).—The *Moutan* or Tree Pæonies do excellently in California. The herbaceous Pæonies are certainly less successful, and though they may by careful attention to certain details be grown in some parts of California, the gardener who has depended so much on them in the Eastern states should not look for the same fine results here. In the warmer and drier sections of California they are hardly worth trying, but the enthusiast whose garden is cool and wet in winter can get fair results by giving them the deep rich soil they require for growth and shade from the hot afternoon sun when they are in bloom. The roots should always be planted in the fall, with the crowns two or three inches under the ground. Everywhere Pæonies need a year or two to become established, and until then they produce poor flowers. There are now innumerable beautiful varieties to choose from. It will be unwise for the California gardener to invest money in expensive novelties until he has tried out the Pæony in his particular garden. In any case, it is not easy to surpass such standard kinds as *Festiva Maxima* and *Mme. Calot*, which are not expensive. As one goes north conditions become more favorable, and from

Oregon north the herbaceous Pæony becomes one of the mainstays of the garden.

PAPAVER (Poppy).—Though not as frequently seen as in Eastern gardens, Poppies both of the Oriental and Iceland types can be well grown on the Pacific coast, very easily in the north, with more care as one gets into southern California. *P. orientale* and its hybrids now furnish huge flowers, from the typical scarlet with black blotch through crimson, apricot, and salmon-pink, to white, in the best forms with tall stiff stems. To be sure of getting any particular variety plants must be secured, preferably in the fall, as they can hardly be handled except in pots in spring. Propagation of the named varieties is by division of the roots. Mixtures may be had from seed, but tend to produce mostly reds. Plant in groups in the border where they can be left permanently. If gophers are in your vicinity it may even be worth while to plant the roots in a chicken-wire basket, for they seem particularly attractive to these rodents. These Poppies enjoy light shade and watering when in growth. Too prominent a place is undesirable, as they die down in midsummer, but after a rest a good watering will start them up again and often give a few fall flowers.

The Iceland Poppy, *P. nudicaule*, is extraordinarily rare, but any one with a cool garden may raise it from seed sown in October. They should be moved to their permanent quarters while still young, or if the place is not ready the plants should be potted up. They bloom from February to April, and more gardeners would grow them if they had ever seen the pretty green tufts surmounted by white, yellow, and orange-red crinkled cups. Their wiry stems fit them well for cutting. In some places it is necessary to protect the young plants by wire from the depredations of linnets and sparrows.

PENTSTEMON.—The prominence given to perennial Phlox in Eastern gardens belongs to other plants in California; first of these are the Pentstemons, plants of outstanding worth for summer effects. The garden hybrids, descendants of native Pentstemons, are best considered as rather short-lived perennials, but this is no drawback, as they are very easily raised from seed, which if sown early in the spring will produce fine flowering plants by late summer. Again, if many plants of one color are wanted for a particular effect, cuttings of the new growth which springs up in the fall after the flowering stems have been removed will readily root in sandy soil and by the following spring may be put in their permanent places. The range of color is from almost pure white through pinks and reds to purple, and in addition there are many varieties whose tubular flowers are white with broad colored edges. Where this plant is used in a border it should be remembered that, as with Gladioli and Foxgloves, the flowers are all on the side facing the sun. In addition to the many garden forms there are several very interesting if less showy wild natives, among them the pinky-lilac *P. heterophyllus*, the lavender and blue

P. spectabilis, and others, some dwarf enough to use in the rock-garden.

PHLOX.—In the gardens of the eastern United States the finest effects of the late summer are given by bold masses of brilliant perennial Phloxes, the garden descendants of wild eastern American plants and so just suited in their conditions. While the north Pacific coast more nearly approximates the climate of the Atlantic coast, the long dry summer of California and the continual bright sunshine are hard on these surface-rooting and moisture-loving plants. Though I have visited many gardens where they are grown, I have never seen perennial Phloxes here approach the splendor of those on the Atlantic coast. Would it not be better to try to get our big effects with other summer-blooming plants, such as the Pentstemons and the finer Geraniums, among the perennials, and the Zinnias among the annuals? This does not mean that the enthusiast or the gardener who desires variety should not have his Phloxes, giving them such special care as a cool situation, a heavy summer mulch of rotted manure or leaves, and thorough irrigation every week or so. With this attention, in many places, particularly near the sea, the returns will be worth the care given. Selections of varieties may be made from catalogues; I would, however, suggest that the beginner always include Miss Lingard, as this is a *suffruticosa*, not a *decussata* seedling, and of unusual vigor in California.

The creeping alpine *P. subulata*, which I have seen

in masses growing in the high Sierras near snow, suffers from the summer drought at lower altitudes in California, and, never particularly vigorous there, it will be best in partial shade and where it will get some moisture.

Phloxes are generally increased by division of the roots, and this should in any case be done every second or third year to improve their growth. In nurseries stock is worked up more rapidly from green cuttings and by sowing small pieces of the roots in flats. Seed is not a satisfactory method, as too large a proportion of the resultant plants will be of undesirable colors.

PHYSOSTEGIA.—*P. virginica* is a summer-flowering plant whose spikes of pinkish-purple flowers are about eighteen inches high. It should be planted between fall and spring, and will get along with quite ordinary treatment. It is not at all outstanding, but adds to the variety in the summer garden.

PLUMBAGO.—The only herbaceous form grown in California is *P. Larpentæ*, a dwarf plant with dark green leaves edged with red. Besides the attractive foliage, in late fall it is covered with deep blue flowers. From its season alone it deserves a place in the rock-garden or for edging a half-shaded path. Increase through division.

PRIMULA (Primrose).—From this very extensive family only a few of the most effective and easiest grown species can possibly be mentioned. The specialist will

want and will try many others.   Of first importance are
the true English Primroses, single flowers on short stems
coming modestly up among tufts of leaves soon after
Christmas.   Allied, and of far greater garden value,
are the polyanthus Primroses, perfectly hardy and very
effective when grown in masses in at least partial shade.
Naturalized in Oak woods, or planted more formally as
beds on the east side of a house, the heads of white,
yellow, orange, red, brown, and blended colors brighten
up the early spring garden.   They are of the easiest
culture, and plants may be raised in quantity from seed
sown in midsummer.   For a beautiful harmony of
white, yellow, and orange there is nothing to equal the
Munstead strain.   Young seedling plants are most
vigorous, but old clumps may be divided in the fall,
when strong growth begins with the rains and cool
weather.   The plants will stand a surprising amount of
drought in summer, when dormant, but are better where
they do not have to be subjected to it but may be kept
green by occasional watering.   A new and already exceedingly popular winter-blooming plant for bedding
is *P. malacoides*, whose heads of miniature flowers are
still limited to lilac-pink and white, though plant
breeders are extending the color range.   From seed
sown in early fall plants will be produced which should
be bedded out about eight inches apart in light, rich
soil in a place which is not too sunny, such as will be
found to the east of a house.   Though perennials, they
practically bloom themselves to death, and it is better
to discard the old plants and raise new ones yearly.

In the nearly frostless sections of the state, *P. obconica* can be treated in the same way, its much larger and often brighter flowers being very effective.

The Auricula is botanically *P. auricula*. The so-called alpine varieties grow readily enough around San Francisco Bay, where the cool summers favor them. Their perfection of shape and color entitle them to good preparation of the ground and to adequate watering. Some gardeners prefer to keep them in pots, where their finer points may be more readily admired. They are raised from seed, a rather slow process, but additional plants are obtained by careful division, preferably after they are through blooming.

PYRETHRUM.—For the average gardener, the only member of this family worth growing is *P. roseum*, which will easily be recognized by the numerous colored Daisies standing a foot or more above the green, feathery foliage through the spring. The range of color extends from white through pink and rose to bright red. The double-flowered forms are less attractive in shape and less bright and gay in color. Like all the Composites, they are good cut flowers. From a packet of mixed seed sown in spring in boxes, a year later one may get many plants in a wide diversity of shades. Increase any desired plant by division, preferably in fall, but for the best results do not disturb the clumps unnecessarily.

RANUNCULUS.—The Double Buttercup, *R. repens flore-pleno*, is distinct and showy enough for gardens, and when colonies have been formed by the rapid travelling of the runners a pleasing effect will be given in early summer by its small yellow flowers. Do not associate it with choice plants in a rockery, as it is too rampant.

The treatment of *R. asiaticus* will be found in the chapter on Bulbs.

ROMNEYA.—Our native *R. Coulteri*, the Matilija Poppy, when once established grows like a weed in any well-drained place, and is quite indifferent to summer drought. When in bloom, a large clump covered with many huge single white flowers, each with its high yellow centre, is a wonderful sight, but as it grows seven or eight feet high and spreads freely by suckers its location should be chosen with care. It is difficult to raise from seed, and the suckers do not generally bear transplanting successfully. It is therefore best to purchase this plant already established in pots.

RUDBECKIA (Coneflower).—These fall-blooming perennials, usually with drooping yellow petals and a high cone-like centre, can readily be grown where ample summer moisture is provided, but in dry places they are quite poor. *R. nitida*, four or five feet high, and single, is an attractive plant for the back of the border, and the double form, Golden Glow, such a common plant in Eastern gardens, is also worth growing and is in no danger of spreading unduly. Both of these are better if frequently divided in winter. A dwarfer yellow form is *R. speciosa* (syn. *R. Newmanni*), an excellent border plant about eighteen inches high.

SALVIA (Sage).—Some day perhaps California gardeners will plant the many hardy perennial Salvias as much as they use the tender Scarlet Sage for fall blooming. Though these plants are many of them of Mediterranean or Mexican origin and therefore well adapted to our conditions, very few species are offered by nurseries. Among them is *S. leucantha*, a very drought-resistant plant with leaves shaped like those of the Willow and bright purple and white bracts carried on tall sinuous stems. From early summer until winter they give their color to the garden. Give them a little attention as to dividing the roots occasionally and cutting back the stems. This is a fine plant for massing in a dry sunny place. *S. azurea* does well under similar conditions and is of a beautiful pale blue color, but the inflorescence is slighter and little mass effect is given. *S. Pitcheri* is quite similar, but with flowers of a deeper blue. Less grown, but desirable for big mass effects in the wilder parts of the garden, is the biennial *S. Sclarea*, the English Clary, which grows four feet high and flowers in summer from seed sown a year earlier. Its cloudy light purple effect is unusual and charming. *S. patens* is less hardy and the flowers soon drop, but the blue color is absolutely unsurpassed in purity.

SANTOLINA (Lavender Cotton).—This finely cut, silvery-leaved plant, *S. incana*, is most useful for its beautiful downy foliage, which will submit to such trimming that it may be used as a formal edging-plant. Single plants, untrimmed, are desirable in a sunny rock-garden but they should not be allowed to bloom, as the yellow flowers are poor and detract from the beauty of the plant. Propagate by cuttings.

SAPONARIA (Soapwort).—The best variety is *S. ocymoides*, a beautiful trailing rock-plant with small pink flowers, well adapted to dry places, easily raised from seed or division of the roots.

SAXIFRAGA (Rockfoil).—The dozens of delightful little Saxifrages grown in English rock-gardens are not for the comparatively careless California gardener, living in a climate which is too bright and dry for them. The collector or enthusiast should try some, but for the average man it will be best to start with *S. umbrosa* (London Pride), with its pretty tufted foliage and spikes of dainty little white flowers, or else *S. Sarmentosa* (Mother of Thousands), a fine trailing species with handsome green-and-white leaves and reddish stems, the flowers also being white. Both these dwarf Saxifrages enjoy a cool, shaded, and preferably moist rock-garden. Very different is *S. crassifolia*, with its large fleshy leaves and rose-pink flowers which always appear in early winter, when color is needed. This also is a shade-loving plant, but more drought-resistant. A good place for it is among Ferns. The Saxifrages mentioned are readily increased by division during the colder, wetter seasons of the year.

SCABIOSA (Scabious).—The most satisfactory perennial form is *S. caucasica*, a fine light blue flat, single flower of the greatest value for cutting. Flowers are continually produced on tall, wiry stems, but as there is no burst of bloom and as the blue is soft rather than brilliant, it is singularly ineffective for landscape effects. Plant in a sunny place and give good cultivation. Plants may be raised from seed, but if not transplanted while very young they should be potted and grown on in that way, as they resent disturbance.

SEDUM (Stonecrop).—There are so many Sedums, and their nomenclature is so baffling, that any one interested should consult special articles and the catalogues of the growers who specialize in these very interesting succulents, so adapted to dry, sunny rock-gardens. Many of them are very small and creeping, with great diversity of leaf-form; the taller ones are excellent border-plants. *S. spectabile*, with its broad glaucous leaves and eighteen-inch stems holding flat heads of pinkish flowers, is a valuable addition to the midsummer garden. Divide them for increase. Somewhat similar to this genus and of like garden use are the succulent Cotyledons and Sempervivums, whose fleshy rosettes are particularly attractive in winter.

SENECIO.—In large gardens where space is not at a premium, *S. petastites*, also called *Cineraria maxima*, should be used for the sub-tropical effect given by its high foliage and yellow heads of bloom. It is also used sometimes for lawn-plantings. It is propagated by suckers, and is impatient of drought.

Shasta Daisy.—See *Chrysanthemum maximum.*

Silene.—The perennial Catchflies are good rock-plants, particularly *S. pendula,* a trailing white kind, and the native *S. californica* (scarlet) and *S. Hookeri* (pink).

Statice (Sea Lavender).—In southern California from Santa Barbara to San Diego the evergreen perennial *S. latifolia,* the great Sea Lavender, is a familiar and beautiful sight, great masses of it being used for landscape effect, particularly along drives and overlooking walls. The large heads of purplish-blue flowers of this everlasting give most effective and unusual color in the warm sunny places and light soil it prefers.

Sweet William.—See *Dianthus barbatus.*

Thalictrum.—The best known of the Meadow Rues is undoubtedly *T. diptocarpum,* whose beautiful Maidenhair foliage and sprays of little mauve flowers on tall wiry stems give a lovely misty effect in the garden. Their preference is for partial shade and moist soil.

Thymus (Thyme).—Why are there so many bare, dry, sunny banks in California when they might be covered at little trouble or expense with one or more of the Thymes? The easiest way to secure the number of plants required to cover a large space is to fill a box of

A corner in the Julian Eltinge place in Los Angeles, interesting in suggesting a possible plan for a small back garden having a fine outlook.

A well-placed flowering fruit tree is an addition to almost any garden. Each year one looks forward to the wonder of its blooming.

sandy soil with cuttings of unbloomed stems in fall. Pieces about two inches long will do. When they are rooted they should be planted a foot or more apart; they will soon spread and cover the ground. *T. Serpyllum* is the common Thyme, with mauve flowers, and of this there is a good form with variegated leaves. *T. albus*, a dainty plant of moss-like growth, and the allied variety with crimson flowers, are only suitable for rock-garden use.

TRITOMA (syn. *Kniphofia*) (Red-Hot Poker).—In summer, fall, and even midwinter there are some Tritomas in bloom, and when several well-grown clumps are planted together they give a bright and yet stately effect in the garden. They also associate well with Bamboos and other large ornamental grasses for sub-tropical and jungle effects, and they are suitably planted near pools. Plant a foot or more apart in good garden soil in a sunny location, and allow them to remain undisturbed as long as they bloom satis-factorily. The nomenclature is badly mixed, and it is best to choose your varieties when they are in bloom. The forms vary greatly in growth. All may be raised from seed, and if sown very early in spring will some-times bloom the same year. Increase of any variety is by division.

VALERIAN.—See CENTRANTHUS.

VERBASCUM (Mullein).—Most of the Mulleins are biennials. They make cushions of large leaves from which, in the year after sowing seed, rise tall stately spikes of generally yellow flowers. They are effective in large gardens, but they cover so much ground and so little of the spike is in bloom at any one time that they can hardly claim a place in a small select garden.

VERONICA.—Though the herbaceous Veronicas are of less importance in the California garden than are the many attractive shrubby ones from New Zealand, a few should be grown in the border, and others in cooler rock-gardens. We have not too many good blue flowers, and *V. longifolia subsessilis* is an addition, with its spikes of deep purple-blue flowers two feet high, borne in midsummer. *V. spicata* is smaller and dwarfer and has clear blue flowers. Of the trailing kinds for the rock-garden, *V. repens* is dwarfest, dainty, and deserving of the moisture it needs.

V. prostrata is a somewhat larger form, and *V. rupestris* is a fine, paler blue trailing plant. For other Veronicas, consult the chapter on Shrubs.

VINCA (Periwinkle).—These evergreen trailers, sometimes also referred to as Myrtles, are of less importance on account of their flat blue or white flowers than because they are so excellently adapted to clothing shady banks, and are so drought-resistant that they are good ground-covers even under trees. Plant a foot or more apart during the rainy season. If kept cut back they will soon spread and cover the ground. The large form is *V. major;* it grows about a foot high. *V. minor* has much smaller leaves and rises only three or four inches from the ground.

Viola (Violet).—In the mild climates along the coast Violets flower all winter, and though not showy are cherished for their very modesty and fragrance. When possible give them a light soil, enriched with rotted manure, and the partial shade such as is found to the east of the house. They are propagated by runners, which should be planted in the fall for blooming a year later. The double varieties are sweetest, but not so graceful as the long-stemmed single kinds such as the popular Princess of Wales.

Zauschneria (California Fuchsia).—In August one bright place in the rock-garden or border is that occupied by *Z. californica,* for once established it will without the least care give an abundance of vermilion tubular flowers a foot or more above its soft gray-green foliage. It spreads by underground growth. Give it a sunny location and an occasional watering to make it do its best.

PERENNIALS FOR SPECIAL PURPOSES

Rock-gardens, Dry Walls, and Path Edges

Aethionema grandiflora
Alyssum saxatile
Arabis albida
Arenaria

Aubrietia
Campanula (dwarf and
 trailing species)
Cerastium

Dianthus plumarius, also Rock Pinks

Erigeron mucronatus

Erysimum Allioni and E. linifolia

Gazania

Gypsophila repens

Helianthemum

Heuchera

Iberis sempervirens and I. gibraltarica

Iris (dwarf bearded)

Linum flavum

Mesembryanthemum

Nepeta Mussini

Primula malacoides

Sedum

Thyme

Veronica (prostrate varieties)

Zauschneria californica

DROUGHT-RESISTANT; EASILY GROWN

Alyssum saxatile

Anchusa italica

Anthemis tinctoria

Cheiranthus (Wallflowers)

Dianthus plumarius

Gaillardia

Gaura Lindheimeri

Gazania

Gypsophila paniculata

Helianthus

Iris (Tall bearded)

Linaria dalmatica

Linum

Nepeta Mussini

Papaver orientalis

Pentstemon

Romneya Coulteri

Salvia (hardy kinds)

Shasta Daisy

Tritoma

Valerian

Zauschneria californica

FOR PARTIAL SHADE

Anemone japonica

Aquilegia (Columbine)

Arenaria

Aster (Michaelmas Daisy)

Begonia (fibrous rooted)

Dicentra spectabilis

Digitalis (Foxglove)
Ferns
Francoa ramosa
Heuchera sanguinea
Primula (polyanthus
  primrose).   Also P.
  malacoides and P. ob-
conica for warmer sec-
  tions
Saxifraga
Thalictrum
Vinca
Violet

CHAPTER VIII

THE INDISPENSABLE ANNUALS

CALIFORNIA is the country of the annual. The great majority of our wild-flowers are annuals; Clarkias, Collinsias, Eschscholtzias, Gilias, Godetias, Lupines, are only a few of the many. We have not even a perennial sod; the grasses which clothe our meadows renew themselves each year from seed. Our climate favors the plant which germinates with the first rains, makes its growth while the soil is cool and moist, flowers through the spring, and when the dry season comes is ready to ripen seed, which will be scattered and repeat the process the next year. In this there is a lesson for our gardeners. We have often to combat nature, but here is a chance to work with her. Even as she does, we should sow hardy annuals in fall, so that they may grow under the most favorable conditions and with the least labor on our part, and in springtime reward us out of all proportion to our slight effort.

If you don't believe this, use some neglected place in your garden, or, if you have none, in the vacant lot next door, for a California wild-flower garden. All that is necessary is to dig and break up the soil (plow and harrow if you are working on a large scale), and give it a good soaking to bring up the weeds. When these have germinated, hoe them off, pulverize the soil, scatter your wild-flower seeds, rake them in, and water the ground thoroughly with a fine spray. If you are lucky enough to get a gentle rain shortly after sowing, germination will be far better than with any watering you can give. Mixtures of wild-flower seeds are offered, but you may prefer to make your own, or to scatter different flowers so that one will predominate in each place. If you do this, allow the colonies to merge into each other as they do in nature.

A few suggestions of varieties for naturalizing will be found at the end of this chapter. While some will doubtless wish to restrict themselves to natives, there is no need to do this. The Sweet Alyssum will naturalize only too readily, and Calendulas, Centaureas, Cosmos, Larkspurs, and the Scarlet Flax, to mention only a few, will take to this treatment quite as kindly as if they were natives. All will perpetuate themselves by self-sowing after the first year.

But there are other uses for annual flowers. Many other varieties, including garden forms of such natives as the Clarkias and Godetias, seem more fitting in beds and in borders where they will supplement the bulbs and perennials. Where Gladioli, Dahlias, and other summer flowers are to be planted, the ground may first be used for early-flowering annuals. Hardy annuals may also be sown in beds devoted to spring bulbs, and among such plants as the tall bearded Irises, to lengthen the season of flowers in those places. It is rather better to sow these in early spring, as the flowers are here wanted somewhat later.

With our forward seasons, hardy perennials bloom so far in advance of their Eastern period that there is a great gap in midsummer to be filled. Here again we may call on the annuals; this time chiefly on the half-hardy kinds, such as Petunias, Zinnias, Stocks, and Marigolds, plants of long flowering season, desirable both in the general flower border and for planting in beds by themselves. The half-hardy annuals are best sown in seed-boxes or in seed-beds, in partially shaded places, in spring. The atmospheric conditions for germination are then less favorable, and this partial shade and considerable attention to watering are necessary to get them started.

Observers will have noted that Eschscholtzias, Petunias, Scabious, and Verbenas often last two years or more, thus in a sense they are really short-lived perennials. But as they bloom the first season from seed and are rarely as fine in succeeding years, they may very well be considered as annuals.

AGERATUM (Floss Flower).—Valuable for its blue flowers, a color not very common in annuals. Is of easy culture and has a very long season of bloom. Is especially useful for edgings. Sow the seed in boxes early in spring, and transplant to about six inches apart in the open ground. In southern California it may be sown in the late summer for winter blooming. Can also be propagated by cuttings in early fall.

Alonsoa.—Attractive little bushes about eighteen inches high bearing many spikes of brilliant, large-lipped little flowers through the summer. *A. War-scewiczii*, vermilion-scarlet, is the variety most grown. Sow in boxes in early spring and plant out a foot apart. Though an annual, it will often live through a second year. Its elegant growth and daintiness fit it for the rock-garden.

Alyssum.—The common Sweet Alyssum, *A. mari-timum*, may readily become a weed under California conditions, but yet many will wish to grow it for its fragrance, its winter bloom, and its absolute indifference to neglect. This last quality is illustrated by the way in which it has become naturalized among the wind-swept rocks along the coast, as for example at Pacific Grove. Fall sowing in the open ground is best, but it may be started at any time and can hardly be prevented from renewing itself. The very dwarf strains are useful for edgings.

Antirrhinum (Snapdragon).—Were it not for the rust which so frequently wipes out Snapdragons in California, this would be our finest bedding plant, but no cure has been found for the rust, though its progress may be somewhat delayed if the first plants affected are pulled up. In greenhouses it has been found that watering only at the roots, instead of spraying, retards the spread of the disease, but no fungicide of any kind has proved effective. In spite of this great drawback, Snapdragons are now available in such lovely colors that they are always worth trying, for in some seasons they practically escape infection or it is delayed until they are nearly through blooming. In new gardens and in places where they have not previously been grown the chances of success are especially good, as there will be no rust spores in the ground. Sow in boxes or seed-beds in either fall or spring. In the warmer parts of California fall sowing gives very effective late winter bedding. The mixtures give rather a bizarre effect; the use of harmonizing named varieties is recommended.

ARCTOTIS.—A family of Daisy-like flowers coming from South Africa and therefore recommended for dry, sunny banks in California. Though there are many showy kinds, *A. grandis*, bluish white with a blue centre, is generally the only one offered. Sow in fall where it is to bloom.

ASTER.—See CALLISTEPHUS.

BARTONIA.—See MENTZELIA.

BRACHYCOME (Swan River Daisy).—*B. iberidifolia* is a dainty little half-hardy annual rather resembling a small Cineraria. The blue form is chiefly grown, but there are also white and rose varieties. Best sown in the open ground in spring. It is especially useful as a follow-up plant for summer blooming in a rockery.

CALENDULA (Pot Marigold).—Though in no sense a fine flower, and with an odor unpleasant to many, the common Calendula (*C. officinalis*) merits growing particularly for its bright orange and yellow flowers which brighten the garden in mid-winter and are then appreciated for cutting. It will stand the poorest treatment, and is therefore best adapted to sowing in the rougher, neglected parts of the garden, where it will continue to renew itself by self-sowing year after year. To start it, the seed may simply be scattered and raked in on ground previously dug. Either in fall or spring in central and northern California, but better only in the fall in the warmer south.

CALIFORNIA POPPY.—See ESCHSCHOLTZIA.

CALLISTEPHUS (China Aster).—Too well known to require description, of great value for summer bedding and for cutting. Sow seed in March or April, either in boxes or in prepared seed-beds of light sandy soil. They should be pricked out and replanted three or four inches apart until large enough to go where they will bloom. For any real success they demand good culture, preferring a cool, rich soil with regular irrigation and cultivation.

CANDYTUFT.—See IBERIS.

CENTAUREA (Cornflower and Sweet Sultan).—*C. cyanus*, the common Cornflower, may be sown either in fall or spring in the open ground and will succeed with very little care, generally renewing itself by self-sowing, but it will of course be much improved by attention to watering and cultivation. Particularly adapted to the wilder parts of the garden, and useful for cutting. Available in rose, white, and light blue as well as in the common and really best color.

CHRYSANTHEMUM (Colored Daisy).—Vigorous spring- and summer-blooming annuals of the most moderate requirements as to culture. This ease of culture and their bright colors recommend them to the less fastidious gardener. They may be sown in the open ground either in fall or spring. They give their best effects when mixtures are not used, but where some variety of simple coloring, such as Morning Star or Evening Star, is grown. The doubles are coarse and the ringed varieties bizarre.

CLARKIA.—A really beautiful California annual, which has been greatly improved by seed growers and is now to be had in lovely shades of pink and scarlet. The double forms of *C. elegans*, such as Salmon Queen and Scarlet Beauty, are best. The main sowing should be made in the open ground in the fall, but by further sowings in spring and early summer flowers may be had until October, as visitors to the flower gardens of the Panama-Pacific Exposition will remember.

COLLINSIA.—California wild flowers of somewhat straggly growth, about eighteen inches high, useful for naturalizing. *C. bicolor*, the most popular variety, is white and lilac-purple. Sow seed in open ground in the fall.

COREOPSIS (Calliopsis, Tickseed).—The bright yellows and maroons of their flowers and the varying heights of different strains, from six inches to two feet, make these summer-blooming plants very desirable. I like them especially for sowing over bulb beds for summer effect. Seed may be lightly raked in where they are to remain, or if preferred they may be sown in seed-beds and very readily transplanted. *C. grandiflora* may be treated as an annual, though it is really a short-lived perennial.

COSMOS.—The California gardener does not have to worry about his Cosmos being cut down by frost. They have always ample time to make their growth of four to six feet and finish blooming before the end of November. They may be sown in springtime, either where they are to bloom or in seed-beds. They are of the easiest possible culture, and where conditions are favorable they will often perpetuate themselves by self-sowing. Sometimes they are planted for an informal and of course quite temporary hedge. Though double varieties are now available, the best effects are still obtained from the finer single strains.

DELPHINIUM (Larkspur).—The annual Larkspur should be much more widely grown in California gardens, as when sown in the fall where it is to bloom it will give beautiful color all through the early summer months if prevented from going to seed. The double tall-branching varieties are by far the best, and their range of colorings, from white through lilac, blue, purple, pink, and rose is far more extensive than is to be found in the perennials. If sown among Tulips and properly thinned out to a foot or more apart they will economize space in the small garden.

DIANTHUS (Chinese, Japanese, and Indian Pinks).— Although *D. chinensis* and *D. Heddewigii* are really biennials and will sometimes under favorable conditions live for two or three years in California, they are best treated as annuals, sown in spring either where they are to bloom or in the seed-bed. Mixed strains, either single or double, give bright and long-continued beds or edgings, but even more attractive results can be obtained where a single color is used, some of the single white and salmon-red selections being particularly fine for the rock-garden.

DIASCIA.—This dwarf little plant with pretty coral-pink flowers, *D. Barberi*, is good for rock-gardens and for edgings and will prove novel and likable. Though listed as a half-hardy annual, with me it lives from year to year, and I have propagated it by division of the clumps. From spring-sown seed it blooms the first year.

DIDISCUS (Blue Lace Flower).—An old plant, the use of which has been much revived of late. *D. cœruleus* is about eighteen inches high and has numerous flat heads of clear blue flowers in shape similar to Wild Parsley. Start seed in boxes and transplant to a sunny position where the plants will be moderately dry. ´ Like many other Australians, it resents over-watering.

DIMORPHOTHECA AURANTIACA.—This rich, glossy orange Daisy from South Africa is very happy under California conditions, but should be in full sun as this is required to keep the flowers open. The type or the hybrids in various shades of warm white, yellow, and salmon, may be sown in spring either where they are to bloom or in seed-beds. As they are low-growing they are best along a path or in a rock-garden.

ESCHSCHOLTZIA (California Poppy).—Everyone knows and loves our glorious native Poppy and regrets that around the cities particularly the fields of it are rapidly disappearing. When seed of the typical form may be obtained for a few cents an ounce, why not scatter it in waste spaces in the fall when the first rains come? As it is really a perennial, and moreover will re-seed itself where the conditions are at all favorable, the sowing may be of permanent value. It should always be sown where it is intended to bloom, as its long tap root makes it very difficult to transplant. In the small garden the orange typical variety is sometimes hard to associate with other flowers, but creamy white, pale yellow, pink, rose, and beautiful Wallflower-red selections can be obtained and grown with equal ease. Keep the seed-pods cut if you do not want it all over the garden.

GILIA.—This attractive native is not as frequently

found in our gardens as its easy culture and the variety of the different kinds would justify. *G. capitata*, about eighteen inches high, and with finely cut foliage and compact heads of light blue flowers, and *G. tricolor* (Birds' Eyes), somewhat dwarfer, lilac and yellow with purple spots, are two of the best kinds, and are particularly adapted to wild gardening where the seed should be scattered and raked in when the first rains come.

GODETIA (Farewell to Spring).—A native annual, the commonest wild form of which has single lilac-pink flowers with a dark centre and will be seen in late spring and early summer throughout the coast ranges. The wild forms are best for naturalizing, but there are many improved varieties in brighter colors, some of them double, which will be more welcome in gardens. The double rose is particularly good. Sow in the open ground in fall for early bloom, or in spring for late flowering.

GYPSOPHILA.—The annual variety, *G. elegans*, is of dwarfer growth and has larger flowers than the perennial *G. paniculata*. It is best used for edging or as a ground-cover on bulb-beds. The white form is much liked for cutting to mix with larger flowers. Make successive sowings in fall and spring where they are to flower; their blooming season is short.

HELIANTHUS (Sunflower).—The common annual Sunflower is too well known to require description, and its

An attractive basin on a brick wall which is largely covered with Ficus repens. In this cool and shady place the Cinerarias and Forget-me-nots look happy.

Flowers are often best in a border, as here. The warmth of the brick path is brought out by the adjoining grass, part of the open central lawn.

easy culture has spread it everywhere. The large-flowering forms are too coarse for most gardens, but the *H. cucumerfolius* varieties should be more grown in California gardens for temporary hedges, screens, and backgrounds, and for cutting. They remain in bloom much longer than any perennial kind and have a wider range of shades of cream and yellow. It is best to sow them in spring where they are to flower, thinning out plants to about two feet apart.

IBERIS (Candytuft).—From a fall sowing in the open ground the hardy annual Candytufts give pleasing drifts of white, lilac, and carmine flowers, in winter in southern California and in late spring and early summer farther north. Their ease of culture—they readily self-sow under favorable conditions—and their adaptability to sandy soil make them especially popular along the seacoast.

LATHYRUS ODORATA.—See SWEET PEA.

LAYIA (Tidytips).—Of the several varieties of this native annual, *L. elegans* seems to be the favorite. It is a pleasing little yellow Daisy with white tips, naturalizing readily from seed sown in the fall.

LEPTOSYNE.—These yellow, Daisy-like flowers, relatives of the Coreopsis, which they resemble, are natives of California, and, like other native annuals, do best from a fall sowing. *L. Douglasii*, one foot high, and *L. Stillmannii*, are both worth growing for their early flowers and bright color.

LINARIA (Toadflax).—No annual in my garden has interested as many visitors as the beautiful Toadflaxes, which seed themselves everywhere but are of such slender growth that their spikes of miniature Snapdragon-shaped flowers never seem weedy or out of place. Sown in the fall, they are among the first annuals to bloom, yet they may be had in midsummer by starting them in spring. The mixed strains usually offered run largely to pink and light purple shades, but by growing all available kinds and letting the bees cross them much greater variation will be secured. This is one annual everyone should try. When my large plantings of bearded Irises are beginning to make strong leaf growth in March, the beds are studded with the jewel-like little flowers of the Linarias, many of which look particularly gay because of their bright yellow blotches.

LINUM (Flax).—The annual Flax most grown is *L. grandiflorum*, a bright red variety which should be sown in the open ground in fall, always choosing a sunny place, as the flowers hardly open anywhere else. Well suited to wild gardening, where it perpetuates itself by self-sowing.

LOBELIA.—Only the half-hardy annuals so much used for bordering flower-beds are considered here. For formal use, compact varieties such as Crystal Palace are needed, but the possibility of using informal, trailing kinds to prolong through the summer the beauty of the rock-garden should not be overlooked. Sow seed in boxes in spring, and bed out for summer display. The blue varieties will always be the most popular, but if other colors are desired white and the red-purple Prima Donna are offered.

LUPINUS (Lupine).—So many kinds of wild Lupines are to be found in California meadows that this flower has been rather neglected in California gardens, though its ease of culture and charming color range certainly recommend it. Catalogues offer a good many annual species, and from these I would especially recommend *L. Hartwegi*, which grows two feet high and can be obtained in white and shades of blue and purple. The pale blue selection is a delightful color. When I saw it massed in a beautiful Santa Barbara garden some years ago it seemed the most attractive feature of the place in May.

MALCOLMIA (Virginia Stock).—This is distinctly a flower to be sown in the fall for winter blooming. Its dainty little blossoms, from white to carmine, are then most attractive. Being very dwarf, it is best used for edgings or as a carpet-plant in beds of such bulbs as Tulips. It deserves greater use.

MARIGOLD.—See TAGETES.

MATTHIOLA.—See STOCK.

MENTZELIA LINDLEYI (syn. *Bartonia aurea*).—The brilliance of this California wild-flower has earned for it the popular name of Blazing Star. Sown preferably in the fall, its golden-yellow flowers, two feet high, give wonderful color in springtime. Prefers a sunny place and resents transplanting.

MIGNONETTE.—See RESEDA.

NASTURTIUM (*Tropaeolum*).—The trailing varieties of these common but beautiful plants should be more used for covering unsightly places, clothing raw banks in new gardens, and as temporary climbers and background plants. The dwarf kinds make effective beds and borders, and are excellent to follow such bulbous plants as Daffodils. In the comparatively frostless sections they may be sown where they are to bloom any time after the first rains and until March or April. Do not sow the seeds too thickly, as almost every one will germinate. The dwarf varieties should hardly be closer than a foot apart, the trailers still farther.

NEMESIA.—South African annuals which are increasing in popularity in California as they are of the greatest value for winter bedding in southern California and for like use in summer on the rest of the Pacific coast. In the frostless sections seed should be sown in fall in boxes or in prepared seed-beds and the plants, when about two inches high, put a foot apart where they are to bloom. The same process in springtime should be gone through for summer bedding in colder places. The mixed strains of *N. strumosa Suttoni* make beautiful beds, while an effect similar to Forget-me-Nots may be had by using Blue Gem alone. It is best not mixed with the others.

NEMOPHILA (California Bluebell).—These pretty little California hardy annuals should be naturalized in half-shady places by scattering and raking in the seed in fall. They may also be used for borders and ground-covers in the garden. If only one is chosen it should be *N. insignis*, whose blue flowers with white centres are commonly called Baby Blue-eyes in California. *N. atomaria*, white with black spots, is much less effective but may be used separately for variety.

NICOTIANA (Tobacco).—These flowering forms of the Tobacco family have a certain value from their sweet-scented, tubular flowers, but because of their rather large and straggly growth they demand a good deal of room. The white *N. affinis* opens on cloudy days and in the evening, while the colored forms of *N. Sanderæ* open during the day. Sow in boxes in spring and transplant to where they will bloom.

NIGELLA (Love-in-a-Mist).—This hardy annual, about eighteen inches high, with feathery foliage is not found in many gardens, though the variety Miss Jekyll is of such a beautiful Cornflower blue that it merits more frequent growing. As with many hardy annuals, the best results are had from a fall sowing where it is expected to bloom.

OMPHALODES (Venus's Navelwort).—Where Lily-of-the-Valley rarely succeeds, a somewhat similar garden effect may be had by scattering in the fall and raking in seed of this beautiful dwarf gray-leaved annual, for in April and May the plants will be a mass of little spikes of pure white flowers, wonderfully appealing during their short season. This sows itself so certainly that it will perpetuate itself wherever the conditions are favorable, yet it is of such slender growth that it never becomes a weed. Good for the wild garden and the rock-garden, and very useful as a follow-up in bulb beds.

PANSY (Viola).—Everyone knows Pansies, and a good many want to have them in their gardens. They are really of very easy culture once certain decided preferences as to conditions are understood.

Pansies dislike heat and drought; it must therefore be obvious that they will do their best growing and make their best show before summer really comes, and also that a border of them on the east side of the house will last in good condition much longer than one on the west side, though the first flowers may not come as soon.

Do not sow the seed in the open ground but in boxes or frames where they can be given that shade during the week of germination which is essential. The seed-boxes must be kept moist until the plants come up, which they will do in great abundance, so that care must be taken not to sow too thickly. When the seedlings have made two or three true leaves, prick them out and replant in other boxes about two inches apart, or in a well-prepared bed which does not get the hot afternoon sun. The best time to sow is in August or September, as this will give plants which can be moved from the nursery bed to their permanent places in late fall. If the soil is light and rich and they are given ample water when the rains do not furnish it, no finer Pansies can be grown anywhere.

Where large size of flowers and variety of colorings are desired it is worth while paying the price of the best mixed seed, but for particular effects of color stockier bedding types such as Lord Beaconsfield or Golden Queen are better. Personally, for this latter purpose I much prefer the closely related Violas, most of them listed as varieties of *Viola cornuta*. They are crosses between Pansies and Violets, and though their flowers lack the size and range of color seen in the well-fed looking Pansies, they have a woodland charm which the Pansy lacks, due to a lengthening and pointing of the petals. The long season in which they keep in good condition and their more compact and stocky growth have given them a tremendous vogue in England. Though less grown here, it is largely because they are not so well known, but since their great success as bedding plants at the Panama-Pacific Exposition in San Francisco their popularity is spreading.

PAPAVER (Poppy).—Brilliant results may be achieved from the use of annual Poppies, all of which do well from fall-sown seed, but care must be taken either to sow very sparsely or to thin out the plants afterward;

they will not stand transplanting. The single Shirley Poppies are deservedly the most admired for their beautiful colorings. The one trouble with their cultivation is that in some sections the sparrows eat the seedlings as rapidly as they come up, so that in such places the beds must be protected with chicken-wire. The varieties of *P. somniferum* are much coarser and weedier in growth, but where a single fine color is used striking effects can be given to the rougher parts of the garden. Along the seacoast, where the soil is shady and summer fogs abound, they may be sown in spring for summer flowering. On the Monterey peninsula I remember seeing in a garden in midsummer a variety of *P. somniferum* five feet high, with huge single mauve flowers having purple blotches at the base. The effect was as wonderful as it was unusual.

PETUNIA.—For its brightness and mass of color, for the long duration of its blooming season, its ease of culture, and its comparative adaptability to drought, the Petunia is one of our best bedding plants, particularly during the summer months. Plants are best raised from seed sown in boxes in spring, the seedlings being moved into their permanent quarters when about two inches high. In southern California similar fall sowings may be made for winter flowering of the bedding type such as Snowball and the bright pink Rosy Morn. With the bedding kinds it is better to confine a planting to a single variety, as the colors are apt to clash. The giant sorts are, however, only offered in mixtures, but fortunately the colors in this section are more harmonious. In California Petunias often prove biennials or short-lived perennials. If some particular variety is wanted in quantity, cuttings may be inserted in sandy soil in a somewhat shaded bed or frame in September.

PHACELIA.—For a beautiful patch of Madonna blue in the rock-garden try *P. campanularia*, the most satisfactory of the varieties of this native annual. It may be sown where it is to flower, either in fall or spring.

PHLOX.—The annual *P. Drummondi*, though an attractive summer bedding plant, seems not to be greatly grown in California. With me it has been less satisfactory here than in the East. Spring is the time to sow it. For the best results the seedlings should be planted out in good soil where they can have attention in the matters of watering and cultivation.

PINK.—See DIANTHUS.

PLATYSTEMON (Cream-cup).—This is another attractive little native annual which should be used in the rock-garden, for edgings, or the seed should be simply scattered in the wild garden in the fall. If thinned out to at least three or four inches apart, its lovely little creamy yellow flowers, resembling tiny Poppies, will begin to appear quite early in the year and will prove an attraction for several weeks.

POPPY.—See PAPAVER.

PORTULACA (Purslane).—For a dry sunny slope on which it is difficult to get any color in midsummer Portulaca is most likely to be successful, particularly in sandy soils. It may be sown where it is to flower, either in fall or spring, but the latter time is better, as it will be most appreciated in summer. These make good fillers of blank spaces in the rock-garden.

RESEDA (Mignonette).—Grown solely for its fragrance, this annual may be had in bloom almost continuously by making successive sowings in the open ground. It transplants badly, enjoys rich soil, and prefers a cool moist place rather than a dry and sunny one.

SALPIGLOSSIS.—For a summer bed or border of unusual colorings try this annual, which grows from two to three feet high and becomes literally covered with beautiful trumpet-shaped blooms. In mixture they give almost the color effect of an oriental rug. They provide excellent cut flowers, though their sticky stems are not pleasant to handle. Sow in seed-bed or box in spring, preferably transplanting the seedlings once before they are put where they are to flower.

SALVIA (Sage).—*S. splendens,* though really a half-hardy perennial, is best treated as an annual. The seed is sown in early spring in a hotbed or in boxes indoors, so that the plants may get an early start. When all danger from frost is over they may be planted out, and in late summer and fall their scarlet spikes will give a showy, though rather hot and garish, effect. For other varieties, see under Perennials.

SCABIOSA (Scabious, Pincushion Flower).—No flower seems to be better pleased with California' than the annual Scabious, they being so adapted to our conditions that they will grow like weeds and may often be found naturalized in fields near gardens. Yet for summer flowers, both for garden effect and cutting, they are admirable, especially where care is taken to restrict one's sowing to the good clear shades of lavender, blue, rose, and cherry, leaving out the dull white and the many other indeterminate shades. As they are wanted chiefly for summer flowers they are best sown in spring, either in the seed-bed or where they are intended to flower.

SCHIZANTHUS (Poor Man's Orchid).—Though Schizanthus are even in California at their best as greenhouse plants, they can be grown very successfully wholly outdoors. If sown in April in good soil where they are expected to flower, they will provide a most interesting display of their dainty flowers. It should be borne in mind that while very floriferous their duration is not long, and successive sowings are necessary for a long display. The little blossoms are of butterfly shape, and have a wonderful range of colors, particularly when grown from the finer and more expensive strains of seed.

SNAPDRAGON.—See ANTIRRHINUM.

STATICE (Sea Lavender).—*S. latifolia,* the best of the Statices, will be found listed under Perennials. The annual *S. sinuata,* which grows about two feet high and may be had in blue, pale yellow, and white, will appeal to those fond of Everlastings. Sow in seed-bed in spring and transplant to the border.

STOCK (Matthiola, Gilliflower).—By a selection of the different kinds of Stocks it is possible to have them in bloom almost continuously. There is no better winter flower than the Stocks of the Beauty of Nice type. Seed of these should be sown in boxes from June to August, and the plants moved out to their permanent quarters in fall. For summer blooming the Ten-Weeks' and Cut-and-Come-Again varieties are excellent from spring sowing in boxes or prepared seed-beds. Though the Ten-Weeks' varieties do not remain as long in bloom, their profusion makes them of special value for summer bedding. As there is no way of insuring that all the plants shall have double flowers it is wise in bedding to plant close enough so that if desired any singles may be pulled out.

SUNFLOWER.—See HELIANTHUS.

SWEET PEA (*Lathyrus odoratus*).—Continual improvements in all the desirable qualities of the Sweet Pea excepting fragrance have kept it for many years the most popular annual plant. Special attention is there-

fore given to its cultural requirements, for though there
is no place better adapted to it than California the best
results can only be expected where fine varieties are
sown and given some care.   Advances in color and size
are so continual that the lists of the best kinds can
only be found in up-to-date seed catalogues.   What the
beginner should note is that there are now two distinct
sections, one of early-flowering varieties and the other
of the standard summer-flowering kinds.   The waved,
or Spencer, type has practically superseded the old
plain, or *grandiflora*, type, and is available in both early
and late sections.   The early section is a particular
boon to those gardening where the summers are warm,
as the Sweet Pea dislikes heat and will there be successful
only when it can be brought into bloom early.   Along
the coast of California, which the summer fogs keep
cool, and north to British Columbia the summer-flowering varieties should certainly be sown.

The preparation of the ground is quite important.
Sweet Peas demand a deep, cool root-run, and should
be encouraged to go deep for their food.   The soil
should be dug to the depth of at least a foot; the best
way to do this is to mark out the row, which should be
dug to the width of two feet, and throw out the soil to
the depth of one foot at the beginning of the row.   This
will leave room so that as the row is dug the soil may
be thrown forward into the empty space.   Wherever
possible, do this digging at least a month in advance of
actual sowing, leaving it rough until that time.   If the

soil is at all deficient in fertility, dig in well-rotted manure or a good heavy dusting of bone-meal. This is for good general culture; the huge flowers raised for exhibition purposes are generally grown in soil which has been trenched to the depth of two or three feet.

Sowing the seed in the open ground is best done from September to December for the early section, and in November and December or in February and March for the summer varieties. The trench in which seeds are sown should be well firmed by treading and the seed put in quite thinly about an inch deep. As the seed-coatings of some varieties are very hard, those of bullet-like appearance should have this coating punctured by chipping or filing on the side opposite to the eye. Soaking the seed is recommended by some for the same purpose.

In localities where birds are troublesome it may be necessary to cover the ground until the plants have made several inches of growth. It is only in their early stages that the birds enjoy them. Fine-meshed wire or a tent-like erection of fly-netting will provide sufficient protection. When the plants have germinated, thin out to as much as a foot apart. Thick planting is responsible in many cases for both poor flowers and short season of bloom. Where the winters are cold, sowing of seed may be done in pots in a coldframe. Paper pots may be used and a single seed placed in each, or three seeds may be sown in a four-inch pot. This plan is particularly desirable where very expensive seed of a novelty is being sown. Planting out should be done when there is no further danger of severe frosts, putting the plants a foot apart or, where a potful of three is left intact, as much as two feet.

When the plants are three or four inches high pinch out the centres to encourage the better side-shoots, and provide small twigs to which the tendrils may cling. Permanent support may take either the form of twiggy tree-branches, five or six feet high, or, where these are not available, chicken-wire trellis or strings stretched between supports. Be sure to use supports which are sufficiently tall and strong. The wire may be of as large a mesh as four inches. Always put the wire on the side away from the prevailing wind, so that the plants will naturally blow into it rather than having constantly to be tied back. After the rains are over, attention should be given to keeping the soil so culti-vated that it will not dry out or crack. A mulch of old strawy manure will greatly assist this. Do not water by a casual sprinkling every day but rather give the plants an occasional thorough soaking. Lastly, keep the flowers cut, or at any rate do not allow them to go to seed. This is the best receipt for prolonging the blooming season.

Tagetes (Marigold).—Both the small French and large African Marigolds are thoroughly satisfactory summer and fall garden annuals. No annual persists in blooming later in the fall than the French Marigold; indeed, in December and January, after being battered about by the heavy fall rains, wherever it has a sunny exposure it will brighten up the garden. It withstands drought extremely well and has no demands in regard to soil, being on the whole more floriferous where not too well fed. Marigolds are not only excellent for beds and, in the case of the dwarf varieties, for edgings, but in the African sorts they are so large that they are well adapted to form a temporary foundation planting while the more permanent shrubs are growing up around the base of a house.

TITHONIA.—Of recent years a very tall, late-blooming annual with orange-colored single flowers has occasionally been seen in California gardens, and the cut blooms have perhaps been noticed in florists' windows. This is *T. speciosa*, a Mexican annual of rather straggling growth up to eight or ten feet. For its color and height there are places, for example, on the sunny south or west side of a house, where it may prove acceptable. Sow in April or May.

TROPAEOLUM.—See NASTURTIUM.

VERBENA.—Their low spreading habit and wide range of bright colors make the annual Verbenas invaluable for beds or for covering sunny slopes, where in the warmer sections they sometimes prove perennial. They are most easily raised from seed sown in a hotbed or in boxes indoors in early spring, but later plants may be secured from an outdoor sowing. Some gardeners find the sparrows very fond of the young growth, and where this is so the seed-bed should be protected with chicken-wire. In transplanting, the plants should be put at least a foot apart where they are to bloom. Colors come reasonably true from seed, but any special variety may be propagated by cuttings in fall or spring, or by pegging down some of the shoots to the ground, thus causing layers.

Viola. See Pansy.

Virginia Stock.—See Malcolmia.

Zinnia.—As a bedding plant in the warmer parts of the state and especially in the Sacramento and San Joaquin valleys there is no summer annual which approaches the Zinnia in effectiveness. For the best results warm weather, rich soil, and plenty of water are necessary, and gardeners along the coast, where cold summer fogs abound, cannot hope for the size and vigor found in warmer places. They may be raised either in boxes indoors, in frames, or in seed-beds, any time during spring, and transplanted out later. In their early stages they particularly resent neglect, and if then allowed to dry out or become starved they do not recover their vigor. Continuous active growth must be kept up. The Zinnia has been greatly improved in size and still more in range of color in recent years, and breeders will certainly continue to make further progress. The colors in the new strains blend beautifully, so that fine mixtures of the giant varieties are perfectly satisfactory. It is a wonderful flower for cutting, particularly in association with dark woodwork. If a small bright flower is needed for edging, the very dwarf Red Ridinghood will be found acceptable.

SELECTIONS OF ANNUALS FOR SPECIAL PURPOSES

For Continuity of Bloom

Spring

Antirrhinum
Calendula
Collinsia
Eschscholtzia
Forget-me-Not
Linaria
Linum grandiflorum

Nemophila
Pansy
Poppy
Stock (Beauty of Nice type)
Sweet Alyssum
Sweet Pea (early flowering)

Summer

Antirrhinum
Aster
Candytuft
Centaurea
Clarkia
Coreopsis
Dianthus

Godetia
Larkspur
Marigold
Nemesia
Petunia
Salpiglossis
Scabiosa

Stock (Ten Weeks')   Verbena
Sweet Pea   Zinnia

Autumn

Cosmos   Scabiosa
Gaillardia   Sunflower
Marigold   Zinnia

Drought-Resistant Annuals

Antirrhinum   Gaillardia
Calendula   Helianthus
Centaurea   Petunia
Delphinium   Portulaca
Dianthus   Scabiosa
Eschscholtzia   Tagetes
           Verbena

Natives for Naturalizing

Clarkia   Layia elegans
Collinsia   Leptosyne
Eschscholtzia   Lupinus
Gilia   Mentzelia Lindleyi
Godetia   Nemophila insignis
      Platystemon californicus

Other Annuals for Naturalizing

Alyssum   Chrysanthemum
Calendula   Coreopsis
Centaurea   Cosmos

Delphinium

Iberis

Linaria

Linum grandiflorum

Myosotis

Nasturtium

Papaver

Reseda

FOR ROCK-GARDENS AND EDGINGS

Ageratum

Alonsoa

Alyssum (dwarf)

Brachycome

Coreopsis

Diascia Barberi

Dimorphotheca aurantiaca

Erysimum

Iberis

Linaria

Lobelia

Malcolmia

Nemesia

Nemophila

Omphalodes linifolia

Phacelia campanularia

Portulaca

CHAPTER IX

A Sequence of Bulbs

FOR the beginner there is no class of flower-pro-
ducing plants with which it is so easy to achieve
success as bulbs and tubers. The reason for this is
that stored up in the bulb is a large quantity of the
necessary plant food, and in most cases, as for example
in Daffodils, the actual bud which will develop into the
blossom may be found in the centre of the fleshy cover-
ings when it is being planted. The result is that, given
reasonably good soil and drainage, bulbs are practically
certain to produce flowers. The quality of these, however, will depend upon how good has been the cultivation and how favorable the conditions. A Daffodil,
even if planted in shallow soil on a hard dry hillside,
in baking sunlight in December if it is of blooming
size will almost certainly flower. However, had the
same bulb been planted with the first rains, say in mid-
October, given good deep soil and a situation where the
root-run would be cool and moist, the flower-stem would
be much taller and the blossom infinitely finer. On this
account I shall have something to say on the culture of
different classes of bulbs.

Apart from their ease of culture, bulbs should be
largely grown because of their adaptability to many

uses in the garden, and for their desirability as cut flowers. Hyacinths and Tulips, for example, are most satisfactory for spring bedding, even in the most formal of gardens; Daffodils have no superior for naturalizing, particularly in the light shade of deciduous trees; Muscari, Scillas, and other small bulbs beautify our rock-gardens; and the South African Irids, of which the Ixias are best known, will grow with the greatest ease in dry sunny places. One of the very best ways to use both the spring- and summer-flowering bulbs is to plant them in groups down the length of the flower-border, as in this way not only will they add greatly to its beauty but when their foliage has died down the gap will be comparatively inconspicuous, and if a light-rooting annual such as Calliopsis or Clarkia be sown among the bulbs in spring these gaps will later be filled. If this result is to be obtained the groups should not be large, yet there should be always enough flowers to give a noticeable spot of color. Never plant bulbs singly or in long straight rows. They need company to look happy.

It is possible to have some bulb in flower every month in the year in California, though spring is their heyday. Rather than to give an alphabetical list of those deserving cultivation I shall roughly follow the calendar, only departing to keep members of a family together.

DAFFODILS FOR EARLY BLOOM

The genus Narcissus gives us our earliest as well as some of our most showy bulbous flowers, for often even before the first of the year, always by January, the early Polyanthus Narcissus, Paper White; the yellow and orange Grand Soleil d'Or; and the popular but less worthy, Chinese Sacred Lily, are in bloom. Where they have been given a sunny exposure the first of the trumpet Daffodils, Golden Spur, will be out by early February, and if some of the latest-blooming kinds be planted in a cold shaded spot you may expect flowers for nearly two months. As long as tastes differ no one can make a selection of varieties that will be satisfactory to every gardener, but from many moderate-priced varieties which I have tried I can recommend the following as fine, vigorous garden flowers, pretty well covering the range of color and shape.

Golden Spur, the earliest of the Yellow Trumpets, fine in color but not as tall and vigorous as Emperor, the standard Yellow Trumpet, a fine doer with large flowers of a lighter yellow. King Alfred is a wonderful flower, a giant in size and of a beautiful golden yellow, a fine grower in California, for it prefers warm soils and mild winters, requirements which have made it less successful in cold English gardens.

Empress, though smaller than Emperor, occupies the corresponding position as a standard among the Bi-color Trumpets, that is, those with white perianths, though Victoria is earlier; and the pale Weardale Perfection by its size and height surpasses both and will doubtless be much grown when cheaper. Of the creamy-white Trumpets, Mme. de Graaff is outstandingly the best.

Among the Incomparabilis or Crown Daffodils the yellow Sir Watkin is largest and most satisfactory in the garden. Other smaller but finer ones are Autocrat, Gloria Mundi, and Lucifer, the last being white with an orange-scarlet cup.

From the Barri section, where the cups are very shallow and generally edged with orange-red, two varieties at least should be selected, the standard pale yellow Barri conspicuous, and the lovely white Sea-Gull.

The Leedsi section contains shallow-crowned white Daffodils sometimes with a suffusion of yellow. Mrs. Langtry, an old and cheap variety, is very vigorous and prolific; but for purity of color and for size one should also grow White Lady. The Barri and Leedsi sections contain the varieties which bloom latest.

Among the Poet's or Pheasant-Eye Narcissus I have found ornatus most satisfactory. There are larger and finer forms, but it is questionable whether they are worth the much greater cost.

In addition everyone should have a few of the true Jonquils, to be distinguished from the Daffodils by their round rush-like leaves. The Campernelle Jonquil, which is the best variety, blooms as early as Golden Spur and in good cultivation has generally two or three flowers on a stem.

The more recently developed Poetaz group, crosses of the poeticus and the polyanthus Narcissus, have three or four large flowers on a single tall strong stem and bloom, in the variety Elvira at least, at the end of the season.

The enthusiast will enjoy trying a few novelties each

year. Culture is very easy. Plant the bulbs four or five inches deep, preferably in late October or November. On the north Pacific coast conditions are ideal for this genus; as one gets into southern California it becomes more important to give them partial shade, a good heavy loam, and generous watering; they cannot be harmed by an over-supply. Under favorable conditions the bulbs of some varieties increase rather rapidly, and should they become crowded the bed should be replanted, but this is hardly likely to occur until the third or fourth year. The poeticus section is dormant for the shortest period, and replanting of these should not be delayed beyond September. Gophers leave Daffodils strictly alone. They do not care for the acrid taste.

THREE EARLY COMPANIONS

Contemporaneous in flowering with the earlier Daffodils are three bulbous flowers deserving of a wider distribution. The first of these in time is *Leucojum vernum*, the Spring Snowflake, far more successful in California than the Snowdrop, to which its flowers are quite similar excepting that they are ornamented at the tips of the petals with a green spot. A clump in the front of the shrubbery or a small group in the rock-garden will be found very fresh and welcome. The quite large bulbs should be planted early, as if left out of the ground too long they have a tendency to rot. Give them half shade and leave them undisturbed and their requirements are satisfied.

The Muscari, or Grape Hyacinths, soon follow, and

under our conditions are most vigorous and prolific
little bulbs. The little spikes of deep blue flowers are
not showy but they are borne so surely and so abundantly that they may always be depended on to give a
beautiful blue note early in the spring. As a ground-
cover in front of some white-flowered deciduous shrub
such as the double-flowered Spiræa or in the rock-
garden, it is most pleasing—for it should be placed
where it is close to the observer. It is seemingly
satisfied with any garden soil and makes no requirements in the matter of shade or moisture.

The last of the triumvirate is *Triteleia uniflora*
(syn. *Milla uniflora*), whose succession of star-shaped
bluish-white flowers will adorn a sunny rock-garden for
several weeks. The curious little white bulbs, rather
resembling teeth, originally came from South America,
but they could not now be more at home than in California. Plant about two inches deep during fall, and
leave them alone so that by their rapid increase they
may make thick patches. Their preference is for a dry
sunny place.

THE DUTCH HYACINTH

Of the larger, so-called Dutch bulbs the Hyacinth is
next in season, March being its particular month.
The stiffness and formality of growth of the Dutch
Hyacinths and their general reputation for lack of
permanence are two reasons why they are eclipsed in
popularity by the Daffodils and Tulips. Neverthe-
less, in their season their very formality adds to their

value as bedding-plants, and their range of color is altogether different from that of other bulbous flowers of their time. They also have a most delicious fragrance.

For those who want Hyacinths but find them too rigid in effect I suggest that the ground between the bulbs be planted in the fall with Forget-me-Nots or Violas, or that seed be sown of such annuals as *Nemophila insignis* or *Omphalodes linifolia*. Then, too, by ordering the smaller and cheaper grade of Hyacinth, smaller but more graceful flower-spikes will be obtained.

For the rock-garden only miniature bulbs should be used. Plant fairly closely in groups of a single color; mixtures give far inferior garden pictures. Hyacinth bulbs should be in the ground by October. Location is of less importance, though in a hot, dry garden they will last longer if somewhat shaded.

THE ELUSIVE CROCUS AND EARLY TULIPS

As the omission to mention Crocuses may have been noticed, I would say that though I have succeeded in growing them they are so uncertain and so much less heartening than where they usher in spring in colder climates, that I do not recommend them for any extensive use here. Similarly, the early Tulips, popular for bedding in parks and gardens on the Atlantic coast, are practically worthless outdoors in California, as the burst of warm weather in February forces them into premature bloom while their stems are still only an inch or two in height.

TULIPS OF ALL SORTS

Choice of Tulips should therefore be restricted to the Darwins, Breeders, and Cottage kinds, as with them there is no such drawback, and given the proper conditions they will flower magnificently in early April on fine tall stems.   Tulips are considerably more exacting in their culture than Daffodils, and have a decided preference for rich, light, well-drained soils.   In hot places they also prefer partial shade such as is given by deciduous trees.   They will not stand the rough treatment accepted by Daffodils and they are unquestionably less permanent, the large bulbs having a tendency to break into several, all too small to bloom. In the case of very vigorous varieties like Inglescombe Pink, where space is available, these small bulbs may be grown on to flowering size.   One advantage possessed by Tulips is that they may be planted very late in the year and still flower perfectly, and though November is to be recommended one need not hesitate to plant them even up to New Year's Day.

The Darwin Tulips are the finest bulbous bedding flowers we have, and merit wide use in formal gardening as well as a careful consideration of color arrangement. Mixtures are very unsatisfactory and collections of one of a kind should be grown only for the purpose of learning which varieties one prefers.   In large plantings a beautiful progression of color groups is possible, as for instance from pale lilac through mauve and purple to maroon, or from blush through pink to rose.   Where clumps of harmonizing or contrasting colors are planted one can have such beautiful combinations as Rev. Ewbank (pale lilac) with Mrs. Potter Palmer (plum), or the rosy-flesh Suzon with the crimson Farncombe Sanders.

The one drawback to Darwin Tulips is that they sometimes "break", that is, the solid colors give place to stripes and according to present taste they become bizarre. Neither the cause nor the control of "breaking" has as yet been discovered.

The true Darwin Tulips contain no yellows nor bronzes. For the rich blends of bronze, brown, old gold, apricot, and purple one must go to the similar large cup-shaped Breeder Tulips, of which the extremely vigorous Clio (syn. Bronze Queen) is the most popular representative. Among the Cottage Tulips will be found not only a greater variety of shape and stature but, in addition to the white, pink, and red range of color, pure yellow such as that of Inglescombe Yellow and Gesneriana lutea. Good examples of the less formal shapes among the Cottage Tulips are the orange-scarlet La Merveille and the white, rose-margined, Picotée.

Greater contrasts in Tulip groups are possible where the Darwins and Cottage Tulips are both used, as for example in a group of the mauve-pink Darwin Sir Harry and the yellow Cottage Gesneriana lutea pallida.

SUCCESSIONS FOR THE TULIP BEDS

To make room for summer-flowering plants it is sometimes desired to remove the Tulips before they have died down. Experiments have shown that, odd as it may seem, this is much less of a shock if done just after flowering than if postponed until the foliage is yellow. Therefore if you want the ground for some other purpose do not hesitate to dig trenches in some out-of-the-way place and as carefully as possible remove the bulbs to them, covering them with soil until their foliage has ripened. An alternative scheme is to carpet the ground between the bulbs with smaller plants having a longer season of bloom, for example Forget-me-Nots, Arabis, Violas, Wallflowers, or *Primula malacoides;* or to sow in springtime, between the bulbs, such annuals for later summer bloom as Larkspurs, Linarias, Clarkias, or Coreopsis.

Tulip bulbs are good eating, and gophers will clean out your beds if they get a chance. Unless you are confident of your ability to poison or trap them it is wiser to protect the plantings with an underground fence of chicken-wire.

ANEMONE AND RANUNCULUS

For a long period in spring, including Tulip time, two groups of tuberous-rooted plants have done much to enliven our gardens, and though they are now less readily obtainable, because of the quarantine, home-grown stock is beginning to be listed. These are the garden varieties of *Anemone coronaria* and of *Ranunculus asiaticus*. They are of somewhat similar culture, both preferring light rich soils and warm sunny beds together with fall planting of their peculiar-looking roots. In both cases soaking for several hours before planting is desirable, in the case of the Anemones this will enable one to distinguish the crown by the fibrous growths which are on the top of the root; the bottoms of the roots are quite smooth. Plant about three inches deep in such a position that they can be thoroughly watered during dry periods.

The Anemones, either in the single Poppy types or the semi-double St. Brigid strain, have a brilliant range of coloring from white through pinks to rose and deep red, as well as blues and purples. They are gayest in mixtures. Few gardeners seem to know that from seed sown in midsummer and thoroughly shaded for two or three weeks until germination occurs plants may be obtained which will bloom profusely the following spring. It is necessary, however, to insure a continuous growth, and to do this the beds must never be allowed to dry out or the plants will become dormant.

In the Ranunculus the range of color is different, including besides whites, pinks, and reds, yellows and scarlet and many blended colors in both single and double forms. Soak the roots in water for two or three hours, and when they have swelled to a much greater size plant them about two inches deep, with the claws pointing downward. In some places the fondness of the sparrows for the young growth of the Ranunculus has made it impossible to grow them without a screen of wire over the young plants.

The exquisite Lily-of-the-Valley (*Convallaria majalis*) can occasionally be grown outdoors in California in a cool, moist, shaded place, but it should not be depended on for the many cut flowers or the beautiful wild garden effect so readily given by it in colder climates.

MEDITERRANEAN BULBS

All bulbs native to the Mediterranean region are happy in California. It is therefore natural that we should grow the larger and taller Spanish Squill (*Scilla campanulata*) rather than *S. sibirica*. It is so well adapted to our conditions and it increases so rapidly that it can unquestionably be grown on a commercial scale and it should soon be more generally available. It is not only a delightful plant for the cooler rock-garden but it should be grown extensively on the margin of shady paths, where its blue, bell-shaped flowers on stems up to eighteen inches high will be wonderfully appealing. There is an excellent white variety and a lilac-pink form of less color value. Drifts of a single color are infinitely more satisfactory than mixed plantings.

As so many kinds of small Mediterranean bulbs are no longer to be had in this country, the Ornithogalums will be the only other genus here to be considered. Several species of this may still be found in old gardens, in particular *O. umbellatum*, the common Star of Bethlehem, which in shaded gardens often naturalizes and in late spring bears its clusters of white flowers striped with green on the reverse. Much more effective from a gardening standpoint and adapted to a more open situation is *O. arabicum*, which from fall-planted bulbs produces in late spring strong stems as high as two feet bearing clusters of large creamy-white flowers rendered very striking by the large shining black ovary in the centre of each; an excellent bulb to add variety in the flower border.

CAPE BULBS

We cannot, however, omit that class of bulbs which is so perfectly suited with our climate, the Cape bulbs, a series of South African irids, including Freesias, Ixias, Sparaxis, and other less known sorts such as Babianas, *Tritonia crocata, Anomatheca cruenta,* and the dwarf early Gladioli. They are all plants for bright sunny gardens, some of them opening only in full sunlight.

Early planting in all cases is desirable, so that growth may begin with the first rains. After blooming in April and early May their small foliage rapidly dries up and may soon be cleaned away. They all increase quickly by offsets and produce seed so readily that under favorable conditions they show considerable tendency to naturalize. Where bulbs cannot be obtained it is quite worth while raising them from seed, as if this is sown in early fall flowers will sometimes be produced the following spring and always the second one.

Freesia.—Of these "Cape" bulbs the Freesias are best known and most widely grown. The pure white *F. refracta alba* and the primrose yellow *F. Leichtlini* are already to be found in many gardens, but the new colored hybrids should be added as they are quite as easy to grow and give a wide range of beautiful pastel shades, including yellow, salmon, pink, lilac, rose, and purple. They make beautiful edgings to paths, and are also very popular for cutting. Freesias particularly appreciate early planting. Try raising some from seed.

Ixia.—Even more important than the Freesias from a gardening standpoint are the Ixias, as their brilliant round blossoms sway continuously on tall, slender, wiry stems and are indescribably gay when the bright sunshine opens them. It is unfortunate that in this country mixtures are so much more frequently offered than are named varieties, for only with the latter can one use them in the finest way for striking color notes. The strong-growing orange-red Vulcan is wonderfully effective, and a good yellow with black centre or a good white with a violet eye will be more appreciated than the heterogeneous assortment too often found. As Ixias need only be planted a couple of inches deep, they may be interplanted with earlier and deeper-rooting bulbs such as Daffodils.

Sparaxis.—These are less important as they lack the height, grace, and variety of color of the Ixias. Being considerably dwarfer they are better for planting further forward, and if good color forms such as the scarlet and yellow Garibaldi or Fire King are procured the result will be very brilliant.

Babiana.—Running in color mostly to purple-blues and magentas, and therefore combining less well with other plants, Babianas come between the Ixias and the

Sparaxis in growth, and have rather stronger foliage than either.

Tritonia—In my own garden no spring bulb has ever been as much admired as the tomato-red *Tritonia crocata*, similar to a dwarf Freesia in growth but more effective as a garden flower on account of its vivid color and long period of bloom. It should be used in the front of the border and in a sunny rock-garden. Never plant it in shade.

Anomatheca cruenta, a starry coral-pink flower with a darker centre, is much less conspicuous than the foregoing but is one of the daintiest and most appealing of small bulbous flowers. If bulbs cannot be procured, remember that it is just about as easy to raise from seed as any annual or biennial, and once secured increases rapidly. Plant an inch deep in a sunny place.

The early Gladioli also belong in this group, but will be found treated with other Gladioli in another chapter where also will be found notes on the Dutch, Spanish, and English Irises, which bloom in succession from early April to late May.

Watsonia is also a South African bulb, but the stalwart growth differentiates the plants from this group. The corms of these allies of the Gladiolus require early planting, as they deteriorate if kept out of the ground after September. Watering or an October rain will bring up the leaves, and in a few weeks they will be two or three feet high, reaching by spring their full height, between four and five feet. If planted in clumps and allowed to remain undisturbed for two or three years this foliage is very effective through the rainy season and until after the flowers are produced in May. Much the commonest variety is *W. O'Brieni*, a fine white form, but there are also good lavender-pinks, salmon-pinks and a coppery red, which last is better planted away from conflicting colors. After flowering the stiff upright foliage begins to turn brown, and when this process is completed the stems should be cut to the ground. On account of the good foliage, very tall flower-stems, and the long period of bloom due to the many sidebranches, Watsonias are good for planting toward the back of a flower-border.

Calla Lily—Another now greatly neglected South African bulbous plant is the Calla Lily (*Richardia aethiopica*). This cherished pot-plant of the East is the easiest of outdoor plants in California, growing into strong hedges where it is given any considerable amount of water. It is best planted in the fall, and for its leaves alone should be considered when tropical effects are being planned on the banks of a pool.

A GROUP OF NATIVES

California has several families of very beautiful, delicate bulbous flowers, unusual in their forms and colorings. These bloom for the most part in late spring. Now that it has become difficult to get many small foreign bulbs we should use our beautiful natives more extensively in our gardens.

Mariposa or Butterfly Tulips—The most striking of these are the Calochorti. There are several sections, the dainty globular Fairy Lanterns quite differing from the larger cup-shaped forms, which have a creamy white, lilac, or yellow ground, the centres often blotched or veined in beautiful and interesting patterns. Good drainage at all times is a prime requisite, and though different species have varying preferences as to soil the majority prefer a light sandy loam with leaf-mold rather than manure to enrich it. If not on a slope, the bed should therefore be slightly raised. Full sun is very acceptable, and though they enjoy water in the late spring while coming into bloom it is essential that they be kept quite dry through the summer, their resting period. They are most attractive and successful in the pockets of a rock-garden which can be kept completely dry in summer.

Fritillaria—The sombre but interesting Mission Bells (*F.biflora*) enjoys full sun, but the brighter *F.recurva* and other varieties, being woodland bulbs, should be given partial shade. The same is true of the Erythroniums, the large Pacific coast Dog's-Tooth Violets, which are at their best in light gritty soil containing leaf-mold and in a rather moist shaded place such as suits many of the newer Chinese Primulas. Commoner and more vigorous are the Brodiaeas, whose tall stems and umbels of purplish-blue, white, or crimson flowers are often seen in our meadows. In cultivation, give them light shade and a gritty soil.

Camassia—Less grown, perhaps because they need a good deal of water while blooming, are the Camassias, which are particularly adapted to the north Pacific coast but in California should be given the damper places on the margins of pools or bog gardens.

A sequence of bulbs for the summer would contain Alstromerias, Agapanthus, Lilies, Amaryllis, Crinums, Tigridias, and Montbretias, with tuberous Begonias, Cannas, Gladioli, and Dahlias in bloom almost continuously. The fall is not a favored time for bulbous plants, but even then we have the little *Sternbergia lutea* and *Zephyranthes Candida*, Nerines, and latest of all the Kafir Lily (*Shizostylis coccinea*).

Alstromeria—A tuberous-rooted plant with the popular name of Lily of the Incas, this is surprisingly little grown considering that it blooms about Decoration Day, when bulbous flowers are few, and that once established it will produce year after year rigid stems from two to three feet high ending in umbels of flowers resembling small Amaryllis. In florists' windows one occasionally sees *A. aurantiaca*, some of its large orange petals striped with red. *A. chilensis* provides a beautiful series of shades, from creamy yellows through buff and apricot to deep pink and red. There is almost no flower which can excel them for house decoration, as the soft-toned flowers last in good condition for over a week. Their rarity is due to the fact that the tubers are not only infrequently offered for sale but also rather difficult to move. It is really easier to raise them from seed sown an inch deep in fall in the places where they are to be grown. In the shade of deciduous trees, where they are at their best, I have seen them naturalize themselves, springing up each fall and dying down in early summer after blooming. They need no summer watering.

Blue African Lily—In Eastern greenhouses you will find *Agapanthus umbellatus*, with its long curving grassy leaves and large umbels of gentian-blue flowers. On the Pacific coast it is a hardy bulbous garden plant, desirable for its strong color note in summer. The tubers should be planted from fall to early spring in a good rich loam, either in a sunny or a partially shaded place. It appreciates plenty of water.

AMARYLLIS

The Amaryllis is splendidly suited to California, yet the variety most grown, the bright pink *A. belladonna*, is probably more often misplaced than not. The broad grassy foliage appears in fall and disappears in spring; about August out of the bare ground come the dark, round flower-stalks, two feet high and capped with umbels of the pink flowers. The effect is naturally very ungraceful, and the habit of using this as a plant to border paths has greatly accentuated its peculiarities. Why not grow this plant farther back in the border, so that the foliage of the plants in front of it may atone for its lack of softening foliage? One possible facer would be Ferns. The heavy bulbs are best moved in the fall and should be planted in groups, in rather light soil if choice can be had. They do well in either sunny or half-shady places, but as they rarely bloom until well established they should not be moved unnecessarily.

By a careful selection of varieties and attention to their cultural requirements, partial shade, a light rich soil, a summer mulch of old manure, and plenty of water while in growth, one may have Lilies in California for some months. *L. candidum* ushers in the Lily season in May, and the beginner might well follow this with the easy native *L. pardalinum* and the old reliable Tiger Lily (*L. tigrinum*). With *L. auratum* and *L. speciosum* he may have flowers as late as August or September. If these prove successful, he may then experiment with the more expensive or more difficult species, including the glorious natives, *L. Humboldti* and *L. Washingtonianum*.

Tigridia—In a warm sheltered garden the gorgeous Tigridias will succeed and in midsummer will give their many three-petaled flowers of white, yellow, and carmine, often wonderfully spotted and marked. While each blossom lasts but a day, if the clump is of any size it will be continuously in bloom for a long time. The bulbs may be planted either in fall or in early spring, and should not be moved until they become too crowded.

Montbretia—In mid-August even neglected gardens will often be brightened with the orange or scarlet sprays of the Montbretias, the least exacting of the summer-flowering bulbs. They deserve better treatment, and will repay dividing and replanting in the fall and an occasional thorough watering through the summer. Over most bulbous plants they have the advantage of pleasing grassy foliage which comes up with the first rains and lasts until September, so that they never leave a bare place. Along the California coast they are perfectly hardy.

Tuberous Begonias are often a failure in California gardens because the grower has not carefully considered their wants. Yet if these are catered to there is no summer-flowering tuberous plant which will give for so long a time as pleasing a show. In California they should not be grown in pots, but in beds of very rich light soil with plenty of moisture and yet so graded that they will drain readily. They are not plants for full sunshine but for a shaded position, one which would be satisfactory for Ferns. The tubers should be started in pots or boxes of fine light rich soil mixed with leaf-mold, and in planting the crown should be about half an inch below the surface. They should be started in a lath-house or similar shaded place where they can be kept always moist until they have made sufficient growth to be transplanted a foot or more apart in the open ground. Where several are started in a single flat, be careful to move the young plants with as little disturbance of the soil as possible. In fall, when the glorious flowers are over, the tubers should be taken up and cleaned, and when dry packed in soil and kept cool until the following spring, when they may be used again.

Canna—No other tuberous-rooted plant gives as

fine tropical effects as the Canna, and the recent developments in addition to the old-time red and yellow
varieties give many fine colors, including brilliant orange
and soft pink shades.   Even if they did not bloom they
would be worth growing for their foliage.   Mediocre
results are generally due to neglecting the essentials in
their cultivation.

Cannas want deeply dug soil, thoroughly enriched
with rotted manure, the warmest situation you can offer,
and regular and very thorough irrigation.   There are
cold, foggy sections on the coast where Cannas are not
happy, and there it is better to do without them.   Other
things being equal, it is always best to choose a plant
that likes your conditions.   New beds should be started
in early spring, when the stock may be increased by
dividing into pieces all of which contain buds.   In
comparatively frostless places Cannas may be left in
the ground as hardy perennials, but with such rapidly
increasing and voracious plants it is better to divide
and replant yearly.

Zephyranthis candida is the little white flower somewhat resembling a Crocus which blooms so abundantly
in September.   It is most commonly planted in the
fall, but spring planting is also possible.   Not being
showy, it is at its best where a number of bulbs are
planted closely in the rock-garden.   Similar in treatment and in use is the less common *Sternbergia lutea*,
whose bright yellow funnel-shaped flowers come as late
as November.   This is supposed to be the "Lily of the
field" alluded to in the Bible.

CYCLAMEN FOR OUTDOORS

Though there are some exquisite little Cyclamens, chiefly from around the Mediterranean, which are hardy in gardens colder than ours, it seems to be news to many Californians that even the Persian Cyclamen can be grown outdoors in our mildest districts, and that so planted they will give many of their distinct and graceful flowers through the spring months. They are reasonably permanent provided that proper conditions are given them. These are a light and porous soil, one in which leaf-mold is the largest constituent, and a sheltered and at least partially shaded position, such as one finds under Oak trees, or in a cool, well-drained rock-garden. Planting may be done from May to early fall, depending on the size of the plants to be used. Great care should be taken not to bury the top of the corm in planting. They like water during the dry weather.

It is really easier for the amateur to grow Cyclamen in this way than in pots, as he cannot as a rule supply the potted plants with the moist greenhouse conditions under which they thrive. It is, however, much easier for him to buy young plants or corms than to raise the Cyclamen from seed, a slow process best left for the professional, who has a greenhouse.

The treatment of *Shizostylis coccinea* is very simple. Its corms, something like those of Gladioli, should be planted in early fall. It seems indifferent as to soil or location. It is not a fine thing, but does give winter color in the border.

CHAPTER X

UNDER this heading have been selected a few of the flowers for which cults exist on the Pacific coast—Chrysanthemums, Dahlias, Gladioli, Iris, Roses. By the omission of others I do not fail to recognize that there are specialists whose chief interest is in succulents, for example, or in Pæonies, the latter unfortunately not sufficiently happy in California to repay undivided attention. The essentials for a fancier's flower are that it offer sufficient variety in color and shape, that it be susceptible to improvement by breeding, that it have a reasonably long season of bloom, and that it be neither too expensive nor too difficult to grow. The specialist is happiest when there are other enthusiasts to share his absorbing interest: these others will only be found where the climatic conditions are adapted to the favored flower. It is interesting to note that the plants selected for special attention in this chapter all find in California more favorable conditions than elsewhere in America.

Specialists might do well to consider one criticism of the general gardener, that is that in their concentration on growing fine individual flowers they give so little consideration to their great possibilities for garden adornment. I often feel that not only the gardener himself but his visitors would derive more pleasure if while still giving his Roses or Dahlias everything that they required in the way of cultivation he so planned as to make his place look less like a nursery than some I have seen. Some attention might well be paid to the grouping and to the color arrangement. This is particularly desirable where the collection is grown in a conspicuous place, in a general garden. Much the easiest way, of course, and this is possible on the larger place, is to have a special little enclosed garden which need not be seen by the casual visitor except when in flower. Other cranks are of course delighted to view it at any time, for they can get a wonderful thrill even from the labels.

I. The Chrysanthemum

On the Pacific coast the Chrysanthemum is a hardy perennial, and its roots will live from year to year in the open ground. The pompons, singles, and the more vigorous of the larger varieties would continue to flower for some years without even being reset, but this practice should never be followed for fine results. All Chrysanthemums are gross feeders, with wonderfully developed root systems, and the ground in which they are to be planted should be deeply dug and well enriched by digging into it horse- or cow-manure, well rotted. They are very thirsty plants, and in choosing a location in the California garden where the summers are dry, it should be in a place where water is close at hand. In most places they should be planted in full sunshine, but in very hot gardens partial shade is better. Both for feeding and to conserve the moisture, a good thick mulch of rotted manure should be put on the beds in early summer. If this cannot be given, a light surface cultivation should follow the day after each watering.

Where the Chrysanthemums are grown mainly for large cut flowers a simple planting arrangement is to have beds about three feet wide and as long as desired and to have a ridge of soil around the entire bed. Such a bed will hold a double row of plants, leaving a foot on each side and between the plants. The ridging is to facilitate watering, as with this arrangement the beds may be thoroughly flooded occasionally. The double line of plants saves room and makes it easier to string the wires to support the tall single stems.

In the propagation of named varieties unquestionably for the finest results cuttings will be used. A greenhouse is unnecessary; I have rooted cuttings without any glass, but quicker and more certain success will come if one has a coldframe, even a very amateurish thing made from a window sash. From the stock plants in the open ground take cuttings of the tops of strong-growing shoots, preferably those with short distances between the joints.

Cuttings may be two or three inches long, and care should be taken to cut them just below a joint and to remove the lower leaves and cut back the top ones, thus preventing rot and reducing evaporation. These cuttings should be planted half their length deep in either beds or boxes of pure sand or very sandy soil. It need not be more than three or four inches deep. In a greenhouse they will root in about three weeks, but they require longer where no bottom heat is given. When by the beginning of growth they show that they are rooted, lift the cuttings gently and either plant them in light soil in a somewhat shaded and protected bed or pot them up for hardening. Cuttings are usually taken from March to May, depending on the varieties and the size of the plants desired. A much simpler method, quite satisfactory for the general gardener but not for the fancier, is to divide the old plants, like any hardy perennial, but preferably to single shoots. In this method both the roots and the tops should be well cut back when the dividing is done in springtime.

When planted in their permanent places, at least a foot apart, and under the conditions previously described, they should be encouraged to make a continuous vigorous growth. When the plants are about a foot high pinch out the centres so as to make them break, and when the new shoots are started decide how many you wish to retain on each plant. For show purposes, that is, the growing of huge flowers, it is better not to keep more than three stems. Where large flowers are being grown, before the plants get too tall they should either be staked or, if planted in rows, they may be tied to wires strung between posts. For exhibition flowers, the time and character of bud to be selected is generally mentioned in the catalogues of Chrysanthemum specialists, for this is essential to success. The term used is to "take" the bud; this really means to keep the bud, removing all others on the same stem.

For protection of the fine colors some growers cover the rows with a tent-like erection of muslin, which has the added advantage of keeping the diabrotica from eating the petals. This green insect, somewhat resembling a large lady-bug in size and shape, may do great damage if it is not either kept off in this way or kept down by hand picking. In the heat of the day the insects are very agile, but before the sun is well up they may easily be picked off and dropped into a cup of kerosene.

Where the object is garden decoration and large sprays of smaller flowers, the plants should be pinched back so as to induce branching and a broad, dwarf growth sought for, so that staking will be unnecessary. In this case also, in the selection of varieties the kinds especially suitable for exhibition should not be used, but rather those of dwarfer and easier growth. Where the nights are cold and foggy and the fall rains are apt to come before the Chrysanthemums have bloomed, the pompon varieties will be found much more satisfactory, both for garden decoration and for cutting. They are everywhere easier to grow than the large Chrysanthemums and give quite satisfactory results with far less attention. It is, for example, quite unnecessary to make cuttings unless you want more plants than can be obtained by dividing the old clumps to single shoots. If these single shoots are planted in good soil in early summer, cut back to within six inches of the ground, and by watering and cultivation induced to make many side-shoots, by pinching these back again in July fine broad bushy plants will be developed. These are naturally easier to use and more effective in the borders, and the yellow, bronze, and terra-cotta shades blend beautifully together to give the autumn-leaf colors our gardens lack. A good selection of these will bloom from September well into November.

Many of the excellent varieties, such as the dark red Julia Lagravère, are very old, but the gardener who is failing to keep track of the recent great improvements in this particular class is missing some fine flowers of large button type, freer and much better placed on the stems. Such a one is the bronze Hilda Canning. Recently also there have appeared a number of seedlings of the tiny yellow button, Baby, and these slightly larger flowers, among them Baby Doll (a bronze yellow), Bright Eyes (pink with a dark rose centre), and the white Dorothy Gish are noticeably good as to placing and are the daintiest cut flowers of their season. Pompons will often be quite good a second year if simply considered as hardy perennials, the clumps being left undivided for a year, not that this is to be recommended.

The early-flowering Chrysanthemums, such as the Marie Massé and Caprice du Printemps types, will be satisfactory only in the north, where they will be valued for blooming before the cold and rain. Even around San Francisco Bay they bloom while the weather is too warm for good garden Chrysanthemums. For garden effect it is much better to grow some of the beautiful single varieties, as these bloom as early as is desirable and with a little pinching back will make bushy plants. Their culture is in no way different from that of the pompons, excepting that where one does not want named varieties or special colors they may be grown very readily from seed. Any one with the space at his disposal should sow a packet of seed in boxes in March or April and thereafter treat the plants just as he would Stocks or Asters or any half-hardy annual. Given the rich soil and the water all Chrysanthemums

love, the little seedlings will grow into fine bushy plants
by fall and will give good fall color. Almost every one
will be different, with a range of color from white
through pinks to crimson, and from yellow through
bronze to terra-cotta. They will vary greatly both in
growth and in quality of flower, and occasionally one
may be produced which is too good to throw away and
should be perpetuated by cuttings or division as with
named varieties. Do not confuse these single perennials with Chrysanthemum coronarium and its varieties, white, yellow, and zoned Daisy-like summer
annuals of rather coarse growth.

II. The Dahlia

Through the length of the Pacific coast but particularly in California the Dahlia enjoys a tremendous popularity and has undergone wonderful development. This is not surprising, for this originally Mexican plant finds here as nowhere in America conditions favorable to its greatest perfection. For large flowers and the retention of fine coloring cool weather during blooming is essential. In the greater part of the United States this means that one must plan to have Dahlias bloom in the fall, with the risk that an early frost may in a single night cut down a season's work. While in the warmer parts of California, away from the coast, it is also better to plant late for fall blooming, the summers in the narrow strip along the ocean are generally so cool and foggy that glorious flowers may be had from early summer to late fall.

These conditions, together with the wonderful recent results of hybridization, are responsible for the well-deserved popularity of the Dahlia in California.

No particular character of soil is demanded by the Dahlia. It grows vigorously in the sands of San Francisco and almost equally well in the heavy adobes of the coast valleys. The essential thing is that the soil be made ready previously for the mass of tiny roots needed to sustain the plants. Where the soil is used exclusively for Dahlias, it should be plowed or dug to a depth of eighteen inches in the fall and

again dug and pulverized a short time before plant,
ing.

Unless the soil is quite poor no fertilizer should be
applied at this stage, as too rich a soil would merely
induce rank growth at the expense of flowers. Where
it really needs it, rotted manure dug in as long as
possible before planting, or bone flour at the time of
planting, will be found best. Where the climate is cool
an open, sunny situation should always be chosen, but
in the hotter sections where there is perpetual summer
sunshine partial shade will be an advantage. Well-
grown Dahlias require much room: three feet apart in
the rows is about right, though the pompons and the
smaller English single varieties may be given less. In
planting, dig a hole about six inches deep and lay the
tuber flat in it, so that the neck containing the bud will
be about four inches from the eventual surface of the
ground. Never place the tuber vertically, though some
growers advise tilting it to an angle of about twenty-
five degrees, the bud being at the higher end. Before
filling in the soil, place a strong stake three or four feet
high at a distance of an inch or so from the bud. If
this is not done until later the tuber is apt to be damaged
during the operation.

The ground should be rather moist, not wet, at the
time of planting. This condition may be obtained by
watering some time previously. Some growers fill in
the soil to the level of the surrounding ground at the
time of planting; others prefer to cover with only two
or three inches, and to leave a depression which may

later be filled in with soil and fertilizer. After planting, cultivate the soil regularly and thoroughly; it is impossible to over-emphasize the value of this continual cultivation throughout the growth of the Dahlia, and particularly before it begins to bloom. In cooler sections no watering will be needed for perhaps a month after planting, for under such conditions flooding is apt to cause rot. But where it is very warm and sunny it is found that at this early stage the ground must be kept moist to secure active growth.

The time of planting depends on when the main crop of flowers is desired. It may begin as early as mid-March and can be continued as late as mid-June. In the latter case, of course, only fall flowers will be obtained. When the plants have made about three sets of leaves pinch out the top to induce branching. The amount of watering done depends on climate and soil. The Dahlia thoroughly likes moisture, but watering once a week or in cool sections once in two weeks is sufficient provided the all-important cultivation follows as soon as the surface has dried out sufficiently to make it possible. When the buds begin to appear, more feeding will be appreciated. The best method is to mulch the plants heavily with well-rotted manure, but where this cannot be given hoe in bone-meal and pulverized sheep- or chicken-manure as a substitute. Be careful, however, not to overfeed and not to put fertilizer so close to the stem that it will cause decay.

It is assumed that by this time the main stem will have been tied by soft, strong cord or strips of muslin to the supporting stake, for otherwise strong winds may blow the plants over when the soil is wet and soft.

To get large blooms, disbudding so as to leave only one on each shoot is quite necessary, but leave young shoots at the base of each stem to carry on the growth when the flower has been cut. Remove all dead flowers by cutting the stems back to a joint from which new shoots will come. Sometimes early planted Dahlias become very woody by August and no longer produce good stems or flowers. To induce a new strong growth to give fall flowers the stems may be cut back to within a foot of the ground.

While the most satisfactory way of supplying moisture is by irrigation and through the mulch after it is applied, an occasional spraying of the plants with the hose freshens them and assists in removing such insect pests as aphis and red spider. If the former become very bad use a nicotine solution.

When, with the fall rains and frosts, growth is completed, the plants may be cut to within a few inches of the ground, and thereafter when it is convenient the clumps should be carefully lifted with the aid of a digging-fork, leaving a considerable amount of soil on the tubers. In cold, wet, poorly drained gardens this had best be done in late fall, but on warm, sunny slopes it is quite possible to leave the plants until February, the only advantage of this being that the tubers of a few varieties, such as Geisha, keep rather poorly and the shorter the time they have to remain in storage the better.

There are parts of California where the clumps may simply be placed on the top of the ground in a sheltered, shaded place, taking care that there is sufficient soil over them to cover them, but for the most part it will be better to store them in a shed or unheated cellar, preferably leaning on the stalks so that any moisture will drain out rather than down on the tubers. Shortly before the planting season the clumps should be divided. By that time the buds will have appeared in the rough knotted portion where the tuber is attached to the main stem. Where by careless handling the tuber has been detached from this head it should be thrown away as utterly useless. Every tuber must have at least one bud, or it will certainly not make any growth.

Now the soil may be shaken off the clump and it may be divided with the aid of a sharp knife into single tubers, each with one or more buds. There is no harm, however, in retaining two or more tubers where no great increase of stock is desired, but the consequent bushy growth is a questionable advantage for anything but garden effect.

With a rare and expensive variety, where dividing with a knife proves difficult though desirable, the aid of a small saw such as is used for fretwork or for cutting keyholes should be had.

It is sometimes almost impossible to get by division the number of tubers wanted. Only in such cases is it worth while to have recourse to cuttings. A greenhouse is the easiest place to root these, but a spent hotbed or later in the season a coldframe will also answer the purpose. The clumps of tubers should be placed on a thin layer of soil and also be covered with soil. When shoots have made a growth of three joints the cuttings should be taken just below the second joint, the lower pair of leaves removed, the upper pair shortened back, and the cutting placed half its length in sand, or, to avoid disturbance after rooting, in pots of fine soil. In this case, make a hole with a round stick in the centre of the soil, larger than the cutting and slightly longer than the amount of it to be buried in the soil. Place it in this hole and pour in sand so that the base of the cutting will be surrounded with it. Cuttings take three weeks or longer to root, depending on the available heat. If one joint has been left on the sprout two further shoots will appear from it. They also may be converted into cuttings, and the process continued, but not indefinitely, as after half-a-dozen cuttings have been taken the stock becomes weak.

While most growers prefer to buy tubers, there is no need to shun rooted cuttings for the rarer varieties if the dealer is careful to supply short-jointed, sturdy plants, properly hardened to outdoor planting, especially as good cuttings will nearly always produce good tubers by fall.

There is no difficulty in raising Dahlias from seed. Sown in boxes in March like any half-hardy annual and planted out when they have made about four leaves, they will bloom gaily through the late summer and fall. This practice is only advised where the gardener has a great deal of room or wishes to invest very little money in tubers, as though the variation is great and interesting, very few varieties will be in any way up to the standard of the named ones. These are the result of patient years of hybridization and selection.

The old stiff, formal show Dahlia is now rarely seen. In California the decorative type, very double flowers full in the centre, seems the most popular. Good examples of this are the huge salmon-rose Dr. Tevis, the perfectly formed pink Mrs. Carl Salbach, and the old standard rose-pink Delice, still unequaled in its color. The broad, flat, informal, semi-double Pæony-flowered class, of which the scarlet and yellow Geisha is a good example, is also much grown. The Cactus Dahlias fall into two classes, the true fluted type, with long, narrow, sometimes twisted petals, such as Mary Purrier or the novel Ballet Girl, and the hybrid Cactus, with their shorter, broader, and flatter petals, examples being Kalif and Ruth C. Gleadell. Both for garden decoration and for cutting the pompons, really miniature show Dahlias, should be largely grown. They combine beautifully in color, are sturdy, and require less attention than any other type. Glow (coral color) and Little Beeswing (golden yellow, tipped red) typify this class. In addition there are the collarette Dahlias and the singles, in several types.

Whether for the garden or for cutting, strong-stemmed varieties only should be grown. It is far better to make selection of varieties from plants growing in a garden than to choose from the huge exhibition flowers seen at the shows. These are often the result of special treatment by expert growers, and are no criterion for the success of the amateur, who wants good sturdy growers with abundant bloom and no bad habits.

The proper time to cut the flowers is in the evening or early morning. Remove all the lower leaves, as Dahlia foliage does not keep well, and hold the stems in boiling water for a minute or two, immediately afterward plunging them as deep as possible into cold water. If this is done in the evening and they are left in a cool place until morning the flowers of many varieties will keep for several days. As an alternative to the hot water treatment some growers believe in burning the ends of the stems in a gas flame. For somewhat wilted flowers, try immersing the stems in boiling water for ten or fifteen minutes.

III. The Gladiolus

It is quite natural that the Gladiolus, being of South
African origin, should find itself well suited with our
California conditions, our same two seasons, the wet
and the dry. While no good gardener would care to
treat them in that way, for inevitably rapid deteriora-
tion would take place, it is possible to consider the
Gladiolus as a hardy perennial plant in California, and
in old gardens I have seen vigorous varieties come up
and bloom year after year. We have, moreover, a
tremendous advantage in the long season of bloom
possible, for in favored places plantings may be made
from December to June, with consequent flowers from
May to October. In this statement only the large
summer-blooming Gladioli are considered, but in addition the California gardener may have greater variety
and length of season by making early fall plantings of
the dwarf spring-blooming Gladioli, small-flowered but
very dainty and desirable. The scale of color is salmon-
red, pink, and white with red blotch, examples being
Peach Blossom and Blushing Bride. These bloom
in late April or early May, and are soon followed by the
related but taller *G. Colvillei*, of which the most familiar
form is pure white, The Bride. These early Gladioli
give the best effect when planted in clumps.

The show is soon continued by the larger summer
varieties. It was at one time the practice to divide
these into groups according to their parentage; the

stiff, erect *G. gandavensis*, with several well-opened
flowers in bloom at one time; the Lemoinei section,
smaller, more hooded, with bright blotches and fewer
flowers open at one time; the Childsi and Nanceianus
groups, quite similar in their tall growth, large widely
opened flowers spaced farther apart, and their tendency
to run to salmon-red in color. But the great amount of
interbreeding done in recent years has made such distinctions too difficult to maintain. We now have huge
hybrids, combining the best qualities of all sections,
and surpassing older varieties in every respect. Improvement is so continuous that selections should be
made from the catalogues of up-to-date dealers.

One quite modern section of summer-flowering
Gladioli still remains absolutely distinct. These are the
Primulinus Hybrids, obtained by crossing the species
G. primulinus, a much hooded, graceful, pure yellow
species, growing by the Victoria Falls in Africa, with
garden Gladioli. These hybrids have smaller flowers,
generally spaced quite far apart, and a new series of
colors, running the gamut from pale yellows through
apricot, salmon-pink, and saffron, to beautiful orange-
reds, all blending together in a harmony never given
by a mixture of the larger Gladioli. These are, moreover, very vigorous, often producing three-branched
stems from a single corm, and because of their thinner
wiry stems and lighter, well-placed flowers they appeal
to many as more beautiful both in the garden and in
vases. Many women will consider no other variety
for house decoration.

In planting Gladioli, their use should be carefully considered. If they are merely for the production of cut flowers unquestionably the best way is to grow them in rows in some less conspicuous part of the garden, for in this way planting, watering, cultivation, and staking are all easier. But for garden decoration they are best planted in groups, far enough back in the border so that the base of the stalks may be somewhat concealed by other plants in front of them and when blooming is over the foliage may not be too conspicuous. For this purpose it is best to plant a dozen or more corms of one inexpensive variety in each group, selecting those of vigorous growth and clear distinct coloring, such, for example, as Mrs. Francis King, Halley, Mrs. Frank Pendleton, or such a primulinus as Alice Tiplady. Varieties with strong, erect stems should be chosen for garden use, as staking is the reverse of ornamental. It should be remembered that the flowers will always face south and west, that is, toward the sun. They are therefore best adapted to a border to the north or east of a path, where they will show their faces, not their backs. They are also quite effective among evergreen shrubbery which is not too rank in growth, lighting up sombre bays between the groups.

Only in very warm sections do Gladioli require partial shade. It is generally best to give them a rather sunny location, and to change this every two or three years, as they do better in new soil. They can be grown in any good soil; if it is poor, dig well and incorporate old manure a considerable time in advance of planting. The corms should never be in contact with any fertilizer. Overfeeding is to be discouraged, but when the shoots are several inches high it is good practice to mulch the ground with well-rotted manure, or to dig in lightly a good commercial fertilizer. Some growers claim that running a furrow about four inches deep between the rows and filling it with fresh manure through which they water every two weeks gives the best results.

Depth of planting will depend on the character of the soil, if it is light six inches is not too much, but if heavy four inches will be better. The advantage of deep planting is that at blooming time the heavy stalks are less likely to cause the plant to topple over. Even in our dry climate overwatering should be guarded against until the plants have made some inches of growth, but thereafter they should have occasional thorough irrigating, followed by cultivation, and as they come into bloom they will welcome an abundance of water. Even after the flowers are over it is advisable to water occasionally for a while, to assist in the production of bulblets.

Unless seed is desired, after flowering the stems should be cut off, leaving as much foliage as possible. When by turning yellow in the fall the plants show that they are maturing, dig them up and after they have been allowed to dry cut off the old flower-stem, and eventually remove the old corm, which will be found under the new one. They may then be stored in any cool, airy place until next planting.

As it is now generally accepted that after a few years of blooming the corms deteriorate in vigor and capacity to bloom, it is well, not only for increasing your stock but for renewing it, to save the bulblets of all fine varieties. If these are sown about three inches deep quite thickly, say two inches apart, some of them will bloom the same season if they have been planted early, and practically all will flower the second year. The hard coat of the bulblet often prevents or greatly delays the beginning of growth, so with valued varieties it is worth while to peel off this coat, using a sharp knife.

New varieties of Gladioli are raised from seed. The results are naturally much more of a gamble than where named varieties are used, but the amateur with plenty of room may be interested in trying his luck, and if hybridizing appeals to him he can make his own crosses and raise seedlings.

The seed may be sown in early spring, either in flats, which should be kept in the shade, or in the open ground, which should be mulched with grass clippings to keep it moist until germination occurs. This is apt to be quite uneven, but with good cultivation it is not uncommon to have some flowers the first year. In any case, there will be many bulblets to re-sow the second spring, and that season the great majority should flower.

If the spikes are wanted for house decoration they should be cut with a knife as the first flowers open, and care should be taken to allow at least three leaves, preferably four or five, to remain on the plant, thus insuring proper ripening of the corm. The cut flowers will open from the bud in water, and will last better if each day an inch is cut off the bottom of the stems when fresh water is given. The faded blossoms should of course be removed.

IV. The Iris

Of all the great popular flowers, the Iris has been the latest to come into its own. Even yet its cult numbers fewer members than that of some other flowers, but it is rapidly spreading. The Bearded Iris particularly is still developing new beauties, and is in a stage of its evolution which makes it very popular with its lovers, who, like all enthusiasts, have their eyes on the future. In California many still think of Irises only as the blue and white "flags" of March, ignorant of the dozens of finer related varieties and of the many other very different species in this genus. This is the more surprising because the climate of California is the envy of Iris cranks the world over, and the joy of those fortunate enough to live here.

It will be noted that the great majority of the Irises come from around the Mediterranean, thus being indigenous to countries having climates rather like that of California and to a somewhat lesser extent of the whole Pacific coast. The important factor is the rainless summer, which far from being a detriment is a boon to most kinds of Irises excepting the water-loving Japanese and Siberian groups. The popular impression that all Irises are bog plants, an impression fostered by the poets, is doubtless due to the fact that the wild Iris of England and western Europe, *I. pseudacorus*, and the related wild Iris of eastern North America, *I. versicolor*, are both plants which will not only grow in marshy ground but actually in the water near banks of streams. But all the bulbous Irises and the great group of rhizomatous Bearded Irises, by far the most important for garden use, positively dislike wet feet and will flourish upon the driest hillsides, even in countries where the summers are rainless. The Iris enthusiast in California has moreover the advantage of being able to grow species not hardy in colder climates, and is thus able to have not only greater variety but a longer season of bloom.

As is often said, the garden year in California begins with the fall rains, and with them also come the first Irises, varieties of *I. unguicularis* (syn. *stylosa*). This Algerian species with grassy evergreen leaves begins in October to throw up day by day its quota of beautiful flowers of varying violet shades, carried on what appear to be stems of from six to twelve inches but are really the elongated perianth tubes of the flowers. When one has a number of well-established plants, the succession of flowers is so constant that one may always have a bowl of them in the house until February, a great boon when flowers, particularly of this color, are so rare.

The best way to gather them is before the buds expand. In the garden, too, they give a pretty note of color, especially when the winter rains do not come down so hard as to batter them to pieces. They should be given an exposure where they will have an abundance of winter sunshine. They are to be recommended for planting along terraces and edging driveways. Culture is of the simplest. Plant preferably in August, but when that is not convenient almost any month from then to spring is possible. Do not water in summer, as they then prefer a thorough baking. If the foliage becomes too thick or untidy it may be cut back in August and will renew itself. In addition to the violet varieties there is a less effective white one. As established plants bloom most freely, do not divide the clumps unnecessarily.

Of all the Irises the Pogoniris or bearded sections are the easiest of growth, the most popular, and the most effective for garden color. Between them, moreover, they provide flowers from March to May, and quite often casual blooms in the fall as well. The first to flower are the very dwarf varieties, usually referred to as pumilas, but really of quite mixed parentage. Their flowers, small and borne on short stems, are usually some shade of yellow or of violet, which restricts their interest, but they are useful for edging, for grouping in the sunny rock-garden, and for covering steep, dry banks, where they demand only freedom from weeds.

I. lutescens Statellae, a white dwarf, is unusually attractive in shape. Soon after these follow the intermediate race, so called because in almost every way they come between the dwarfs and the tall Bearded Irises. Here again there is no wide range of color, white, somewhat indeterminate pale yellows, and violet being all.

About the same time the early members of the tall bearded group begin. These include *I. germanica*, the misnamed blue-purple type so commonly seen;

I. albicans, the contemporaneous white variety; the really fine red-purple *I. Kochii*, and several similar varieties. Of this last, some forms, especially Crimson King, bloom also quite regularly during the fall.

In April and May the grand procession of tall Bearded Irises goes by. Older catalogues divide these into sections such as the lavender to violet pallidas, the white plicatas with their frilled edges of lavender or purple, the yellow and maroon variegatas, and the squalens, indescribable blends including many bronze varieties. But so much cross-breeding has been done in recent years that many of the newer varieties find no place in these sections.

Among these Pogoniris there is great variety of habit, size, and color, depending on the predominance of certain wild parents in the garden hybrid. The tallest, most vigorous, and widest branching kinds are descendants of species such as *I. trojana, cypriana*, and *mesopotamica*, indigenous to the countries bordering the eastern Mediterranean. This strain, because of its tendency to make winter leaf growth, is often unsatisfactory in eastern North America, and varieties such as Kashmir White, Lady Foster, Caterina, Isoline, Alcazar, and the Ricardi hybrids are often mentioned by Eastern Iris growers as being delicate. This criticism should never be considered as affecting California, where they are the most successful and admired of all Bearded Irises. Indeed, it is from breeding with such parents that our California hybridists are raising further novelties of astonishing vigor and size, destined, when they become more widely distributed, to glorify our gardens and landscapes. As yet the colors are mostly lavender, mauve, and purple, including many with paler standards than falls, but this range is being extended.

The descendants of *I. pallida* largely retain the tall, stiff, unbranched flower-stems and fine, broad glaucous foliage of their ancestor. They are very floriferous, and the well-shaped flowers, lavenders, lilac-pinks, and violets, are most effective in the garden. The *I. variegata* progeny do not give us either the tall stems or the large flowers of the pallidas, but we need them for their very different series of colors, mostly contrasting arrangements of yellow with brown or maroon.

Between these there are intermediate types quite worth growing for their added variety of color, furnishing white flowers, sometimes frilled, veined, or with purple falls, and many beautiful blended colors from pale pastel shades through buff and bronze to smoky violet and dusky purple, most of them with some yellow in the make-up. The few pure yellows have until recently tended to be very dwarf and weak in growth in California, but breeders have already had considerable success in raising larger and more vigorous yellow cross-bred seedlings, and from the many efforts being made we shall doubtless get entirely satisfactory Irises in this color.

Nothing could be easier than the culture of the Bearded Iris. It will stand unbelievable neglect, but if its few wants are supplied it will repay the gardener amply. No particular kind of soil is required, and unless it be very poor indeed no fertilizing is necessary. If manure is given it should be well rotted before being dug into the soil which will be well below the bottom of the rhizomes, as contact is likely to cause their decay. Bone-flour or bone-meal, either mixed with the soil or hoed in as a top dressing, is about the best method of feeding them. Where lime is lacking in the soil this should be supplied, as these Irises are lime-lovers. All Irises love sunshine, and the bearded ones, though they will make lots of leaf growth in the shade, will not bloom there. If you have no other place, do not grow Iris. Shun also swampy or wet, sour land. There are generally many available places in the average garden. If you have a particularly dry border or bank they will take care of it very nicely.

It is possible to divide or plant Iris any month of the year, but naturally if the disturbance takes place within the two or three months before they bloom the flowers will be relatively poor. In my experience the best time to plant is immediately after blooming, as they then begin to make an entirely new set of roots. This, however, involves some summer watering, and many therefore prefer to postpone planting until the fall. In planting dormant rhizomes, particularly any which have travelled far, great care should be taken not to give too much water until growth begins.

In setting the plants, the top of the thick, fleshy rhizome should be level with the surface of the soil. If buried too deep they rot. The distance apart depends entirely on the vigor of the variety and its rate of increase. As the finest show comes from established plants, do not divide oftener than alternate years and in many cases they may be left for a third year, but be sure to divide and replant when the rhizomes become very crowded or they will fail to bloom.

I know by experiment that the Bearded Irises may be left absolutely dry through the summer months and yet give excellent bloom the following year. But growth is certainly more vigorous where an occasional soaking of the ground is given from July until the rains begin and this practice is particularly recommended for southern California. Should the spring be a dry one it is advisable to water them occasionally before and during bloom.

Irises of variegata parentage and also the white and purple amoenas thrive better if given more water than other Bearded Irises, and are better in California in a cooler place in the garden, giving taller stems under these conditions.

Bearded Irises do not readily set seed unless crossed. New varieties are always raised from seed, but this is not the business of the average gardener. The hybridizer sows his cross-bred seed in the fall, in a specially prepared bed, and when the tiny seedlings appear next spring he transplants them into rows where some of them will bloom the following season. The less vigorous ones will take two years from germination to blooming. The seed germinates irregularly, and the bed should be in a place which can be left undisturbed for two years or more, as seedlings will continue to appear each spring.

To obtain real advances over good named varieties thousands of seedlings must be raised and only the best named.

In answer to a frequent question I would say very positively that the varieties do not deteriorate or revert to the common purple as many people imagine. The disappearance of fine varieties planted among the sturdy common type is unquestionably due to the ability of the latter to supplant the higher-bred forms when left to compete for space in a crowded border.

The Bearded Irises are too often used as continuous edging for paths, an unsatisfactory place because these flowers look best when massed and because such a prominent position should not be given to plants whose season of bloom is comparatively short. Where only a few are used, they should be planted in clumps of a single variety in the flower border, where if they are placed at rather regular intervals they give a certain unity to the planting. Where a large collection of many kinds is grown it is best to have part of the garden set aside for them where they will not be in too great evidence after blooming. One possible arrangement is to have them in wide borders on either side of a path, and to soften the contact with the path by informal edgings of permanent rock plants such as Helianthe-mums, Aubrietias, Pinks, *Nepeta Mussini*, *Alyssum saxatile*, or Violas. Another plan is to sow in fall between the forward clumps and along the path seeds of light, dainty annuals such as the annual Linarias and *Omphalodes linifolia*.

Where it is especially desired to keep up the color in the Iris garden, either leave spaces between the clumps and plant Gladioli in them in the spring or else dig up this ground in quite early spring and scatter among the Irises seed of annual Larkspurs, or of the taller annual Coreopsis. These two are chosen because their basal foliage is sparse and will not shade the rhizomes, a condition which must be avoided in interplanting. A beautiful color arrangement is quite possible even in a collector's Iris garden, if instead of planting in rows and conspicuously labelling each variety he will take the trouble to group them in an informal way, putting several similar varieties together when he wants a strong color note or very different ones for contrast. A diagram of the planting, or inconspicuous metal labels, will make it possible to identify any variety.

There are literally hundreds of named varieties, many of which should be discarded in favor of the fine new ones which are yearly being added. A good guide to selection is the symposium published by the American Iris Society. Many dealers are now quoting its ratings in their catalogues. Even better, visit in Iris time the garden of a grower or collector who has the latest and sometimes finest, though still ungraded, novelties.

It is regrettable that rhizomes of the Oncocyclus, Regelia, and their offspring, the Regelio-cyclus crosses, are not readily to be procured, for they are rare plants of an almost weird beauty which can be induced to bloom and continue in California better than elsewhere in America. *I. Susiana* is the huge Oncocyclus which attracts so much attention in our florists' windows in early springtime, its white ground speckled closely with black, its black beard, and its deep purple style-arms making it very sombre and unusual. For all Oncocyclus and Regelia Irises a specially prepared bed should be made in full sunlight. The soil should be of a light sandy character, incorporated in the lower parts with gravel to provide thorough drainage. With this should be mixed either lime or powdered plaster. The bed should be raised, not only for drainage but so that after the flowers are gone they may be absolutely dried off until October. The Regelias and the Regelio-cyclus Irises are easier to grow and less liable to disease than the true Oncocyclus.

Two beautiful Irises from Japan are *I. tectorum* and *I. fimbriata* (syn. *japonica*), both of which bloom in April. *I. tectorum* gets its name from the circumstance of its being used as a roof-covering in Japan: it will therefore be understood that it likes a sunny place and good drainage. Give it the same conditions as the tall bearded section and its rather flat blue or white flowers will reward you. *I. fimbriata*, though it will do well in sunshine, is one of the few Irises which are quite as successful in partial shade. It is popularly called the Orchid Iris, and will be recognized by its long stem on which are scattered small flat lavender flowers, the style-arms of which are fringed or fimbriated.

Through March and April many mesas and hillsides are covered with our beautiful native Irises, mostly forms of *I. Douglasiana* and *I. macrosiphon*, the taller *I. longipetala* being more generally found in places which are marshy in spring. They are not showy flowers, being mostly in tones of buff, lilac-pink, and shades of lavender and violet, but they are charming in their daintiness and are quite worth growing in gardens. It is practically useless to dig them up when they are in bloom, as they particularly resent disturbance at that time. Plants from the wild move fairly readily when growth is beginning after the first fall rains, but these Irises are so easily raised from seed sown in the fall, and so many interesting variations in color are thus secured that this method should be preferred. Plants are offered by a few specialists.

Of late years the bulbous Irises have been much less in evidence than before the quarantine. California-grown bulbs are now being offered, and doubtless in time we shall again have Dutch and Spanish Irises at least in our gardens. These two classes of bulbous Irises are almost indistinguishable in type of blossom from each other. The Dutch ones bloom about the beginning of April, and are taller, larger, and more vigorous than the Spanish Irises, but their color range is restricted to white, yellow, lavender, and blue, while the late April-blooming Spanish type has also bronze and more combinations of the colors mentioned. It is advisable to grow both classes so as to extend the blooming season.

As the bulbs do not keep well out of the ground it is well to plant them as soon as they are offered in the

fall, putting them about three inches deep and five or
six inches apart in a dry sunny location. The narrow,
inconspicuous foliage which appears in the fall is in-
adequate as background for the beautiful butterfly-like
blossoms. They are therefore better not planted along
paths but in groups against a background of hardy
plants or shrubs. In cutting the flowers leave as much
of the stalk as possible, to enable the bulbs to ripen
properly. *I. tingitana* is the earliest of the xiphium
type, blooming two weeks before the Dutch. The
English Irises are not frequently seen. Unlike the
Spanish Irises they prefer a cool spot with very much
more water during growth. As they do not get this so
readily in California, they usually die out. They are
later and larger than the Spanish Irises.

With larger flowers of somewhat similar shape to the
Spanish Irises are the members of the spuria group, but
these are rhizomatous and have fine, tall, stiff leaves,
narrower and of a darker green than the Bearded Irises.
Many of them are peculiarly adapted to California, as
will be seen from the huge clumps of *I. ochroleuca*
(syn. *gigantea* and *orientalis*) which persist for years in
neglected yards, and continue to send up in May rigid
stems, five or six feet high, along which are set the
creamy white flowers, blotched with yellow on the falls.

Less familiar but of stronger, purer color are the
bright yellow *I. Monnieri*, the darker yellow *I. aurea*,
and the blue *I. monspur*, of which there are several quite
similar forms. This last is a cross between *I. Monnieri*
and *I. spuria*. The latter is a smaller Iris, of which

there are blue and also white forms. Give all these a sunny place where they will dry out in summer. During their growing season, the winter, they will appreciate any amount of water. By far the best time to plant them is when they begin to make new growth, about October, as they resent disturbance least at that time. Established clumps bloom best; do not disturb them unnecessarily.

I. pseudacorus and the Siberian and Japanese Irises are water-lovers. *I. pseudacorus* will grow right in water, yet even where it is exposed to summer drought it will live and give its small bright yellow flowers, the falls of which are slightly lined with black. The Siberian Irises, though not large, are cherished for their dainty purple or white flowers, often beautifully veined. They are extremely floriferous when allowed to remain undisturbed and given plenty of water; they will not endure drying out in summer. Similar in their requirements but far more effective for garden adornment are the large Japanese Irises, commonly called varieties of *I. laevigata* or *I. Kaempferi*. Some of the flowers of these, particularly the doubles, are of great size, but the single forms, with only three falls, are much more graceful. They are at their best when used on the edge of a pool or where they will get the run-off from an artificial streamlet such as the Japanese are so fond of putting in their miniature landscape gardens. In the Japanese tea-garden at Golden Gate Park in San Francisco they are grown not only on the banks of a stream but right in the water, being planted in deep redwood boxes which are taken out of the water in fall and stored outdoors in a dry place until the next spring. Though these Irises prefer much water in summer, no pool or swamp is necessary to grow them, for if the bed is heavily mulched with manure and so arranged that it may be given an occasional thorough watering in summer great success is quite possible. They are great feeders, and take readily to a rich soil and plenty of manure, but they hate lime, either in the soil or in the water, and failure is sometimes wholly due to its presence in excess.

Planting is best done in the fall, when they are dormant. Do not disturb them while they continue to flower well. A sunny place is best in most gardens, but where very hot spells are likely to occur during the months of bloom, June and July, a partially shaded position or some artificial protection from the heat of the sun should be given to prevent the burning of the blossoms.

After the Japanese Irises cease blooming there is a hiatus in the Iris year, but in October *I. foetidissima*, the Gladwyn Iris, ripens and opens its pods of bright scarlet seeds, a note of brilliant color in the garden and very popular for house decoration. At this time also a number of the tall Bearded Irises are apt to send up occasional blooms. Kochii, Crimson King, and Archeveque will almost invariably do so, and there are others, among them Iris-King, which have also considerable tendency to fall flowering.

Though not a true Iris, *Morea irioides* is related to the

genus and is so generally mistaken for an Iris that I make mention of it here. Above its dark evergreen foliage appear taller jointed stems producing beautiful Iris-like flowers, white with a golden blotch. It blooms at intervals, and has the peculiarity of bringing out new flowers on the old stems, which should not therefore be removed while still green. It is hardly desirable for cutting, as the flowers last but a day.

V. The Rose

There can be no question that the Rose is deserving of special consideration and treatment, for it is doubtful if it will anywhere do better than on the Pacific coast when it is given proper care. For example, Portland, Oregon, is justified in its title of the Rose City, as all the bush Roses and notably Caroline Testout reach perfection there, while in the parts of California which are not affected by too close proximity to the sea climbing Roses are of almost unbelievable vigor and in springtime nearly cover many houses. Whether or not he may specialize in growing fine Roses, the California gardener should always recognize the value which climbers have in hiding architectural defects of an old house or softening the angles and rawness of a new one, being always careful not to overdo such planting. In our warm climate pergolas and summerhouses have a reason for existence, and they may be further justified as supports for climbing Roses Again, the ugliness of wire fences will disappear when they are clothed in the foliage of some of the less rampant climbers, the pink Cherokee or Tausendschön, for example. Banks may also be covered with the trailing Wichuraiana Roses, best on account of their glossy evergreen foliage.

Where no special place is set apart for bush Roses they may be used to a limited extent in groups among shrubs. They mix less well with other flowers in the border. Bush Roses make their finest garden effect where they are used in bedding and a limited number of tested kinds are grown, each bed restricted to a single variety. Where many Roses in numerous varieties are to be grown much the best plan is to set apart a place for a Rose garden. As Roses lend themselves very well to planting in rows or beds, most special Rose gardens are formal in design. In the geometrical beds the plants are readily accessible and may be given every care; they look well when in bloom and will not be conspicuous when finished blooming. It is not essential to use any other plants in this garden, though an edging plant, such as Violas or *Nepeta Mussini*, will serve to soften the margins of the beds. The requirements of digging and cultivation have mitigated against the use of carpeting plants in California. The location of a Rose planting should always be in full sunlight, shade being decidedly conducive to mildew. For the same reason, a damp or drafty place should be avoided.

Roses will grow in any good soil, provided it be properly prepared. Their preference is for the heavier loams, as will be seen in the ease with which good Roses can be grown in the heavy adobe of the Santa Clara Valley or the stiff red soil of Redlands. But the Tea Roses particularly are happy in much lighter soils. The important thing is that the soil be thoroughly dug to a depth of at least eighteen inches; too many gardeners merely tickle the surface, few are willing to dig more than the depth of a spade or fork. Do this digging in fall, incorporating in the soil a quantity of rotted manure, that from the cow-pen being best. In planting the Roses good generous holes should be dug, and the roots spread out and surrounded with fine soil. Gardeners looking for the very finest results sometimes put a layer of six inches of well-rotted manure in the bottom of the deep hole, cover it with several inches of good soil, and then plant their Roses. If budded stock is used, the place where the bud was inserted should be about three inches below the surface. If it is dry during planting, water thoroughly. In no case should Roses be planted in wet, sticky soil. Three feet apart is not too far for vigorous Roses, though some varieties can be put as close as two feet.

The immediate after care is restricted to irrigation and cultivation. One can hardly do worse than sprinkle Roses every evening with the hose. Instead of this useless, often injurious, practice, give them a thorough watering once a week or every alternate week, depending on the temperature and sunshine. Individual plants are best handled by hoeing out a basin around the base, or rows may have a trench running parallel to them. In either case let the hose run long enough to saturate the subsoil, and as soon as the surface has dried out sufficiently, cultivate to conserve the moisture. It is best to water in the morning, particularly in cool sections where dampness at night is an inducement to mildew.

Some gardeners make the mistake of trying to keep their Roses in bloom continuously, wearing them out and unfitting them to develop the finest flowers. They should have two rests each year, the first from December to March, which they will take themselves, and the second in July and August, which will be induced by withholding practically all water. After the first will come the great flowering of the spring and early summer; after the summer rest, the secondary flowering of autumn. To provide continual plant food a dressing of rotted manure should be spread on the beds and dug in during the winter. Bone-meal is also an excellent fertilizer and may be hoed into the soil around the bushes.

Bush Roses should be heavily pruned about January. Exact rules cannot be given, as varieties differ in growth. In general, the practice is to cut back all strong canes to within two or three buds of the previous year's growth, to remove the dead wood and small twiggy branches which are incapable of bearing flowers, and as the plant grows older to keep its centre open by removing all crowded growth. The second pruning, after the midsummer rest, is much less drastic, being chiefly to cut out dead wood and to head back long canes. Tea Roses need less pruning, and climbers merely enough to keep them in bounds and prevent the accumulation of dead branches.

Mildew is best controlled by spraying with a lime-and-sulphur mixture, or by dusting the leaves in the morning with sulphur. The green fly, or aphis, which feeds on the young growth, may be greatly discouraged by vigorous use of the hose on the infested parts, or more thoroughly eliminated by spraying with a nicotine solution or powder.

Some varieties do not give the best results on their own roots; such, for example, are the recent developments in the Pernetiana class, and many of the best growers insist on having budded plants, claiming that the added vigor far more than compensates for the very occasional case where the wild stock suckers. But there remain a great many Roses—very vigorous kinds such as Frau Karl Druschki, General MacArthur, and Mme. Abel Chatenay, Teas such as Lady Hillington, and all the real climbers—which are perfectly satisfactory on their own roots. Where this is so it is easy to increase the stock by cuttings. Make a bed of quite light and sandy soil in a cool, partially shaded place, and put the cuttings in it from September to December, starting with the Tea Roses and taking the Hybrid Perpetuals latest. The cuttings should be of the previous season's wood, in lengths of about eight inches, six inches of which should be buried in the soil. Water the soil to settle it around the cuttings, and leave them until rooting takes place or until the succeeding fall if that is most convenient. The swelling of the buds in spring does not necessarily indicate that the cuttings have formed roots.

Selection of varieties should be dependent, first, on the use which it is proposed to make of the Roses, and, second, on their adaptability to the section in which one is living. It is quite futile for the gardener in such a cold, drafty climate as that of San Francisco to grow the white Cherokee or the glorious Beauty of Glazenwood, although these make a wonderful show in such warmer and more protected places near by as San Rafael and Saratoga. Unless one enjoys experimenting it is wise to make inquiry regarding its adaptability to one's local conditions before planting any variety very extensively.

Among the several classes of vigorous climbers are the small-flowered Banksias, the easy-growing and floriferous Noisettes, such as Lamarque and Rêve d'Or, the single Cherokees, white, pink, and cerise, the climbing Polyanthus, like Cecile Brunner, the Multiflora and Wichuraiana hybrids, valuable in that they bloom in late May, and many climbing sports of garden Roses and new varieties of complicated parentage.

Bush Roses are divided into several classes, of which the chief are—the Hybrid Perpetuals (for example, Ulrich Brunner), the Hybrid Teas (for example, Antoine Rivoire), the Teas (for example, Maman Cochet), the Pernetianas (for example, Los Angeles). As new cross-bred novelties are yearly being added, these divisions are becoming of less importance.

CHAPTER XI

Rock and Water Gardening

THE interest in and enthusiasm over rock-gardens and the planting of dry rock walls have grown greatly in recent years, and in England particularly has the man with a small place found in it his greatest pleasure. It must of course be recognized that an arrangement of rocks and plants which aims to imitate nature is best when the garden is large enough to isolate it from more formal things and to keep it away from the house, but this can often be done in some corner even of the little place, and where it cannot, there are other ways of growing many of the plants. One reason why rock-gardening has been so taken up by the little gardeners is that in it they may have a great variety of plants—perennials, bulbs, annuals, and small shrubs—and may with a few of each make beautiful and interesting pictures.

In the large open garden thousands of Tulips and hundreds of Aubrietias or Primroses may be necessary to make an adequate show, while in the rock-garden half-a-dozen bulbs of *Tulipa Didieri alba*, a pocket with the same number of plants of *Primula malacoides,* and a single well-grown deep rose Aubrietia trailing over a rock will be quite as beautiful a picture, for it will be just as much in scale. It is indeed a special field for the interest and art of the individual who does all his work himself, and one in which he may excel his wealthier neighbor who cannot hire the love and attention needed to give the best results and to return the greatest pleasure.

Rock-gardening will, moreover, enable him to grow successfully many dainty or difficult things which appreciate the special conditions and soil provided, the sun, or drainage, or the shade of a large rock, and the cool root-run beneath it. It is also true that by rock-gardens and planted walls, slopes may be made the most interesting parts of a garden instead of eyesores or a source of great expense for terracing and upkeep of grassy banks. In America there is no section so well adapted to this kind of gardening as is the north Pacific coast, with its moist climate and comparatively cool summers, but even farther south in California the coastal sections are capable of splendid results and of even greater variety of plant materials, though more attention needs to be given to exposure and watering.

In laying out a rock-garden, where possible screen it off somewhat by shrubs or trees from the other more formal parts. It will then seem more natural and the element of surprise will be added when it is found by the visitor. Where irregular ground or a slope is available this should be chosen, as it is more suitable and makes the laying out much easier. The exposure is not a matter of moment, because success may be quite as great facing west as east if only the gardener will select his plants for their preference for the position available. Facing west or south he will plant more of the sun lovers from the Mediterranean or South Africa, facing east or north rather the real alpines, which prefer a cool place with no summer baking. Two main types of arrangement will be found—the rocky slope, coming down in successive much broken terraces to a bordering path, and the ravine, where the path runs through the garden and the ground is naturally or artificially higher on either side and this height further emphasized by rear planting. Variations and combinations of these will also be found. Use that most natural to your conditions. If your garden is quite level the latter plan is better as the artificial ravine is the easier to make. For the placing of the rocks study the outcroppings on a stony hillside and note the horizontal lines of the strata and the way in which the stones are generally found lying on their widest side, partly buried in the soil, never in a regular manner and never sticking up out of the ground like almonds placed on end, and with less bulk in the soil than out of it. Stones should slope back, never forward, as you want the water to run back to the roots of the plants, not drip over the front edges of the rocks. As the paths are reached have some of the stones come right down to them, but leave occasional spaces where a pocket of soil on the margin will be occupied by some dwarf plant. Above all, avoid the ghastly pile of round rocks raised in the centre of the lawn, on which some earth is thrown and then a few miserable plants are put to die of the inevitable drought.

Where the labor and cost of regrading level ground would seem to be unwarranted because the result would always appear unnatural and forced, many rock plants may still be grown by edging the paths of the flower garden with flat stones of varying size and height and putting in your rock plants so that they will grow partly over them in some cases, between the rocks in others, thus having the benefit of the cooler root-run under them. Delightful informal edgings to paths may be had in this way, using Sedums and Cotyledons for their interesting foliage, *Alyssum saxatile*, the hardy Candytufts, Thymes, Armerias, Helianthemums, *Erysimum allioni* or *E. linifolium* in bright sun, and in the shady places such things as *Arabis albida*, *Plumbago Larpentae*, Saxifrages, and creeping Veronicas and Bellflowers.

Again, where the ground is very steep and perhaps the only available place is near the house or along the main path up or down to the house, why not make narrow terraces, held up not by hard, unlovely concrete walls, but by facing each terrace with a wall built of large stones, as warm in color and pleasing in texture as possible and with the interstices filled with good soil instead of mortar? The dry walls should slope back slightly as they rise and the separate stones should be so tilted back that the moisture will tend to run back to the roots of plants growing between them. These plants are best put in during construction and should then be small, but in favorable places they may often be added later or started from seed sown in fall in the crevices.

In planting be sure no air spaces are left, good soil being rammed tightly around the plant roots. On the terraces taller rock plants and small shrubs may be grown, while for trailing over the walls from the top there is a wide choice of plants. I have in mind a place where a formal Rose garden has such a wall on one side; in springtime it is a delightful sight when draped with pink, white, apricot, and red Helianthemums, creamy-white Silene, and gray-leaved Cerastium, while at the base are found a few grassy Pinks and the bright yellow *Alyssum saxatile*. Stone steps where the mason has not been allowed to fill the joints with mortar offer many opportunities for alpine Pinks, the smaller Campanulas, Arenarias, Thymes, and other low-growing plants, best put in the corners and at the back of the treads for they should not be in the walkers' way.

Experience will teach most about the planting and care of rock-gardens. As they are naturally best when not often disturbed, proper soil should be provided at the beginning. Few rock plants like heavy clay or adobe soils, their tastes running rather to lighter loams enriched with leaf-mold. Many are lime lovers, some fewer need peat, which may be put in the special pocket they fill. All demand good drainage and many like the cool, moister root-runs they get under rocks or where stone chips are mixed with the soil. There are lots of easy ones for the beginner, and these are the ones I shall mention. Few if any will object to summer watering and some demand it. The best way to provide for those wanting much of it is to put them near the drip of a pipe or overflow of a pool, or facing north where the sun dries out the ground more slowly. Of the larger species, a single plant may sometimes be sufficient, but in nature a group of the same kind will generally be found, and in planting it is well to follow this suggestion.

The rock-garden will be most varied and interesting where the owner places no narrow limits on his plant materials, but uses shrubs, herbaceous perennials, succulents, bulbs, and small annuals, always taking only those of appropriate size and growth and eliminating straggly, weedy things.

Shrubs will be needed for two purposes. They will add, firstly, to the permanence of the rock-garden, and being practically all evergreens they will provide it with varied and interesting greenery at all seasons of the year. Secondly, they will add diversity of height and will not only furnish the best materials for backgrounds but often also for trailing over the front of a large rock or a wall. Some give beauty by their flowers, berries, or colored leaves. In the rock-garden there are places for even a few small deciduous flowering shrubs, such as *Spiræa Thunbergi*, the California red-flowering Currant (*Ribes sanguineum*), or the dwarf double almond (*Prunus japonica*). Among evergreens we have several forms of the broad-leaved *Aucuba japonica*, a shade lover, the various Boxes, and *Lonicera nitida*, a more rapid grower of similar foliage. These

are best for their foliage as are also *Raphiolepis japonica* and the shrubby Veronicas and Myrtles. The
smaller Brooms, such as *Cytisus præcox* and *C. albus*,
kept cut back give different twiggy growth and early
flowers. There are dwarf forms of the native Ceanothus, fine for sunny places, and a whole host of new
evergreen Barberries with lovely berries, of which
Berberis Wilsoni and the taller *B. subcauliolata* are best
known. For deep pink or red berries we want also the
trailing, spreading Cotoneasters, especially *C. microphylla* and *C. horizontalis*. In midwinter the unusual
orange and rose flowers of *Chorizema ilicifolium* will
be found in warm places, and the best of the Heathers,
Erica melanthera, though there are many other good
ones. In early spring come *Daphne odora* and *Diosma
ericoides* (Breath of Heaven), both sweet-scented, and
these are soon followed by the Azaleas, of which the
Japanese Kurume type will be found easier to grow and
less formal than the Indian Azaleas of the Eastern
greenhouse. Most valuable for their foliage are the
gray-leaved Rosemary, the prostrate Junipers, and the
smaller Hypericums, all useful ground-covers.

Among the herbaceous plants, described more fully
in their special chapter, are many suitable for rock-
gardens and at their best there. For dry sunny places
we have the perennial Candytufts, *I. sempervirens*
and *I. gibraltarica*, and the related *Aethionema grandiflorum*, the Helianthemums or Sun Roses, Aubrietias,
the perennial *Alyssum saxatile* in its compact form, and
also the paler *A. saxatile citrinum*, *Achillea millifolium*

roseum and *A. tomentosum,* the dwarf Rock Pinks, wild
forms of Dianthus, *Iris pumila* and dwarf forms of
Iris unguicularis (syn. *stylosa*), green and variegated
leaved Thymes, Armerias, shrubby Mesembryanthemums, *Mahernia odorata, Gypsophila repens, Sisy-
rinchium bellum,* Heucheras (even better in part shade),
starved garden Wallflowers or preferably the wild
Cheiranthus Allioni and allied *Erysimum linifolium.*
Of gray-leaved plants we can use among others dwarf
Lavenders, Santolina (Lavender Cotton), Cerastiums,
and the native Zauschneria with its midsummer
flowers of vermilion.   More rampant and so needing to
be kept within bounds are the yellow Gazanias, *Felicia
rosea, Lippia repens, Erigeron mucronatus,* the blue
Convolvulus mauritanicus, and the lovely lavender
Cat-mint *Nepeta Mussini,* all of them best planted at
the top of a wall or on the edge of the path, where they
may readily be controlled.   In dry sunny sections
rock-gardens may be made almost alone of succulents—
Sedums, Cotyledons, Cacti, small Aloes, and other
desert plants.

In a warm garden many sun lovers will do well in
partial shade.   Experiment must show what is best,
but if your rock-garden has only morning sun it should
be well adapted to the sand-loving Arenarias, *Arabis
albida, Anemone sylvestris,* and the lovely creeping and
trailing Campanulas, of which *C. Portenschlagiana* and
C. isophylla are best known and valued for their
summer flowers.   *Aster subcaeruleus, Phlox subulata,*
the perennial Silenes, *Plumbago Larpentae, Saxifraga*

umbrosa (London Pride), and *S. sarmentosa*, creeping Veronicas such as *V. repens* and *V. chathamica*, small Columbines, and Ferns, are all fine in cool, shady rock-gardens. For larger groups there are some very easy and effective plants—Forget-me-Nots, Violas, and Primulas. Among the last one of the easiest is the dainty *P. malacoides* in white or lavender-pink, also the true English Primrose and the related polyanthus Primroses, but for this purpose it is best to choose colors of the last carefully as several plants of a variety will give a better effect than a mixture. Of Violas the wilder types such as *V. cornuta* or *V. gracilis* are here to be preferred to garden forms. Pansies are altogether out of place, being so obviously cultivated plants. Of trailers *Vinca minor* is the toughest and yet can be kept in control. The Kenilworth Ivy (*Linaria cymbalaria*) flourishes in complete shade, and though it has light violet flowers it is worth growing for its leaves alone.

For winter and spring especially, bulbs should be planted in the pockets in the rock-garden. Avoid the larger gardenesque kinds such as the Darwin Tulips or the big trumpet Daffodils. Yet even in these families can be found suitable varieties, wild Tulip species such as *Didieri alba* or the Lady Tulip, *T. Clusiana*, or among the Narcissus the Campernelle Jonquil with its narrow reed-like foliage. Even little Hyacinths make a pretty group, but only the small bulbs should be used. Snowdrops are hardly worth while in the average California garden, but Snowflakes, *Leucojum vernum*, easily take their place. Other small early-flowering bulbs are the Scillas, Muscari, Cyclamen, and *Triteleia uniflora*, and, for later flowers in shady, moist, but well-drained pockets, the native Fritillarias and Erythroniums. The many South African bulbs all prefer a warm sunny spot, a fact which should be kept in mind in using Freesias, Sparaxes, *Tritonia crocata*, or early dwarf Gladioli in the rock-garden. Oxalis are alluring but easier to get than to get rid of. For fall flowering the white *Zephyranthis candida* is fine; so are *Sternbergia lutea* and the fall Crocuses, but the bulbs are now very difficult to obtain.

It is easy to have a beautiful and well-filled spring rock-garden. The trouble comes when bare places appear because many of the perennials are over and the bulb foliage has died down. Unless you intend it only for a spring garden be sure to leave places for later plants. To keep it going have some pockets for spring-flowering annuals which will be replaced by summer ones. For example, *Nemophila insignis* may be followed by the dwarf blue *Nemesia*. Bulbs may also be covered during summer with small, shallow-rooting annuals. Among those for spring effects select from the dwarf Sweet Alyssum, Virginia Stocks, *Phacelia campanularia*, *Omphalodes linifolia*, or the annual Candytufts. For summer try the *Alonsoas*, *Brachycome* (Swan River Daisy), *Diascia Barberi*, *Dimorphotheca aurantiaca* and its hybrids, the annual Linarias, Nemesias, Portulaca, Lobelias, and single dwarf French Marigolds. All these are more fully treated under Annuals.

This fine piece of what practically amounts to rock gardening is a stairway in the Duncan McDuffie estate in Berkeley. Toward the edges larger drought-resistant subjects such as Cistus, Valerian, and Nepeta Mussini are used, while toward the centre Thymes, Helianthemums, Rock Pinks, and Sedums give the chief effects.

This small formal rose garden in the grounds of Mr. and Mrs. Wm. C. McDuffie, Berkeley, shows that with a proper arrangement and selection of varieties, roses may be grown for garden adornment as well as for cutting.

Water gardens are not very common on the small California place though they would be especially appreciated, for the whole Pacific coast has dry summers and as one goes south their length increases. European gardeners under similar conditions in Spain and particularly in Italy have made much use of water, and the fine formal gardens in the latter country have an abundance of fountains, rivulets, and pools. We recognize how refreshing are its sight and sound in rainless regions, but it unfortunately has to be paid for in California and that deters most of us.

It is, however, worth considering whether, for instance, in a little formal court or patio one cannot afford a small fountain, basin, or pool. In the forecourt of an attractive Pasadena cottage a little fountain comes out of the plastered wall and falls into a basin. A pipe, running underneath the house, carries away the water to a pool in the back garden, an economical arrangement, as the overflow of the pool may be used to provide moisture-loving plants with their needs. In any case, it is unnecessary to keep the water running at all times.

Directions for the making of such garden ornaments as pools and fountains cannot be given here, but I would emphasize their value in formal work and the pleasure to be derived from them in gardens in which we live. Water can also be used in a less formal manner, and is both useful and ornamental when it becomes an added feature of a well-planned rock-garden, trickling down over stones and ending up in a pool, in and around which water-loving plants may be grown.

The Japanese are adepts at making the most of a little
water in their picturesque gardens, and any gardener
interested in the problem would do well to study the
examples found in public parks and private places.
The largest of these which I have seen is in Golden
Gate Park, San Francisco, and it illustrates the regular
plan of having a waterfall, the water from which wends
its way by a tortuous, narrow channel to a wider ex-
panse where it forms either a little lake or a marsh, the
latter a perfect home for bog plants and Japanese and
Siberian Irises. Where an informal pool or pond is
planned, the planting of its banks merits much attention. Small Bamboos, Tritomas, Day-Lilies, and other
plants of rush-like foliage should be combined with low,
moisture-loving creepers and shrubs which will lean
over the banks. One of the chief values of water is
for the reflections possible in it where interesting planting has been done.

CHAPTER XII

GARDEN CALENDAR

THE excuse for attempting a calendar of gardening operations for a state over eight hundred miles from north to south is to prevent the California gardener from using planting guides intended for eastern North America or for western Europe, guides which are in many instances quite inapplicable to the conditions here. Besides, in spite of the many degrees of latitude, differences in temperature from north to south are astonishingly small, and general directions, if interpreted in a broad and discriminating way, may readily be of assistance. Certain difficulties must, however, be recognized.

It is colder and wetter in northern California than in the south, the summers on the coast are cooler than in the interior, and the winters in the interior are less favorable to plant growth than those on the coast, while anywhere the altitude may make the difference between January fruit and flowers and long-continued ice and snow. Further, the variations from season to season are great. Our garden diary shows years when the first rains came in late September or early October and were heavy enough to start everything into growth and to allow of all kinds of planting, while the records of other years show little or no rain until as late as Christmas or even early January.

Again, the quantity of rain in any section varies so much in different years that gardening operations are greatly affected. Lastly, the gardener should recognize the length of the different seasons in California and the long periods over which the same operation may be undertaken. There is an absence of the need of haste to get certain work done before the ground freezes, or before warm summer follows quickly on a short spring, conditions familiar to all those who have gardened east of the Mississippi. Thus, the planting of trees and shrubs may extend from November to May, and even later where the materials are evergreens, balled or in pots.

Tulips may be put in from October to New Year's with almost equally satisfactory results. The Bearded Irises may be divided and replanted in June, before their new root growth begins, or any time thereafter until the winter rains start them into very active growth.

The sowing of hardy annuals may be done during any month from October to May, depending very largely on when the flowers are preferred, and Gladioli and Dahlias are often planted in batches a month or so apart so as to have a succession of bloom from May to October.

It will therefore be understood by any one who consults the calendar here given that discrimination must be used in applying it to his particular location. The notes are merely to be considered as general guidance. Some task which might be undertaken in any one of several successive months will not be reiterated in the instructions.

JANUARY

Certain publicity agencies have spread abroad the fairy tale that even in January millions of Roses and other flowers are to be seen on every hand in California. As a matter of fact, this month and December are the months of the year when there is least bloom in our gardens, though any well-planned garden along the coast may still be attractive and provide a few flowers at this dull time.

When or where the rains are very heavy and the season is cold it is not a period of great activity. This is particularly true of the amateur, who finds the shorter and colder days unsuitable for garden work. When the soil is not cold and soggy and the weather permits, it is a good month to plant deciduous trees and shrubs, and such evergreens as are quite hardy. Plant also Roses. Choose the warmer, balmier days for this work, avoiding times when cold, drying winds are present.

Everywhere it is a propitious time for the pruning of deciduous trees, climbers, shrubs, and Roses. Cuttings of ripened wood of Roses may also be put in at this time.

When the ground is not too wet, dig empty flower-beds and borders, incorporating manure with the soil if possible, but in any case leaving them rough so as to expose the soil to the action of the sun and air.

Dig and fertilize lightly around trees and shrubs.

Cannas and Dahlias should now be lifted and stored until they are to be replanted.

In southern California this is a good month to sow certain hardy annuals for summer flowers, such as Snapdragons, Coreopsis, Centaureas, Dianthus, and Sweet Peas.

FEBRUARY

February is a better gardening month. The ground is now moist, and warm sunny days favor plant growth and make work in the garden more attractive. It is in one sense the first month of spring, for, though much natural germination occurs with the first rains in October or thereabouts, between that time and February normally occurs the coldest time of the year.

The planting of deciduous material and hardier evergreens should be continued. Cuttings of deciduous shrubs such as the Weigelas, Hydrangeas, Fuchsias, and Lilacs may now be planted in sandy soil in a partially shaded place.

Many hardy perennials may now be divided and planted, and hardy annuals, such as the California and the true Poppies, may be sown in the open ground. It is also well to get Hollyhock seed in by now.

Start Verbenas, Pentstemons, and similar summer-blooming plants, preferably in a frame.

MARCH

With the warmer weather which comes in March deciduous trees and shrubs can no longer be kept dormant, and plantings of these and also of Roses with bare roots should be completed this month. The assurance that from now on there will be little cold weather makes this one of the best months for the planting of the more tender broad-leaved evergreens, such as the Eucalyptus and Acacia. The planting of these may really be extended from this on until summer where water can be readily given. Not later than this month should be completed the pruning of deciduous shrubs which bloom in summer or fall, those most grown being Hydrangeas and Fuchsias for summer and Poinsettias for late fall. Do not prune spring-flowering shrubs at this time.

March is the best spring month in which to sow a lawn. Grass will make a better stand now because the soil retains much of its natural moisture and yet is warm enough to encourage germination. Established lawns should at this time receive attention by scattering over them well-rotted manure, and after its value has leached into the ground raking off the strawy residue. This is the best fertilizer, but if it is not available substitute a good commercial fertilizer such as bone-flour, scattering it on the surface and washing it in.

Give great attention now to weeding, as plant growth is vigorous and weeds left at this time will crowd and rob garden plants and draw to themselves moisture which should be left for more desirable tenants.

Ground which has been left rough from earlier digging should now be hoed and raked in preparation for planting.

Divide and replant perennials which bloom in summer and fall, such as Michaelmas Daisies, Shasta Daisies, Helianthus, and Chrysanthemums. With all these it is best to use single shoots of the fresh young growth from the outer side of the clumps. If you expect to have Hollyhocks this summer, the seed should now be in the ground where they will bloom. Fall sowing is even better.

Among the plants which may be well put out into the garden beds are Carnations, always in a lighter soil and one with good drainage, Pentstemons, and in half-shady spots the fibrous-rooted Begonias.

Where the rainy season is cold this is the first month in which to make a planting of Gladioli for early bloom. Plantings for succession may be made until June.

There is no better time than now to make sowings of the chiefly half-hardy annuals on which we must so largely depend for our summer flowers. These should include Asters, Ten Weeks' Stocks, Salpiglossis, Zinnias, Petunias, and Marigolds. Though they may be started in seed-beds outdoors a safer and easier plan is to sow them in flats.

Start also cuttings of such summer bedding plants as Marguerites, Heliotropes, and Salvias. With bottom heat success is easy, but even without it a certain percentage will root.

Where the possession of partially shaded beds enables one to have fine tuberous Begonias in summer, they should now be started in pots or in flats, choosing a shady place, a lath-house if possible.

Begin as early as this the campaign against pests. Snails and slugs are getting active, and they should be sought under leaves, stones, boards, or any litter.

APRIL

April is to California as June is to the Eastern states— the most beautiful garden month of the year. It is therefore desirable not to have left oneself too much work to do, but to have the garden in order and to enjoy it. In any case, it is getting late for the planting of many things, but one may still make sowings of annuals, or, preferably, plant out those already started in boxes, affording them protection from wind and sun if these are strong.

Such tuberous-rooted plants as Cannas, Dahlias, Tigridias, and Begonias may now be planted out with perfect safety. The plantings of Dahlias may extend through May and June as well.

Summer-blooming plants such as Fuchsias, Geraniums, and Heliotropes, if in pots, should now be put out where they are to bloom.

This is the last month during which summer- or fall-blooming perennials should be planted if one expects them to bloom the same year.

Chrysanthemum cuttings will now root in sand without any artificial heat. In the latter part of the month, Dahlia cuttings should also be started; the latter will root even better in May where the great assistance of bottom heat is not available.

Do not neglect to water occasionally trees and shrubs

planted this season, remembering that a thorough soaking followed by surface cultivation is far better than innumerable sprinklings.

The fight against pests must continue. With warmer days come the aphides, or plant lice. A strong stream from the hose will discourage them but will not kill them off as thoroughly as will the nicotine or other insecticides offered for this purpose.

MAY

It is now getting late for planting, but the warmth-loving subjects from pots can still be put out and bulb-beds can be filled with annuals previously raised in boxes.

Summer-flowering annuals which have been sown in the open ground should now be ruthlessly thinned; only if this is done will their season of bloom extend for a long time. In preparation for the succeeding spring, first sowings should be made of such perennials as polyanthus Primroses and Columbines.

During this month or the next take up and divide Violets for next winter's bloom.

The spring-flowering bulbs are now over as far as bloom is concerned, but it is essential to their future flowering that they be allowed to mature their foliage. Do not remove it until it turns yellow. If you need the space, they may be transplanted to trenches in some out-of-the-way place, there to be left to ripen. Surprising as it may seem, experience has shown that it is generally better to do this just after flowering than three or four weeks later.

JUNE

In June and the months immediately succeeding the chief work is maintenance—watering and cultivation, the removal of spent flowers, the tidying up of plants which have gone out of bloom, and the staking of those still to come. As the gardener wants flowers rather than seed, he must be careful not to allow the latter to form.

About the only plants which may still be put out are Dahlias, Chrysanthemums, and Salvias, all fall bloomers. Pinch back Chrysanthemums to encourage bushy growth.

Delphiniums will now have completed their first blooming. Cut them back to the ground and water them to encourage another crop.

Where it is convenient to do so, divide and replant Bearded Irises, so as to obtain the maximum of growth and the longest undisturbed period before next blooming season. But they can be moved with ease and success any month until the end of the year.

This is a good time to make cuttings of Pinks, Carnations, and Nepeta Mussini, using in all cases the fresh growth which comes from the base.

Early in June the pruning of spring-flowering deciduous shrubs should be attended to.

JULY

In July a first sowing may be made of biennials for spring flowering, as an early start will of course give larger plants. Canterbury Bells, Wallflowers, *Anemone*

Coronaria, and Stocks of the Beauty of Nice type should be included.

During this month give particular attention to the watering of Gladioli and Dahlias, as both appreciate much moisture as they come into bloom.

Allow the Roses to dry off in July and through August. This period of rest will greatly improve the fall crop of flowers.

Keep weeds from going to seed, and remember that in our dry summers many of them will still ripen if merely cut down. They should be put on a compost heap where they will rot.

Dig, water, and cultivate around trees, shrubs, and vines which were moved this year. As they become more thoroughly established in other years this is less necessary, though it will always stimulate greater growth.

AUGUST

It is well to start not later than this month the biennials for spring flowering mentioned under July, and to include also the sowing of Pansies, Violas, Forget-me-Nots, *Coreopsis grandiflora,* Cinerarias, and *Primula malacoides.*

This month and the next are both good times to start raising perennials from seed, for example, Delphiniums sown thus early will flower next summer.

This is a good time to make or renew a planting of Ferns in a shady place. Remember that they prefer a light soil in which there is much humus. Leaf-mold is the easiest form in which to get it.

Amaryllis belladonna is best separated and replanted shortly after blooming. Do this now.

Two quite different bulbs profit by early planting, indeed are much less successful when deferred. One of these is *Lilium candidum*, the familiar Madonna Lily, the other the dainty little Freesia, so much at home in California.

Where Roses are to be propagated from half-ripe wood this is a good time to put in the cuttings.

Do not forget that Gladioli need some attention after blooming, and that an occasional watering will help them to complete their cycle of growth and to produce more and larger bulblets.

Some of the Dahlias have been now long in bloom and seem worn out. Cut these back hard to induce new growth strong enough to bear later flowers.

SEPTEMBER

In the warmer parts of California it is possible to have Sweet Peas in January if seed of the winter-blooming strains is sown this month. Give them a sunny place and protect the sprouting seedlings by mosquito-netting or wire.

In southern California sow Linaria, Nemesia, Lobelia, and the small-flowered Petunias for winter bloom.

If the Wallflowers, Pansies, Violas, and Forget-me-Nots sown a month or more ago are now large enough, they should be transplanted and grown on until it is desired to plant them where they will bloom.

In those districts favorable to their growth outdoors

set out now growing plants of Cyclamen, remembering their preference for shady places.

Watsonia bulbs deteriorate if not planted early. There is no better month than September to get them into the ground.

The planting of Freesias should now be completed.

Roses which have been given a rest during July and August should now be moderately pruned and the ground around the bushes should be dug and well watered to stimulate them into growth for fall flowers.

Exhibition Chrysanthemums should now have attention. They should be mulched with rotted manure and disbudded.

September is often a very warm month. Do not, just because the rains may soon come, cease watering and cultivating.

Many Dahlia shows occur in this month. Those interested in novelties should visit them, but they would be wise to check up on their selections by seeing plants in bloom.

OCTOBER

Our first good rains often come this month, and usher in a period of great garden activity. These rains practically make the month of their appearance the first one of spring, though it must be remembered that the coldest weather of the year will follow so that some spring operations have to be held over until the second or real spring, which begins in February.

In this month begin planting Dutch bulbs, a process

which the Tulips may extend until Christmas. Most of these bulbs will be the better for being in the ground by November. In the order of planting give preference to the Narcissus and Daffodils, and to bulbous Irises.

Get in also as early as is convenient such Cape bulbs as the dwarf Gladioli, Ixias, and Sparaxis. Anemones and Ranunculus, not strictly bulbs, may be planted any time from October to the beginning of the New Year.

Sow in the open ground seeds of hardy annuals— Eschscholtzias, Lupines, Godetias, and Nemophilas, all natives, and Poppies, Larkspurs, Scarlet Flax, and the multitude of others in this class. Sow Hollyhocks where they are to flower, as an early start is a great help.

Plant out where they are to bloom Primroses of the polyanthus, malacoides, and obconica classes, also Cinerarias, Pansies, and other biennials and perennials which you have been raising from seed.

October is a fine month to divide and replant perennials including particularly those which like the cool and wet months to become established, among them hardy Phlox, Bearded Iris, and Tritomas. Montbretias, though bulbs, should be given the same treatment now.

October is the best of the fall months in which to seed a lawn. Do not delay this until later, as the ground gets too cold.

This is a good time to put in cuttings of Geraniums, Pentstemons, and Lavender.

After the first rains, weeds will spring up everywhere. Much time will be saved by getting rid of them while

they are still small. Hoeing over beds filled **with**
dormant bulbs is time well spent.

NOVEMBER

The sowing and planting operations of last **month**
may be continued. Now also the really hardy evergreens, such as the Laurels and Rhododendrons, may be
transplanted. The conifers especially will appreciate
it this month or next, so as to get the advantage of
winter growth.

Dahlias, Gladioli, and tuberous Begonias will now be
through blooming and should be lifted and dried off.

This and next month are the best ones for planting
Irises of the spuria, Sibirica, and Japanese groups.

Do not burn up the fallen leaves which are now
strewing your garden. Keep them raked up as they
smother growth, but gather them into piles for the
compost heap. They are a most valuable source of
humus.

DECEMBER

The ground is now getting cold, and it is a less favorable time for seed-sowing outdoors, but Sweet Peas,
which germinate at a low temperature, should still be
put in. The ones to sow now are the regular Spencer
varieties for spring and summer bloom.

It is rarely that one wants all the Chrysanthemum
plants which have bloomed. Dispose of surplus, and
if the ground in the garden is wanted heel into some
out-of-the-way place one or two plants of each variety
to provide stock next year.

Propagating of deciduous trees, shrubs, and Roses from hard wood cuttings may be done this month, and these same may very well be pruned at this time.

The pruning of many evergreens may also be accomplished this month and next. One may also prune and thin out climbers which are getting beyond bounds.

The native Toyon, or Christmas Berry, is popular at this time for decoration. As it does not transplant well but is easily raised from seed, save some of the berries now. Bird-lovers should grow this native plant, as it attracts many of our most desirable birds.

Seeds of Cotoneasters and Pyracanthas may also be collected at this time.

The end of the year seems a fitting time for a thorough clean-up of the garden, cutting off the dead stalks of herbaceous plants, clearing off weeds, and tidying up the place so as to give vermin little chance to hide.

This is also an excellent time for the spraying of trees and shrubs affected with scale.

THE END

INDEX

INDEX

(For the convenience of the reader, the first page reference after the name of each species in most instances indicates the principal one of a group of references.)

314 *Index*

Daffodil, Trumpet, 219, 291
  Victoria, 219
  Weardale Perfection, 219
  White Lady, 220
  Yellow Trumpet, 219
Dahlia, 248, 4, 10, 11, 35, 47, 61, 62, 187,
    234, 240, 241, 296, 298, 301, 303, 304,
    305, 306, 308
  Ballet Girl, 254
  Delice, 254
  Dr. Tevis, 254
  Geisha, 251, 254
  Glow, 254
  Kalif, 254
  Little Beeswing, 254
  Mary Purrier, 254
  Mrs. Carl Salbach, 254
  Ruth C. Gleadell, 254
Daisy (see Bellis)
  Colored (see Chrysanthemum)
  Michaelmas (see Aster)
  Mexican (see Erigeron mucronatus)
  Paris (see Chrysanthemum frutescens)
  Shasta, 67, 68, 143, 184, 300
  Swan River (see Brachycome)
  Transvaal (see Gerbera Jamesoni)
Daphne, 98
  odora, 98, 112, 289
  odora marginata, 98
Day Lily (see Hemerocallis)
Delphinium (Larkspur), 146, 193, 13, 20, 29,
    31, 34, 61, 62, 67, 129, 130, 143, 187,
    215, 216, 226, 270, 303, 304, 307
  Belladonna, 147
  cardinale, 147
Deodar (Cedrus deodara), 81
Deutzia, 87
Dianthus (Pink), 147, 194, 21, 31, 35, 70, 214,
    215, 269, 287, 290, 298, 303
  barbatus (Sweet William), 148, 72, 128
  caesius (Cheddar Pink), 148
  chinensis, 194
  deltoides (Maiden Pink), 148
  Heddewigii, 194
  plumarius (Pheasant-eyed Pink), 147, 70,
    184
Diascia Barberi, 194, 70, 216, 292
Dicentra spectabilis, 184
Dictamnus Fraxinella (Fraxinella), 148
Didiscus caeruleus (Blue Lace Flower), 194
Diervilla (see Weigela)
Digitalis (Foxglove), 149, 43, 185
Dimorphotheca, 195, 75
  aurantica, 195, 216, 292
Diosma ericoides (Breath of Heaven), 98, 32,
    69, 74, 289
Diplacus glutinosus (see Mimulus glutinosus)
Dog's-Tooth Violets (see Erythronium)
Dolichos lignosus (Australian Pea Vine), 117
Doronicum Clusi, 149
Duranta, 98
  Plumieri, 98, 112
Dusty Miller (see Centaurea candidissima
    and C. officinalis)

Elm, Huntington, 79
Empress Tree (Paulownia imperialis), 79
Erica (Heath), 99, 32, 112, 289
  mediterranea, 99

  melanthera, 99, 69, 289
  persoluta alba, 99, 69
Erigeron, 149
  grandiflorus, 150
  mucronatus (syn. Vittadenia triloba)
    (Mexican Daisy), 150, 70, 290
  salsuginosus (Beach Aster), 150
  speciosus, 150
Eryngium (Sea Holly), 150, 71
  amethystinum, 150
  Oliverianum, 150
Erysimum, 143, 216
  Allioni, 150, 184, 286
  linifolium, 143, 184, 286, 290
Erythronium (Dog's-Tooth Violet), 233, 292
Escallonia, 99, 31, 60, 75, 112
  Berteriana, 99
  montevidensis (syn. floribunda), 99
  rosea, 99
  rubra, 99
Eschscholtzia (California Poppy), 195, 15,
    62, 75, 77, 186, 188, 214, 215, 307
Eucalyptus, 74, 6, 82, 299
  ficifolia, 74, 83
  polyganthema, 82
Eugenia, 100, 104
  myrtifolia, 100
Euonymus, 100
  japonicus, 100, 112
Evening Primrose (see Oenothera)
Exochorda grandiflora (Pearl Bush), 86

Fairy Lanterns (Calochortus), 233
Farewell to Spring (see Godetia)
Fatsia (Aralia), 100
  japonica, 100
  papyrifera, 100
Felicia (syn. Agathea), 151
  celestis, 151, 70
  rosea, 151, 70, 290
  Trailing, 151
Ferns, 24, 43, 129, 185, 235, 291, 304
Ficus (Fig), 82, 117, 120
  microphylla (the Moreton Bay Fig), 82
  repens, 120, 117
Fig (see Ficus)
Fig, Hottentot (see Mesembryanthemum
  edule)
Fire Thorn (see Pyracantha coccinea)
Flax (see Linum)
Floss Flower (see Ageratum)
Forget-me-Not (see Myosotis)
Forsythia, 86
Foxglove (see Digitalis)
Fragraria chilensis, 55
Francoa (Maiden's Wreath), 151
  ramosa, 151, 185
Fraxinella (see Dictamnus)
Freesia, 229, 14, 71, 75, 292, 305, 306
  Leichtlini, 229
  refracta alba, 229
Fremontia californica, 100, 74
Fritillaria, 233, 292
  biflora (Mission Bells), 233
  recurva, 233
Fuchsia, 87, 88, 4, 23, 43, 60, 90, 112, 298,
    299, 301
  California (see Zauschneria)

Index